Sacred Scriptures

o

'o be returned on or before the day marked above, subject to recall.

Also available from Continuum:

Christianity as a World Religion, Sebastian Kim and Kirsteen Kim
An Introduction to Religion and Literature, Mark Knight
An Introduction to Religious and Spiritual Experience, Marianne Rankin
The Study of Religion, George D. Chryssides and Ron Geaves
Religious Diversity in the UK, Paul Weller

Sacred Scriptures of the World Religions

An Introduction

Joan A. Price, Ph.D.

continuum

Continuum

Continuum International Publishing Group
The Tower Building   80 Maiden Lane
11 York Road   Suite 704
London SE1 7NX   NY 10038
                          New York

www.continuumbooks.com

British Library Cataloguing-in-Publication Data
A catalogue record for this book is available from the British Library.

ISBN: HB: 978-0-8264-2471-6
     PB: 978-0-8264-2354-2

Library of Congress Cataloguing-in-Publication Data
Price, Joan A.
   Sacred Scriptures of the world religions : an introduction / Joan Price.
      p. cm.
   Includes bibliographical references.
   ISBN-13: 978-0-8264-2471-6 (HB)
   ISBN-13: 978-0-8264-2354-2 (pbk,)
   ISBN-10: 0-8264-2471-6 (HB)
   ISBN-10: 0-8264-2354-X (pbk.)
   1. Sacred books--History and criticism. 2. Sacred books. 3. Religious literature--History and criticism. 4. Religious literature. 5. Religions--Textbooks. I. Title.

BL71.P75 2009
208'.2--dc22

                                                                           2009010230

Typeset by Free Range Book Design & Production Limited
Printed and bound in Great Britain by CPI Antony Rowe, Chippenham, Wiltshire

Contents

Preface

Once upon a time there were six blind men who wanted to know what an elephant looked like. The first blind man felt the elephant's side. 'The elephant is like a wall.' The second blind man ran his hands along the elephant's tusk. 'The elephant is like a smooth, taut spear.' The third blind man stroked the elephant's trunk. 'A snake,' he said. 'The elephant is like a snake.' The fourth blind man ran his hands down the elephant's leg. 'The elephant is like a tree.' The fifth blind man stroked the elephant's ear. 'The elephant is like a fan.' The sixth blind man grasped the animal's tail. 'The elephant is like a rope.' The blind men disputed loud and long. Although each was partly right, all were actually wrong.

This ancient story of the 'Blind Men and the Elephant' goes to the heart of our theological wars. So often religious disputes are waged in ignorance of what each other means, thus, like the blind men and the elephant, we fight about an Ultimate Reality that none of us has seen. When we are opinionated or ignorant of our limitations because of insufficient knowledge or smug mentality, we are as blind as if we had no eyesight. The possibility that arises here is that in dogmatic theology, as we usually understand it, we settle for our limitations by transforming them into absolute truths.

The mountain simile may help us to understand the ultimate unity of the various religions of the world: There are many paths starting at the bottom of the mountain leading up the mountain to the top. Each path starts from a different geographical location with respect to climate, terrain, and biological and social conditions. One path up the mountain proceeds from the jungle, another from the desert, another from the Arctic, and another from a large city. The jungle is wet with dense growth, the desert dry and barren, the Arctic cold and remote, and the city crowded and noisy. It is the ultimate task of religion to help their inhabitants find their way up the mountain to the top. Those starting from the desert need to carry large quantities of water, which would not be necessary for those in the jungle – in fact, would hinder them. Arctic climbers need warm, heavy clothing, which would inhibit both the desert dwellers and the jungle inhabitants. City residents might take mobile phones and GPS navigators to find their way in unfamiliar terrain.

Each group would need its own set of instructions for traveling through their particular region. For the Arctic inhabitants to insist that everyone must take warm, heavy clothing to reach the mountain top, for the desert dwellers to advise climbers in all regions to carry large quantities of water, or for the city residents to insist that all climbers text-message daily would show a lack of understanding of the other paths.

Sacred Scriptures of the World Religions: An Introduction is a book to help us understand that there are other paths as well as our own. And as the paths get closer to the top of the mountain, the terrain becomes more and more similar for everyone no matter where they started. As we climb higher up the mountain we begin to see some of the other paths and the people traveling them. Only then can we recognize that the various religions lead to a common goal.

Understanding religious roots is of particular importance in the twenty-first century because of our growing interest in multicultural diversity, global, and international affairs. The Internet and TV news take us around the world daily. We meet people of different faiths and we want to comprehend their roots, beliefs, and the meaning of their holy scriptures. The scriptures I have chosen to broaden and deepen our understanding of other cultures and religious belief systems include the oral wisdom of primal mythologies, and the written wisdom of Hinduism, Buddhism, Jainism, Sikhism, Taoism, Confucianism, Judaism, Christianity, and Islam. This is not a definitive list of all the religions in the world, nor even a rounded view of the religions considered, for we need only think of Christianity and the different meanings it has for all Christians: Catholic, Protestant, Orthodox, Evangelical, and so on. Is it even possible to say what Christian scriptures mean to all Christians? The scriptures and their explanations included in this book are an introduction to the wisdom of the world religions that will hopefully inspire further investigation and study of other religions and worldviews.

I have arranged the book by tradition with scriptural passages and subject explanations. Each chapter begins with an introduction of how the religion originated, followed by clear and readable interpretations and commentary on the topic relating to specific scriptural passages such as dependent origination, nirvana, and the skandhas associated with the Buddhist tradition, or the meaning of the Torah and the Talmud in the Jewish tradition. For each religious founder, I have included an account of his life and the culture in which he lived.

In presenting the sacred scriptures of the world religions, I have chosen not to include my own ideas and evaluations. I have placed short 'Reflections' questions throughout the book to capture your important ideas and stimulate your curiosity about issues discussed in the main selections and that pertain to your everyday life. The end of each chapter has a summary to help you refresh your memory. Following the summary is a short section that tells you what is happening in that religion today, and a timeline of its sacred scriptures and important events. At the very end of the chapters are suggested readings and study questions for your consideration, as well as a list of sources for the scriptural quotations used throughout the chapter.

I want to thank my students, colleagues, and friends. Their support and enthusiasm have played a major role in my writing of this book. For their helpful suggestions and comments on the manuscript, I would like to thank the reviewers: Ronald Leonard, Ph.D. and Ann Mahoney, Ph.D. I extend deep gratitude to Continuum's editor Kirsty Schaper for her insightful ideas and to her assistant Tom Crick. A very special thanks goes to Natalie Giboney for her professional help with permissions.

There is a divine light that leans over the world.

Sri Aurobindo

Primal Wisdom

Horned and Feathered Serpent
Horned and feathered serpent deities can be benevolent
or malevolent beings. They are often associated with rain,
lightning, thunder, and waterways.

The Earliest Humans

The earliest human beings roamed from place to place, hunting animals and gathering roots, seeds, and stalks of wild plants for sustenance. When food and water became scarce or unavailable because of seasonal change, drought, floods, or over-consumption, people simply moved on to settle elsewhere. The earliest cultures that we call civilized were those first permanent settlements capable of surviving nature's normal cycles of change.

Primal Religions

Primal (meaning 'first') religions are basically oral religious traditions that rely on word-of-mouth myths (stories) handed down from generation to generation. We call them primal or prehistoric religions because they began before human beings developed a written language. Primal religions abound and include among them African tribal, Australian Aboriginal, Polynesian, and Native American Indian religions.

Understanding these oral traditions means exploring their myths and symbols. In some sense their practices and beliefs are open to us in their simplicity. Native American Hopi Indians, for example, greet the Sun with 'singing cornmeal,' a prayer for a long and happy road for themselves and their families. However, explored within the context of the whole – their worldview, their relationship with the natural and the supernatural, and their complex ceremonial life – these oral traditions take on a dynamic and deeply esoteric (or secret) nature.

> **Reflections**
> Can you recall listening to stories about your own religion?
> How important were these stories in forming the beliefs you hold today?

No single primal tradition exists, but as many religions can be found as there are tribes and societies. Each has its own spiritual tradition of ancestral homelands, the waters upon them, the skies above them, and the creatures that inhabit them. Although each tradition has its own life patterns, all share some common beliefs:

- Belief in a supreme divine Creator.
- Belief that the universe is an orderly system of interrelated elements.
- Belief in animism (all nature has spirit or soul).
- Belief in the unity of the human body with nature.
- Belief in the power of the Shaman or medicine man or woman.

African Tribal Religions

Africa, home to the million-year evolution of human beings, has archeological evidence of religious observances practiced by human beings from as early as 30,000 BCE. We know, for example that Africans were burying human corpses in a manner that showed concern for the body after death. Ancient rock paintings of masked figures and serpent-like creatures suggest other kinds of religious activity as well, mainly fertility rites.

Vast distances and geographical barriers such as broad deserts, dense forests, and high mountains have always made contact between Africans living in different regions difficult and infrequent. The many languages, between 800 and 1,700, and their countless dialects spoken throughout the continent have further hampered communication. The countries north of the great Sahara Desert have a long association with the cultures of the Mediterranean Sea. The neighboring countries south of the Sahara, however, have had their own distinct cultural histories.

Because of the lack of written records, we know little of the sub-Saharan experience before the colonial period, which began in the 1400s. Rock paintings and engravings, and other early art forms reveal primal African culture and civilization. The sub-continent's sense of timelessness suggests that the religious experiences recorded by the first Europeans differed only slightly from those of the earliest period and were more in the manner of expression than in the substance of religious belief.

Common Threads

Each sub-Saharan culture developed its own separate customs and creeds, but certain ideas appear to have been shared by all, including creation myths that not only deal with the origins of the world and of the human race, but also with the cause of death. According to most myths, at first there was order in the universe and divine and human beings communicated freely. Then humans made mistakes and were disobedient. This led to the separation of heaven and earth and the withdrawal of the High God.

Reflections

Do you remember stories about the disobedience of the first human beings? What happened to them and how did their disobedience affect humankind today?

All African religions are *holistic*, which means that individuals and their communities believe their religions strengthen their mental, physical, and emotional health by keeping matter and spirit in balance. Each culture's rich ceremonial life also included celebrations of the rites of passage into adulthood, praying for fertility, and seeking tribal ancestors' protection against evil forces.

The High God

According to the religious instruction that young Africans received orally from their parents and from shamans, the High God, who created the world and everything in it, mixed freely at first with human beings. When human disobeyed, however, the High God moved beyond the sky – too high and too distant for humans to comprehend. Because he had little contact with the world and its inhabitants, the High God was not the subject of intimate worship.

Sacred Wisdom of the African Oral Traditions

1. **Nzambi, the High God of the Bakongo (Lower Congo River Area, Africa)**

   Nzambi Mpungu is a being, invisible, but very powerful, who has made all, men and things, even fetishes which he has given to men for their good. 'If he had not given us our fetishes, we should all be dead long ago.' He intervenes in the creation of every child, he punishes those who violate his prohibitions. They render him no worship, for he has need of none and is inaccessible. On earth man lives with his incessant needs to satisfy; the aged have there a privileged position. Above all is Nzambi, the sovereign Master, unapproachable, who has placed man here below to take him away some day, at the hour of death. He watches man, searches him out everywhere and takes him away, inexorably, young or old .... Among the laws there are nkondo mi Nzambi, 'God's prohibitions,' the violation of which constitutes a sumu ku Nzambi [a sin against Nzambi], and an ordinary sanction of this is lufwa lumbi 'a bad death.'

2. **Basonge Creation Myth (Zaire, Africa)**

   The Creator, Fidi Mukullu, made all things including man. He also planted banana trees. When the bananas were ripe he sent the sun to harvest them. The sun brought back a full basket to Fidi Mukullu, who asked him if he had eaten any. The sun answered 'no,' and the Creator decided to put him to a test. He made the sun go down into a hole dug in the earth, then asked him when he wanted to get out. 'Tomorrow morning, early,' answered the sun. 'If you did not lie,' the Creator told him, 'you will get out early tomorrow morning.' The next day the sun appeared at the desired moment, confirming his honesty. Next the moon was ordered to gather God's bananas and was put to the same test. She also got out successfully. Then came man's turn to perform the same task. However, on his way to the Creator he ate a portion of the bananas, but denied doing so. Put to the same test as the sun and the moon, man said that he wanted to leave the hole at the end of five days. But he never got out. Fidi Mukulla said, 'Man lied. That is why man will die and will never reappear.'

3. Leza, the High God of the Ba-ila (Northern Rhodesia, Africa)

Long ago the Ba-ila did not know Leza as regards his affairs – no, all that they knew about him, was that he created us, and also his unweariedness in doing things. As at present when the rainy season is annoying and he does not fall, when then they ask of Leza different things: they say now: 'Leza fall too much.' If there is cold they say 'Leza makes it cold.' And if it is not they say, 'Leza is much too hot, let it be overclouded.' All the same Leza as he is the Compassionate, that is to say, as he is Merciful, he does not get angry, he doesn't give up falling, he doesn't give up doing them all good – no, whether they curse, whether they mock him, whether they grumble at him, he does good to all at all times, that is how they trust him always. But as for seeing always his affairs, no, the Ba-ila do not know, all they say is: Leza is the good-natured one; he is one from whom you beg different things. We Ba-ila have no more that we know.

4. Dinka: Human Disobedience (Sudan, Africa)

In the beginning God was very close to man, for the sky then lay just above the earth. There was no death, sickness, sorrow, or hunger, and men were content with one grain of millet a day granted them by God. One day, a greedy woman, who wanted to pound more than the one grain permitted, used a long-handled pestle and struck the sky. This angered God, who withdrew with the sky to its present position far above the earth. Since then the country has become spoiled, and men are now subject to death, sickness, hunger, and disease.

5. Hutu: The Origin of Death (Rwanda and Burundi, Africa)

In the olden days, when Imana (God) still lived among men, Death did not live among men. Whenever he happened to stray onto the earth, God would chase it away with his hunting dogs. One day during such a chase, Death was forced into a narrow space and would have been caught and destroyed. But in his straits he found a woman, and promised her that if she hid him he would spare her and her family. The woman opened her mouth and Death jumped inside. When God came to her and asked her if she had seen Death, she denied ever seeing him. But God, the All-seeing One, knew what happened, and told the woman that since she had hidden Death, in the future Death would destroy her and all her children. From that moment death spread all over the world.

6. Fon: Male/Female God (Benin, West Africa)

The world was created by one god, who is at the same time both male and female. This Creator is neither Mawu nor Lisa, but is named Nana-Buluku. In time, Nana-Buluku gave birth to twins, who were named Mawu and Lisa, and to whom eventually dominion over the real thus created was ceded. To Mawu, the woman, was given command of the night; to Lisa, the man, command of the day. Mawu, therefore, is the moon and inhabits the west, while Lisa, who is the sun, inhabits the east. At the time their respective domains were assigned to them, no children had as yet been born to this pair, though at night the man was in the habit of giving a 'rendezvous' to the woman, and eventually she bore him offspring. This is why, when there is an eclipse of the moon, it is said the celestial couple are engaged in love-making; when there is an eclipse of the sun, Mawu is believed to be having intercourse with Lisa.

7. Ngombe: God Leaves Man (Central Africa)

Akongo (God) was not always as he is now. In the beginning the creator lived among men, but men were quarrelsome. One day they had a big quarrel and Akongo left them to themselves. He went and hid in the forest and nobody has seen him since. People today can't tell what he is like.

8. Pygmy: God (Zaire, Africa)

In the beginning was God,
Today is God
Tomorrow will be God.
Who can make an image of God?
He has no body.
He is as a word which comes out of your mouth.
That word! It is no more,
It is past, and still it lives!
So is God.

9. Yoruba Song of God (Nigeria, Africa)

The sun shines and sends its burning rays down upon us,
The moon rises in its glory.
Rain will come and again the sun will shine,
And over it all passes the eyes of God.
Nothing is hidden from Him.
Whether you be in your home, whether you be on the water,
Whether you rest in the shade of a tree in the open,
Here is your Master.

Did you think because you were more powerful than some poor orphan,
You could cover his wealth and deceive him,
Saying to yourself, 'I cannot be seen'?
So then remember that you are always in the presence of God.

Not today, not today, not today!
But some day He will give you your just reward
For thinking in your heart
That you have but cheated a slave, an orphan.

10. Zulu Proverb (South Africa)
Without proverbs, the language would be but a skeleton without flesh, a body without a soul.

11. A Bushman Demands the Help of His God (South Africa)
Gauwa must help us that we kill an animal.
Gauwa, help us. We are dying of hunger.
Gauwa does not give us help.
He is cheating. He is bluffing.
Gauwa will bring something for us to kill next day.
After he himself hunts and has eaten meat,
When he is full and is feeling well.

Australian Aboriginal Religion

The early Aborigines were nomadic hunters and food gatherers who roamed the arid Australian land more than 40,000 years ago. They wore few clothes and lived in simple shelters of wood or stone. Today they make up only 2.5 percent of the Australian population and largely live their traditional way of life of hunting and gathering.

The word *aborigine* means 'from the beginning,' and it refers to the descendants of an oral culture whose civilization continues to remain relatively unaffected by other foreign cultures. Today's Aborigines are the surviving members of the earliest inhabitants of Australia and among the few people whose religion has remained primarily intact.

Approximately 500 distinct Australian Aboriginal peoples and more than 200 Aboriginal languages have been identified. Despite the vast differences in terrain and climate that separate these individual groups, the Aborigines throughout Australia follow similar religious practices.

The Dreaming

The Dreaming is the Aborigines' term for the founding of the universe and the evolution of its spiritual, natural, and moral order. The Dreaming dates from the primordial past and continues in the worldly and supernatural realms of the present. It is the source of life and the spiritual power that underlies and sustains the world. 'Dreamtime' is the period from the beginning of the universe to the present or until the coming of Europeans, which some Aborigines consider the end of the sacred period. They do not believe that there is nothing more to learn from the Dreaming, only that they no longer live in it.

According to a traditional Dreamtime legend, in the beginning the Father of all Spirits was the only one awake. Gently he awoke the Sun Mother and when she opened her eyes warm sun rays spread out upon the sleeping earth. Following the Father of all Spirits command, Sun Mother went down to the bare earth and everywhere she walked plants grew. The bright light that radiated from her woke the spirits of the insects, the birds, and the animals. She was happy to see the creatures of the earth come to life. Then the Father of all Spirits told her to make rivers and streams and bring the fish spirits to life. She did as He commanded.

The Sun Mother instructed all her creatures to enjoy the earth and to live in peace with each other. Then she returned to the sky and became the sun. At first the earth creatures lived in peace, but soon desire crept into their hearts and they began to argue. The Sun Mother did not like what she saw, so she came down from the sky to stop their arguing. She told each creature, 'If you are not happy with the form I gave you, choose any form you wish.' Fish changed into frogs, frogs changed into bats, bats changed into lizards, lizards grew big ears, and other animals changed their color, until everything was in chaos.

The Sun Mother was very upset, because she knew the Father of all Spirits would be angered by what had happened. So she gave birth to a god and a goddess. The god was the Morning Star and the goddess was the moon. The god and goddess gave birth to two children, which Sun Mother sent to earth as the first two human beings. Because they were part god and goddess, human beings were superior to other earth creatures and would always be happy with their forms.

12. Dreamtime Story of Creation (Australia)
(Told by Aunty Beryl Carmichael)

This is the creation story of Ngiyaampaa country, as well as the land belonging to Eaglehawk and Crow.

Now long, long time ago of course, in the beginning, when there was no people, no trees, no plants whatever on this land, 'Guthi-guthi', the spirit of our ancestral being, he lived up in the sky.

So he came down and he wanted to create the special land for people and animals and birds to live in.

So Guthi-guthi came down and he went on creating the land for the people – after he'd set the borders in place and the sacred sights, the birthing places of all the Dreamings, where all our Dreamings were to come out of.

Guthi-guthi put one foot on Gunderbooka Mountain and another one at Mount Grenfell. And he looked out over the land and he could see that the land was bare. There was no water in sight, there was nothing growing. So Guthi-guthi knew that trapped in a mountain-Mount Minara-the water serpent, Weowie, he was trapped in the mountain. So Guthi-guthi called out to him, 'Weowie, Weowie,' but because Weowie was trapped right in the middle of the mountain, he couldn't hear him.

Guthi-guthi went back up into the sky and he called out once more, 'Weowie,' but once again Weowie didn't respond. So Guthi-guthi came down with a roar like thunder and banged on the mountain and the mountain split open. Weowie the water serpent came out. And where the water serpent travelled he made waterholes and streams and depressions in the land.

So once all that was finished, of course, Weowie went back into the mountain to live and that's where Weowie lives now, in Mount Minara. But then after that, they wanted another lot of water to come down from the north, throughout our country. Old Pundu, the Cod, it was his duty to drag and create the river known as the Darling River today.

So Cod came out with Mudlark, his little mate, and they set off from the north and they created the big river. Flows right down, water flows right throughout our country, right into the sea now.

And of course, this country was also created, the first two tribes put in our country were Eaglehawk and Crow. And from these two tribes came many tribal people, many tribes, and we call them sub-groups today. So my people, the Ngiyaampaa people and the Barkandji further down are all sub-groups of Eaglehawk and Crow.

So what I'm telling you – the stories that were handed down to me all come from within this country.

Reflections
Why do you think the Aborigines refer to the source of life and the spiritual power that sustains the world as 'The Dreaming'? Is there anything similar in your own belief system?

Shamans

To restore themselves to a healthy state, the people turn to medicine men or shamans. These gifted individuals must go through an extraordinary initiation period to prove they have the ability to tap into unseen mysterious forces beyond the knowledge of ordinary people. Shamans cast out disease, emotional guilt, and mental uncleanness; they can turn away curses and spells, and ensure victory in war. To help them exorcise a disease whose origin they consider psychological, the shaman may implore the aid of higher spiritual forces.

13. Shamanic Initiation (Unmatjera, Central Australia)
Following are the words of Ilpailurkna, a famous shaman of the Unmatjera tribe.

When he was made into a medicine man, a very old doctor [medicine man] came one day and threw some of his *atnongara* stones* at him with a spear-thrower. Some hit him on the chest, others went right through his head, from ear to ear, killing him. The old man then cut out all his insides, intestines, liver, heart, lungs – everything in fact – and left him lying all night long on the ground. In the morning

---

* These *atnongara* stones are small crystalline structures which every medicine man is supposed to be able to produce at will from his body, through which it is believed that they are distributed. In fact it is the possession of these stones that gives virtue to the medicine man

the old man came and looked at him and placed some *atnongara* stones inside his body and in his arms and legs, and covered his face with leaves. Then he sang over him until his body was all swollen up. When this was so he provided him with a complete set of new inside parts, placed a lot more *atnongara* stones in him, and patted him on the head, which caused him to jump up alive. The old medicine man then made him drink water and eat meat containing *atnongara* stones. When he awoke he had no idea as to where he was, and said, 'Tju, tju, tju' – 'I think I am lost.' But when he looked round he saw the old medicine man standing beside him, and the old man said, 'No, you are not lost; I killed you a long time ago.' Ipailurkna had completely forgotten who he was and all about his past life. After a time the old man led him back to his camp and showed it to him, and told him that the woman there was his lubra, for he had forgotten all about her. His coming back this way and his strange behaviour at once showed the other natives that he had been made into a medicine man.

Reflections
When the old medicine man said to the initiate, 'No, you are not lost; I killed you a long time ago,' what do you think he meant?

Initiation Rites

Initiation into the mysteries and sacred life of the tribe is an important part of Aboriginal ritual practice. Initiation into adulthood follows from one religious ritual to the next. Each initiation rite is of equal importance to every other and is performed under the guidance of a medicine man, or shaman, to portray the creative powers and activities of the Sky Being. The religious rituals performed at various stages of life keep human beings spiritually connected with the deities and the Dreaming. Each step in ritual initiation is a chance for the tribe to provide the initiate with formal instruction in moral behavior.

At puberty, boys learn the myths of their tribe and live for a period of time in isolation, where they undergo physical ordeals and tests of self-reliance. After the isolation period, they are ritually initiated into their group by circumcision. After the circumcised boy's ritual death, the village women mourn as if he had truly died. Throughout their lives, males continue to receive ritual initiation into the complex laws of their religion. Although women are not initiated into religious law, they undergo an initiation into adult secular society when they have their first menstrual period.

14. Initiation into Adulthood (South-East Australia)
… The Australian initiation ceremony comprises the following phases: first, the preparation of the 'sacred ground,' where the men will remain in isolation during the festival; second, the separation of the novices from their mothers, and, in general, from all women; third, their segregation in the bush, or in a special isolated camp, where they will be instructed in the religious traditions of the tribe; fourth, certain operations performed on the novices, usually circumcision, the

extraction of a tooth, or subincision, but sometimes scarring or pulling out the hair. Throughout the period of the initiation, the novices must behave in a special way, undergo a number of ordeals, and be subjected to various dietary taboos and prohibitions. Each element of this complex initiatory scenario has a religious meaning.

The separation of the novices from their mothers takes place ... in accordance with the customs of different tribes ... Among the Kurnai ... the mothers sit behind the novices; the men come forward in single file between the two groups and so separate them. The instructors raise the novices into the air several times, the novices stretching their arms as far as possible toward the sky ... The neophytes are being consecrated to the Sky God. They are then led into the sacred enclosure where, lying on their backs with their arms crossed on their chests, they are covered with rugs. From then on they see and hear nothing. After a monotonous song, they fall asleep; later, the women withdraw. A Kurnai headman explained... 'If a woman were to see these things, or hear what we tell the boys, I would kill her.' When the neophytes wake, they are invested with a 'belt of manhood' and their instruction begins.

Polynesian Oral Traditions

The Polynesian islands are found within a vast 3,000-mile-long triangle extending from Hawaii in the north Pacific, New Zealand in the southwest, and Easter Island in the southeast.

During pre-historic times, their language consisted of stories and songs about gods and heroes that had many of the strengths and weaknesses of human beings. The people praised their great chiefs, warriors, and especially the navigators who led the canoe parties to find new lands. Their prayers summoned the gods to protect the canoe-builders, house-builders, and fishermen. Everything depended on correct ritual. The master-craftsman of every occupation taught his successor both his technical skills and the proper use of charms, invocations, and spells. These rituals were so powerful that if any step was omitted or if their hearts were not pure, disaster and death would follow.

The oral traditions followed the Polynesians wherever they settled because they carried with them their gods, their heroes, and their sacred myths. Some of the names of the gods and heroes changed with the language of the different island people, but on almost every island favorite stories had the same characters: Hina, the woman who beat tapa cloth in the moon; Maui who fished up the island and snared the sun; Timirau whose pet whale was murdered by Kae; Tawhaki who visited the sky; and Rata whose canoe was built by the little people of the forest.

The High God of Tahiti, Polynesia was Ta'aroa, an all-knowing creator who brought the world into existence from nothing – the night or darkness. Ta'aroa lived alone in the void and made all things.

15. Ta'aroa, the Creator (Tahiti, Polynesia)
He existed, Ta'aroa was his name
In the immensity

There was no earth, there was no sky.
There was no sea, there was no man.
Above, Ta'aroa calls.
Existing alone, he became the universe.
Ta'aroa is the origin, the rocks.
Ta'aroa is the sands,
   It is thus that he is named.
Ta'aroa is the light;
   Ta'aroa is within;
   Ta'aroa is the germ.
Ta'aroa is beneath;
   Ta'aroa is firm;
   Ta'aroa is wise.
He created the land of Hawaii,
   Hawaii the great and sacred,
   As a body of shell for Ta'aroa.

16. Hina, the First Woman (Tahiti, Polynesia)

After the creation peace and harmony everywhere existed for a long time. But at last, discontentment arose and there was war among the gods in their different regions, and among men, so Ta'aroa and Tu [male divinities] uttered curses to punish them.

They cursed the stars, which made them blink; and they cursed the moon, which caused it to wane and go out. But Hina, the mitigator of many things, saved their lives ... the host of stars are ever bright, but keep on twinkling, and the moon always returns after it disappears.

They cursed the sea, which caused low tide; but Hina preserved the sea, which produced high tide, and so these tides have followed each other ever since.

They cursed the rivers, which frightened away the waters, so that they hid beneath the soil; but Hina reproduced the shy waters, which formed springs, and so they continue to thus exist.

[According to Tahitians, the man and not the woman caused people to lose eternal life.]

17. Maori Creation Myth (New Zealand)

Io dwelt within the breathing-space of immensity.
The Universe was in darkness with water everywhere.
There was no glimmer of dawn, no clearness, no light.
And he began by saying these words,
... 'Darkness become a light possessing darkness.'
And at once light appeared.
(He) then repeated those self-same words in this manner,
That He might cease remaining inactive:
   'Darkness become a light-possessing darkness.'
And at once light appeared ...
   'Light, become a darkness-possessing light.'

And again an intense darkness supervened.
Then a third time He spake saying:
> 'Let there be one darkness above,
> Let there be one darkness below.
> Let there be one light above,
> Let there be one light below,
> A dominion of light,
> A bright light.'

And now a great light prevailed.
(Io) then looked to the waters which compassed him about,
> and spake a fourth time, saying:
> 'Ye waters of Tai-kama, be ye separate.
> Heaven be formed.' Then the sky became suspended.
> 'Bring forth thou Tupua-horo-nuku.'

And at once the moving earth lay stretched abroad.
Those words (of Io) became impressed on the minds of our ancestors, and by them were they transmitted down through generations, our priest joyously referred to them as being:
> The ancient and original sayings.
> The ancient and original words.
> The ancient and original cosmological wisdom (*wananga*).
> Which caused growth from the void,
> As witness the tidal-waters,
> The evolved heaven,
> The birth-given evolved earth.

18. The Creation of Woman From the Earth Mother (Maori)

To produce man it was therefore necessary for the god Tane, the Fertilizer, to fashion in human form a figure of earth upon the Earth Mother's body, and to vivify it. This event transpired in the following way: Tane proceeded to the puke (*Mons veneris*) of Papa [the Earth] and there fashioned in human form a figure in the earth. His next task was to endow that figure with life, with human life, life as known to human beings, and it is worthy of note that, in the account of this act, he is spoken of as Tane te waiora. It was the sun light fertilizing the Earth Mother. Implanted in the lifeless image were the *wairua* (spirit) and *Manawa ora* (breath of life), obtained from Io, the Supreme Being. The breath of Tane was directed upon the image, and the warmth affected it. The figure absorbed life, a faint life sigh was heard, the life spirit manifested itself, and hine-ahu-one, the Earth Formed Maid, sneezed, opened her eyes, and rose – a woman.

Such was the origin of Woman, formed from the substance of the Earth Mother, but animated by the divine Spirit that emanated from the Supreme Being. Io the great, Io of the Hidden Face, Io the Parent, and Io the Parentless.

Reflections

Do you, like the Polynesians, refer to nature or Earth as 'Mother'? Is there a reason people refer to nature as feminine?

19. A Tahitian Family Prayer
(In ancient times, this ancient prayer was repeated each night).

Save me! Save me! It is the night of the gods. Watch close to me, my God (*atua*)! Close to me, oh, my Lord (*fatu*)! Protect me from enchantments, sudden death, evil conduct, from slandering or being slandered, from intrigue, and from quarrels concerning the limits of land. Let peace reign about us, oh, my God! Protect me from the furious warrior, who spreads terror, whose hair bristles! May I and my spirit live and rest in peace this night, oh my God.

Native American Religions

The first people to inhabit the North American continent lived in close affinity with the earth and sky, changing weather, and open spaces. Their descendants retain a strong reverence for and a sense of oneness with the natural world that permeates their religious beliefs, artistic expression, and 'lifeways,' as Native Americans term their system of moral living.

The origin of these people mistakenly identified by Christopher Columbus as 'Indians' because he thought he had arrived in India remains controversial. Several theories of migration have been proposed, but most scholars accept the theory that America's first inhabitants had their ancestral roots in East Asia. The scholars base this appraisal on evidence of relationships among physical appearance, social customs, religious beliefs, and languages. The ancestral migrations to the North American continent may have begun to arrive in the Americas as many as 40,000 to 60,000 years ago, as hunting and gathering groups crossed from Siberia to Alaska across a land bridge that then existed in what is now the Bering Straits. While some groups spread gradually south and east across North America, others moved down into Central and South America, whose southern tip they reached at least by 8000 BCE. As they moved, the groups achieved cultural and linguistic diversity with each society speaking its own unique language. Some cultures remained primarily nomadic hunting societies, while others developed advanced agricultural communities. Even tribes living in close proximity to each other differed in their beliefs, ceremonies, and 'lifeways.'

Because these early cultures kept no written records, much of the information we have about the origins of Native Americans derives from legends and myths passed down by oral tradition within their own tribes. Even today, some of this information is never shared with outsiders. The vast majority of our knowledge of Native American religion comes from public dance ceremonies and other evidence of Indian culture and experience offered to the non-Indian population. American literature begins with this Native American Indian lore, a collection of myths, legends, humorous stories, songs, and poems passed from one generation to the next by the spoken word.

Religious Beliefs and Customs

For Native Americans, religion is a vital and inherent aspect of society. It permeates human activity and links individuals to the orderly system of the universe. All Native Americans share belief in a supreme High God or Great Spirit, who holds together all things in the universe. Associating supernatural powers with the sun and with animals and birds, Native Americans share a profound respect for Mother, or Grandmother, Earth.

Native Americans have a deep sense of mystical unity. All things in the universe depend on each other. Each entity has its individual significance but is dependent on and shares in the growth and work of everything else. Native Americans deeply respect the natural order of things and seek to achieve in their lives the orderly pattern that they see in nature. Everything in the Indian's world is potentially suffused with spiritual meaning, and each person's basic goal in life is to be in harmony with the Great Spirit and the vital forces of nature.

Reflections

Do you, as the Native Americans, believe the world is potentially suffused with spiritual meaning?

---

20. Creation Myth (Hopi, North America)

[At] first, they say, there was only the Creator, Taiowa. All else was endless space. There was no beginning and no end, no time, no shape, no life. Just an immeasurable void that had its beginning and end, time, shape, and life in the mind of Taiowa the Creator.

Then he, the infinite, conceived the finite. First he created Sotuknang to make it manifest, saying to him, 'I have created you, the first power and instrument as a person, to carry out my plan for life in endless space. I am your Uncle. You are my Nephew. Go now and lay out these universes in proper order so they may work harmoniously with one another according to my plan.'

Sotuknang did as he was commanded. From endless space he gathered that which was to be manifest as solid substance, molded it into forms, and arranged them into nine universal kingdoms: one for Taiowa the Creator, one for himself, and seven universes for the life to come.

Taiowa was pleased. 'You have done a great work according to my plan, Nephew … Now you must create life and its movement …'

Sotuknang … [then] created her who was to … be his helper. Her name was Kokyangwuti, Spider Woman.

When she awoke to life and received her name, she asked, 'Why am I here?'

'Look about you,' answered Sotuknang. 'Here is this earth we have created. It has shape and substance, direction and time, a beginning and an end. But there is no life upon it. We see no joyful movement. We hear no joyful sound. What is life without sound and movement? So you have been given the power to help us create this life. You have been given the knowledge, wisdom, and love to bless all the beings you create. That is why you are here.'

... [Spider Woman] then created from the earth trees, bushes, plants, flowers, all kinds of seed-bearers to clothe the earth, giving to each a life and name. In the same manner she created all kinds of birds and animals – molding them out of earth, covering them with her white substance cape, and singing over them ...

... 'It is very good,' said Taiowa. 'It is ready now for human life, the final touch to complete my plan.'

21. Mother Corn Creation Story (Pawnee, North America)
(From the ritual account given by the Pawnee Indian, Four Rings, to Dr. Melvin Gilmore.)

Before the World was we were all within the Earth.
Mother Corn caused movement. She gave life.
Life being given we moved towards the surface:
We shall stand erect as men!
The being is become human! He is a person!
To personal form is added strength:
Form and intelligence united, we are ready to come forth –
But Mother Corn warns us that the Earth is still in flood.
Now Mother Corn proclaims that the flood is gone, and the Earth [is] now green.
Mother Corn commands that the people ascend to the surface.
Mother Corn has gathered them together, they move half way to the surface;
Mother Corn leads them near to the surface of the Earth;
Mother Corn has gathered them together, they move half way to the surface;
Mother Corn leads them near to the surface of the Earth;
Mother Corn brings them to the surface. The first light appears!
Mother Corn leads them forth. They have emerged to the waist.
They step forth to the surface of the Earth.
Now all have come forth; and Mother Corn leads them from the East towards the West.
Mother Corn leads them to the place of their habitation ...
All is completed! All is perfect!

22. Tirawa, the Supreme God of the Pawnee (North America)
'The white man,' said the Kurahus, 'speaks of a heavenly Father; we say Tirawa atius, the Father above, but we do not think of Tirawa as a person. We think of Tirawa as in everything, as the Power which has arranged and thrown down from above everything that man needs. What the Power above, Tirawa atius, is like, no one knows; no one has been there.'

When Kawas explains to the Kurahus the meaning of the signs in the East, 'she tells him that Tirawa atius there moves upon Darkness the Night, and causes her to bring forth the Dawn. It is the breath of the new-born Dawn, the child of Night and Tirawa atius, which is felt by all the powers and all things above and below and which gives them new life for the new day ...'

The Universe

Most Native American Indians regard the universe as a series of worlds that are set one above the other, with the world inhabited by human beings at the center. Six points of space or direction – north, south, east, west, zenith (top), and nadir bottom) – link this series of worlds or cosmic sectors. Each world is associated with a sacred mountain, animal, plant, and color.

While all supernatural beings and spirits possess ambivalent powers and intentions, Indians generally distinguish between those of a good nature, including the mythical Thunderbird, mountains, rivers, minerals, and flint, and evil spirits such as monsters and water serpents. The tiny malicious creatures that haunt the woods, deserts, and waterways, and the spirits of the dead that come to inflict pain, sorrow, or death also belong to the corps of evil beings.

23. The Web of *Wakan* (Ogalala Sioux, North America)

Every object in the world has a spirit and that spirit is *waken*. Thus the spirits of the tree or things of that kind, while not like the spirit of man are also *waken*. *Wakan* comes from the *waken* beings. These *waken* beings are greater than mankind in the same way that mankind is greater than the animals. They are never born and never die. They can do many things that mankind cannot do. Mankind can pray to the *waken* beings for help. There are many of these beings but all of four kinds. The word *Wakan Tanka* means all of the *waken* beings because they are all as if one. *Wakan Tanka Kin* signifies the chief or leading *Wakan* being which is Sun. However, the most powerful of the *Wakan* beings is *Nagi Tanka*, the Great Spirit, who is also *Taku Skanskan*. *Taku Skanskan* signifies the Blue, in other words, the Sky.

24. That We May Walk Fittingly (Tewa Pueblo, North America)

O our mother the Earth, O our father the sky,
Your children are we, and with tired backs
We bring you gifts that you love.
Then weave for us a garment of brightness;
May the warp be the white light of morning,
May the weft be the red light of evening,
May the fringes be the falling rain,
May the border be the standing rainbow.
Thus we may walk fittingly where grass is green,
O our mother the earth, O our father the sky!

25. Good and Evil Spirits (Mohawk, North America)

… The Good Spirit created many things which he placed upon the earth. The Evil Spirit tried to undo the work of his brother by creating evil. The Good Spirit made tall and beautiful trees such as the pine and hemlock. The Evil Spirit stunted some trees. In others he put knots and gnarls. He covered some with thorns, and placed poison fruit on them. The Good Spirit made animals such as the deer and the bear. The Evil Spirit made poisonous animals, lizards and serpents to destroy the animals of the Good Spirit's creation. The Good Spirit made springs and streams of good, pure water. The Evil Spirit breathed poison into many of the springs. He put snakes into others. The Good Spirit made beautiful rivers protected by high hills. The Evil Spirit pushed rocks and dirt into the rivers causing the current to become swift and dangerous. Everything that the Good Spirit made, his wicked brother tried to destroy …

… That is why every person has both a bad heart and a good heart. No matter how good a man seems, he has some evil. No matter how bad a man seems, there is some good about him. No man is perfect.

Ceremonies

Native American Indians express their close, mystical unity with all forms of existence through visual representations, songs, dances, games, and ceremonies that they believe join them with the forces of nature. This concept of balance versus imbalance supersedes good and evil in the Native American conscience. What the Westerner defines as evil, the Native American recognizes as an imbalance that can be adjusted or corrected through ceremony or ritual. For example, if a hunter must kill an animal, he explains his need to the animal through ceremony. He offers a prayer and profound gratitude to the animal for the gift of its life – a sacrifice the animal makes willingly for the good of the tribe. Dying in peace, the animal's soul will come back with goodwill; otherwise it could avenge itself on the tribal community for an unjust act of killing.

Reflections

Do you find any similarities between the Native American offering gratitude and prayer to the animal he must kill for food and giving thanks before you eat a meal?

Ceremonies also mark important times of the year, such as the winter and summer solstices and the spring and fall equinoxes, thus reminding people of their responsibilities during planting and harvesting, and of other behavior that is appropriate to the changing seasons. Agricultural societies stress communal ceremonies that are interwoven with the seasonal cycle. Among nomadic societies curing ceremonies are predominant. Song, dances, games, and religious ritual express the people's closeness with their deities, who appear in visual form to share in the celebration. Such physical expression of mystical experiences brings people closer to the mysteries and unseen powers of the world – the creators, the spirits, and one's ancestors. Also, through complex initiation ceremonies tribal members teach young people their societies' views about sickness, death, and the hereafter.

26. Voices of the Spirits (Yakima, North America)

Some day the great chief above will overturn the mountains and the rocks. Then the spirits that once lived in the bones buried there will go back into them. At present those spirit live in the tops of the mountains, watching their children on earth and waiting for the great change which is to come. The voices of these spirits can be heard in the mountains at all times. Mourners who wail for their dead hear spirit voices reply, and thus they know that their lost ones are always near.

Reflections

Do you believe that ghosts or spirits of the dead can affect people who are living in the world?

---

27. Mountain Chant Ceremony (Navajo, North America)

The voice that beautifies the land!
The voice above,
The voice of the thunder,
Among the dark clouds
Again and again it sounds,
The voice that beautifies the land.

The voice that beautifies the land !
The voice below,
The voice of the grasshopper,
Among the flowers and grasses
Again and again it sounds,
The voice that beautifies the land.

28. Grandmother Earth (Sioux, North America)

We shall burn the sweet grass as an offering to *Wakan-Tanka*, and the fragrance of this will spread throughout the heaven and earth; it will make the four-leggeds, the wingeds, the star peoples of the heavens, and all things as relatives. From you, O Grandmother Earth, who are lowly, and who support us as does a mother, this fragrance will go forth; may its power be felt throughout the universe, and my it purify the feet and hands of the two-leggeds, that they may walk forward upon the sacred earth, raising their heads to *Wakan-Tanka*!

29. An Arapaho Ceremonial Prayer (North America)

(A Woman, consecrated by a priest, impersonates the Mother of creation.)

My Father, have pity upon us! Remember that we are your children since the time you created the heavens and the earth, with a man and woman!

Our Grandfather, the Central Moving Body, who gives light, watch us in the painting of the belt which our Father directed, as it is before us! Now speak to your servant who is to wear the belt! Look at her with good gifts, and may she do this for the benefit of the new people (children) so that this tribe shall have strength and power in the future!...

We cannot cease praying to you, my Father, Man-Above, for we desire to live on this earth, which we are now about to paint on this occasion. We have given this belt to the sweet smoke for our purity hereafter. May our thought reach to the sky where there is holiness. Give us good water and an abundance of food!

Shamans

All Native American tribes recognize the importance of shamans, or medicine men or women. These individuals are powerful and dangerous mediators between the human and spirit worlds. Shamans are healers and diviners – holy men and women – who have the ability to become transformed into animals, birds, and mythical beings. They can travel to the homes of these creatures, commune and sometimes do battle with them, gain new knowledge from them, and form new power relationships.

The people depend on their shaman, whose role combines the functions of a holy healer, prophet, and priest. Shamans communicate with the gods, perform religious ceremonies, and treat illness with medicine, magic, and religion. Prophesy, clairvoyance, spiritualism, herbs, roots, pollen, leaves, and religious practices all form part of the shaman's powers and techniques. Only he or she has the holy power to exorcise evil forces that consume body and mind with sickness, and to restore impaired individuals as productive members of society through the performance of appropriate rituals.

Reflections

Do you, as Native Americans, think that healers (medicine men and women) should be holy? Would it make any difference to a patient's well-being if their doctor is or is not holy?

---

30. The 'Enlightenment' of the Eskimo Shaman (Siberia)

The *angakoq* (lighting or enlightenment) consists 'of a mysterious light which the shaman suddenly feels in his body, inside his head, within the rain, an inexplicable searchlight, a luminous fire, which enables him to see in the dark, both literally and metaphorically speaking, for he can now, even with closed eyes, see through darkness and perceive things and coming events which are hidden from others: thus they look into the future and into the secrets of others.'

The candidate obtains this mystical light after long hours of waiting, sitting on a bench in his hut and invoking the spirits. When he experiences it for the first time 'it is as if the house in which he is suddenly rises; he sees far ahead of him, through mountains, exactly as if the earth were one great plain, and his eyes could reach to the end of the earth. Nothing is hidden from him any longer; not only can he see things far, far away, but he can also discover souls, stolen souls, which are either kept concealed in far, strange lands or have been taken up or down to the Land of the Dead.'

31. A Powerful Shaman (Apache, North America)

'My white brother,' an Apache shaman told Reagan, 'you probably will not believe it, but I am all powerful. I will never die. If you shoot me, the bullet will not enter my flesh, or if it enters it will not hurt me … If you stick a knife in my throat, thrusting it upwards, it will come out through my skull at the top of my head … I am all powerful. If I wish to kill any one, all I need to do is to thrust out my hand and touch him and he dies. My power is like that of a god.'

32. Is This Real, This Life I am Living? (Pawnee, North America)

Let us see, is this real,
Let us see, is this real,
This life I am living?
You, Gods, who dwell everywhere,
Let us see, is this real,
This life I am living?

33. You Cannot Harm Me (Dakota, North America)

You cannot harm me,
    you cannot harm
    one who has dreamed a dream like mine.

Sacred Pipe

The sacred pipe, symbol of the oneness of all existence, is accorded a high place of honor. Essentially a medium of prayer, it is used for religious ceremonies, the ratification of contracts and treaties, the reception of important guests, and the declaration of war and peace. The sacred pipe invokes spirits for a safe journey, and for all activity that requires the bond of sincerity and brotherhood. When Native American Indians pray with the pipe, it is believed that the smoke rising from it will carry their message to the spirits.

34. The Meaning of the Sacred Pipe (Sioux, North America)

With this sacred pipe you will walk upon the Earth; for the Earth is your Grandmother and Mother, and She is sacred. Every step that is taken upon Her should be as a prayer. The bowl of this pipe is of red stone; it is the Earth. Carved in the stone and facing the center is this buffalo calf who represents all the four-leggeds who live upon your Mother. The stem of the pipe is of wood, and this represents all that grows upon the Earth. And these twelve feathers which hang here where the stem fits into the bowl … represent the eagle and all the wingeds of the air. All these peoples, and all the things of the universe, are joined to you who smoke the pipe – all send their voices to *Wakan-Tanka*, the Great Spirit. When you pray with this pipe, you pray for and with everything.

Songs and Prayers

35. Prayer (Blackfoot, North America)
Mother Earth, have pity on us and give us food to eat!
Father, the Sun, bless all our children and may our paths be straight!

36. Song (Cheyenne, North America)
The solid sky,
the cloudy sky,
the good sky,
the straight sky.

The earth produces herbs.
The herbs cause us to live.
They cause long life.
They cause us to be happy.

The good life,
may it prevail with the air.
May it increase.
May it be straight to the end.

Sweet Medicine's earth is good.
Sweet Medicine's earth is completed.
Sweet Medicine's earth follows the eternal ways.
Sweet Medicine's earth is washed and flows.

37. The Peace Hymn (Iroquois Nation, North America)
To the great Peace bring we greeting!
To the dead chief's kindred, greeting!
To the warriors round him, greeting!
To the mourning women, greeting!
These our grandsires' words repeating,
Graciously, O grandsires, hear us!

Summary

Primal religions are basically oral traditions that include stories (myths), symbols, and ceremonies handed down from generation to generation. There is no single primal religion, but as many religions as there are tribes and societies. Each has its own spiritual tradition, but all primal religions believe in a divine creator, an orderly universe, animism, the interrelationship of humans with nature, and the power of the shaman.

Africa, the evolutionary home of human beings over the course of more than a million years, reveals archeological evidence of religious practices as early as 30,000 BCE. Although sub-Saharan culture developed separate customs and values, they all share belief in a High God, rites of passage, prayers for fertility, ancestor worship, and witchdoctors or shamans.

Most African religions believe that after the High God created the world and all things in it, human beings disobeyed him and the High God withdrew. Although he continues to sustain the world, human beings cannot find him. Lesser gods and spirits are now in closer touch with the people. If people want good crops, good hunting, and a large population, they must appease the lesser gods and spirits with worship and sacrifice to keep them happy.

Early Aborigines roamed the Australian continent 40,000 years ago. For thousands of years, Aborigines have believed that 'The Dreaming' is the source of life and the spiritual power that sustains the world. Within the Dreaming, the High God and powerful deities created the world and all of its inhabitants. The universe is made up of a social structure that allows interplay between the spiritual and natural worlds. In the Dreaming, deities, humans, and animals share a common totemic bond.

Aborigines turn to medicine-men or shamans for healing. Shamans are gifted individuals who have the ability to tap into unseen mysterious forces. Shamans cast out mental, emotional, and physical diseases and they can ensure victory in war.

The Polynesian islands are found within a 3,000-mile-long triangle extending from Hawaii in the north Pacific, New Zealand in the southwest, and Easter Island in the southeast. The oral traditions followed the Polynesians wherever they settled because they carried with them their gods, their heroes, and their sacred myths.

Through ritual and prayer, the Polynesians summoned the gods to protect the canoe-builders, house-builders, and fishermen. If the heart of a Polynesian was not pure, disaster and death would follow.

Native American Indians began to arrive in the Americas approximately 40,000 years ago. Religion is a vital aspect of all Native American societies. They share belief in a High God, usually called the Great Spirit, and have a profound reverence for Mother, or Grandmother, Earth. They deeply respect the natural order of things and seek in their lives the orderly pattern that nature possesses. Their basic goal in life is to be in harmony with the Great Spirit and with the vital forces of nature.

Native Americans express their relationship with all existence through songs, dances, games, and ceremonies. Ceremonies also mark important times of the year. Death is included as part of the recurring cycle of events.

Primal Religions Today

After contact with Christianity and Western European culture, few people in the primal traditions live as their ancestors did. Urban culture has spread over the earth destroying native habitat and their religions. Some of the greatest threats to oral religions are mining interests, logging, oil drilling, creation of artificial snow, and the expansion of proselytizing religions, especially Christianity and Islam.

However, some of their basic beliefs remain strong, and they retain their identity as they participate in modern society. For example, in Africa, Australia, the Pacific, and North America, the people are attempting to renew the practices of their traditional ways. In Africa there is a reawakening of tribal ceremonies and dance. Independent African churches have sprung up throughout the land blending elements of Christian scripture with traditional African rituals. Australian Aborigines continue to view themselves as caretakers of the land by strongly protesting the destruction of the environment. Recent political achievements have strengthened the Aborigines' ability to assert their own culture and mores. In New Zealand there is a revival of Maori culture in canoe-building, language and dance. In Hawaii hula schools are flourishing as are traditional Hawaiian religious services. Despite the vast changes in most aspects of their lives, Native Americans' basic beliefs and elements of their traditional 'lifeways' remain strong. Many seek to maintain or re-establish the customs of their forebears. Reservation schools and Indian colleges offer curricula that are now designed to serve the needs of Native Americans who intend to participate in modern society while retaining their tribal identity. The sensitivity of the oral traditions to the environment and their ability to see nature as sacred is having a deeply positive influence on civilization today.

Timeline

African

c. 5 to 2.5 million BCE	Evidence points to a common human ancestry originating in Africa from the emergence of a humanlike species in eastern Africa.
c. 6000,000 to 200,000 BCE	The earliest true human being in Africa, Homo sapiens. Hunters and gatherers, nomadic groups throughout Africa.
c. 25,000 to 10,000 BCE	Rock paintings. May depict religious objects.
c. 6,000 to 4000 BCE	River people along Nile, Niger, and Congo rivers. Cyclopian stone tombs for the dead. Mathematical abacus. First domestication of animals.
c. 4500 BCE	Ancient Egyptians begin using burial texts to accompany their dead – first-known written documents.

Australian Aborigines

c. 120,000 years ago	People clear land by using fires.
c. 60,000 years ago	Three human remains found near Lake Mungo.
c. 56,000 years ago	Use of rock shelters, stone tools, and red ochre pigments for rock painting or body decoration.
c. 45,000 years ago	Rock engravings made in South Australia – the earliest dated petroglyphs.
c. 30,000 years ago	Evidence of bread making – oldest in the world. Man buried in a shallow grave with forearm bones

	stained pink from ochre. Signs of spiritual and creative life.
c. 26,000 years ago	The body of a woman provides the earliest evidence of ritual cremation in the world.
c. 8,000 years ago	Earliest visible evidence of Aboriginal belief connected with the rainbow Serpent. This became the longest continuing belief in the world

Polynesian

Ancient Polynesians belonged to the stone-age culture. They may have descended from the ancient sailing peoples of Southeast Asia known as Austronesians. During their migrations the Polynesians carried their oral traditions with them.

c. 4,000 BCE	Voyaged around the archipelagoes of the Western Pacific, expanding eastward. Passed the Solomon Islands.
c. 1100 BCE	Arrived at Tonga and Samoa. Migrated eastward.
c. 300 BCE	Reached the Marquesas Islands (Hiva). Migrated east.
c. 300 CE	Arrived at Easter Island. Migrated north.
c. 400 CE	Arrived in the Hawaiian Islands. Migrated south.
c. 1000 CE	Arrived in New Zealand.

Native American

Timeline refers to general characteristics of the Native American people – north, south, east, and west.

c. 60,000 to 30,000 years ago	Arrival of groups of people from northeast Asia. Hunting culture. Religion: animal ceremonialism, shamanism.
c. 8000 to 5000 BCE	Religious rituals around the gathering of plant foods. Also shamanism, sacred songs, and dances.
c. 5000 BCE	Settlement in villages. Constructed burial mounds. Religious beliefs in plant spirits and ancestor spirits. Sacred songs and dances.
c. 1500 BCE to 100 CE	Evidence of burial mounds. Mother Earth statuettes.
c. 300 BCE to 700 CE	Ceremonial centers and cosmological symbolism. Sacred objects, songs, and dances.
c. 1 to 500 CE	Pueblo houses and ceremonial chambers.
c. 700 to 800 CE	Beginning of basket-maker period. Ceremonial symbolism and fertility religion. Sacred objects, songs, and dances.
c. 1000 to 1400 CE	Mississippian culture enters the eastern plains and prairies introducing cosmological symbolism and ceremonialism. The belief systems become common to eastern and western tribes.

c. 1100 to 1200 C E   Founding of the Hopi pueblo of Oraibi – the oldest
                             living village in the United States.

Study Questions

1. What motivated the earliest humans to move from place to place?
2. What is the meaning of the world 'primal'?
3. Why does no single primal religion exist?
4. According to archeological evidence, how long have religious observances been practiced by human beings?
5. Explain the significance of the shaman in primal religions.
6. Why did the African High God have little contact with the world and its inhabitants?
7. How many years ago were Africans burying human corpses in a manner that showed concern for the body after death?
8. What art forms reveal primal African culture and civilization?
9. According to the Maori, how did woman originate?
10. Explain the meaning of the word 'aborigine.'
11. Why is 'The Dreaming' important to the Aborigines?
12. What is the significance of initiation rites to the Aborigines?
13. Today, the Aborigines make up what percent of the Australian population?
14. How many Aboriginal languages have been identified?
15. Name the major Polynesian islands.
16. During a Polynesian ritual, what could cause disaster and death?
17. Name three of the characters found in all primal Polynesian stories.
18. Who were the first people to inhabit the North American continent?
19. In Native American mythology what are the ambivalent powers of supernatural beings?
20. What is the importance of ceremonies among Native Americans?
21. What is the role of the shaman in Native American societies?
22. What is the significance of Spider Woman in the Hopi creation myth?

Suggested Reading

African Tribal Religions
1. Mbiti, John (1986), *Introduction to African Religion*. London: Heinemann.
2. Murphy, Joseph M. (1994), *Working the Spirit: Ceremonies of the African Diaspora*. Boston: Beacon Press.
3. Mutwa, Vusamuzula Credo. (1998), *Indaba My Children: African Folktales*. Northampton, MA: Interlink Publishing Group.
4. Voeks, Robert A. (1997), *Sacred Leaves of Candomble: African Magic, Medicine and Religion in Brazil*. Austin: University of Texas Press.
5. Willett, Frank, (1993), *African Art*. Rev. ed., London: Thames and Hudson.

Australian Aboriginal Religion
1. Barwood, Lee and Ehrich, Joanne (2007), *Klassic Koalas: Ancient Aboriginal Tales in New Retelling*. Australia: Koala Jo Publishing.

2. Berndt, Ronald M. and Berndt, Catherine H. (1994), *The Speaking Land: Myth and Story in Aboriginal Australia*. Rochester, VT: Inner Traditions.
3. Smith, Ramsey W. (2003), *Myths and Legends of the Australian Aborigines*. New York: Dover Publications.
4. Thomas, William Jenkyn. (2007), *Some Myths and Legends of the Australian Aborigines*. http://www.forgottenbooks.org: Forgotten Books.

Polynesian Oral Traditions
1. Beckwith, Martha W. (1997), *Hawaiian Mythology*. Honolulu: University of Hawaii Press.
2. Dixon, Roland B. (2007), *Oceanic Mythology*. BiblioBazaar.
3. Kirch, Patrick Vinton (1997), *The Lapita Peoples: Ancestors of the Oceanic World*. New Jersey: Wiley-Blackwell.
4. Trompf, Garry. (1995), *The Religions of Oceania*. New York: Routledge.

Native American Religions
1. Brown, Joseph Epes. (1989), *The Sacred Pipe: Black Elk's Account of the Seven Rites of the Oglala Sioux*. Norman: University of Oklahoma Press.
2. Nerburn, Kent. (1999), *The Wisdom of the Native Americans*. Navato, CA: New World Library.
3. Mcgea, Ed. (1990), *Mother Earth Spirituality: Native American Paths to Healing Ourselves and Our World*. San Francisco: HarperOne.
4. Waters, Frank. (1969), *Book of the Hopi*. New York: Viking Press.

Sources

1. Edwin W. Smith, ed. (1950), *African Ideas of God: A Symposium* (second edition). London, p.159, quoted in Mircea Eliade, (1967), *Essential Sacred Writings From Around the World*. San Francisco: HarperSanFrancisco, p. 6.
2. Dominque Zahan (1979), *The Religion, Spirituality, and Thought of Traditional Africa*, trans, K.E. Martin and L.M. Martin. Chicago: University of Chicago Press.
3. Edwin W. Smith and A.M. Dale. 1920), *The Ida-speaking People of Northern Rhodesia*. II. London, p. 199, quoted from *Essential Sacred Writings*, Mircea Eliade, pp. 8–9.
4. Alfonso M. d'nola, comp. (1961), *The Prayers of Man: From Primitive Peoples to Present Times*, ed. Patrick O'Conner, trans. Rex Benedict. New York: Ivan Obolensky.
5. Ikenga-Metuh, Emefie (1987), *Comparative Studies of African Traditional Religions*. Onitaha, Nigeria: IMICO Publishers.
6. Melville J. Herskovits. (1958), *Dahomey*, vol. 2. New York: J.J. Augustin, p. 101.
7. Susan Feldman, ed. (1963), *African Myths and Tales*. New York: Dell Publishing, pp. 37–39.
8. N. Smart and R.D Hecht, eds. (1982), *Sacred Texts of the World: A Universal Anthology* New York: Crossroad, p. 384.
9. Paul Radin. (1937), *Primitive Religion: Its Nature and Origin*. New York: Viking Press.
10. Ikenga-Metuh. *Comparative Studies*.
11. Lorna Marshall. 'Kung Bushman Religious Beliefs.' *Africa*, XXXII (162), p. 247. quoted from Eliade, ed., *Essential Sacred Writings*, p. 268.
12. Aunty Beryl Carmichael. (2004), Australian Museum. http://www.dreamtime.net.au/creation/text.htm

13. Spencer and J. Gillen. (1904), *The Northern Tribes of Central Australia*. London, pp. 480–481, quoted in Eliade, ed., *Essential Sacred Writings*, p. 428.
14. A.W. Howitt. (1904), *The Native Tribes of South-East Australia*. London, pp. 406–408. Quoted in Eliade, ed., *Essential Sacred Writings*, pp. 424–426
15. E.S. Craighill Handy (1927), *Polynesian Religion*, Bernice P. Bishop Museum Bulletin 34.
16. E.S. Craighill Handy. *Polynesian Religion*.
17. Hare Hongi. (1907), 'A Maori Cosmogony.' *Journal of the Polynesian Society*, XVI, pp. 113–114.
18. Elsdon Best. (1923), 'Maori Personifications,' *Journal of the Polynesian Society*, XXXII, pp. 110–111.
19. J.A. Moerenhout. (1837), *Voyages aux iles du Grand Ocean*. II. Paris, p. 83.
20. Frank Waters. (1969), *Book of the Hopi*. New York: The Viking Press. pp. 3–5.
21. H.B. Alexander. (1953), *The World's Rim*. Lincoln: University of Nebraska Press, p. 89.
22. H.B. Alexander. *The World's Rim*, p. 132.
23. J.R. Walker. (1917), *The Sun Dance and Other Ceremonies of the Oglala Division of the Teton Dakota*. American Museum of Natural History, Anthropological Papers 16, pt. 2, pp. 152–153.
24. Herbert J. Spinden. (1976), *Songs of the Tewa*. Santa Fe: Sunstone Press.
25. Andrew Wilson, ed. (1995), *World Scripture: A Comparative Anthology of Sacred Texts* (New York: Paragon House, pp. 311–312.
26. Richard Erdoes and Alfonso Ortiz. (1984), *American Indian Myths and Legends*. New York: Pantheon, p. 118.
27. Washington Matthews, trans. (1994), *Navaho Legends*. Salt Lake: University of Utah Press, p. 27.
28. Joseph Epes Brown. (1971), *The Sacred Pipe*. Baltimore: Penguin, p. 69.
29. G.A. Dorsey, (1903), 'The Arapaho Sun Dance,' Field Columbia Museum Anthropology Series, IV, p. 74.
30. Knud Rasmussen (1930), *Intellectual Culture of the Iglulik Eskimos*. Copenhagen, pp. 112–113, quoted in Roger Walsh, *The Spirit of Shamanism*. 1990, Los Angeles: J. Tarcher, p. 52.
31. Albert B. Readen. (1930), *Notes on the Indians of the Fort Apache Region*. American Museum of Natural History, Anthropological Papers XXXV, p. 391.
32. D.G. Brinton. (1890), *Essays of an Amricanist*. n.t., p. 292.
33. William Brandon, ed. (1971), *The Magic World*. New York: William Morrow.
34. Brown, *The Sacred Pipe*, pp. 5–7.
35. Walter Mc Clintock. (1968), *The Old North Trail, or Life, Legends, and Religion of the Blackfeet Indians* (reprint). Lincoln: University of Nebraska Press.
36. Truman Michelson. 'Notes from the Bull Thigh, Sept. 4, 1910,' MS 2684–a Smithsonian Institute, Washington D.C.
37. Paul Wallace. (1994), *The Iroquois Book of Life: White Roots of Peace* (Santa Fe: Clear Light Publishers, p. 86.

2 Hindu Wisdom

Om

*The Sanskrit word Om or (Aum) is the primordial sound
by which the earth was created. The Om symbol represents
the waking state, the deep sleep state, and the dream state.*

Early Religions In India

India's earliest known inhabitants came from the Indus River Valley in present
day northwest India and Pakistan. They were nomadic hunters and food gatherers
who wintered in the lush valley and moved each summer to the nearby cool hills.
They began to change their pattern of living in approximately 4000 BCE, gradually
settling into relatively stable agricultural communities. In another thousand
years, they had developed a village culture, and by 2500 BCE, an advanced urban
civilization existed in the region, named after the city of Harappa.

The Harappans, whose civilization covered an area wider than either ancient
Mesopotamia or Egypt, abandoned nomadic life to settle and populate several
large cities that were each methodically designed and well organized. Many
archeological findings indicate that religions in this early culture viewed the earth
as the giver of life and that they worshipped a mother goddess.

The Harrapans' burial customs confirm their belief in an afterlife. Sometimes
adorned with personal ornaments, bodies were carefully buried in cemeteries with
pottery placed beside them in their graves. At one burial site, pairs of skeletons
found in several graves suggest that wives practiced self-cremation, or 'suttee.' By
throwing themselves on their husband's funeral pyres (fires), the wives sought to
join their mates in life beyond death.

The Harappan civilization declined during the nineteenth century BCE, and
finally fell to invaders from the north in approximately 1500 BCE. However, its
contributions to Indian culture and religion lasted far longer. Succeeding Indian
societies retained the Harrapans' reverence for animals and mysticism, both of
which characterize the predominant Indian Hindu experience today.

The Aryan Invasion

About 2000 BCE, northern invaders known as Aryans ('noble') crossed the Iranian plateau and entered India through canyons gouged by melting snows in the Hindu-Kush Mountains of the northwest. As they spread further into India along the Indus and Ganges Rivers, the tall, fair-skinned Aryans relentlessly pushed the dark-skinned original inhabitants, called Dravidians, into southern India, where the Dravidians finally established their own society. The Aryans then dominated northern India for two thousand years, until 500 CE or about the time that the Roman Empire fell to invaders from northern Europe.

The Aryan Language

The Aryans appear to have been a practical, optimistic, and fun-loving people who attributed to their gods personal characteristics that were similar to their own. Although warlike, the Aryans clearly had a philosophical turn of mind, devoting detailed thought to the mysteries of the origin of the universe. They asked the 'hows' and 'whys' that form the root of philosophical speculation and religious belief in every age and culture. They addressed such provocative questions in terms of human personality and morality, and they attributed events in nature to superhuman persons or gods who possessed the personalities of human being.

Reflections

Like the Aryans, do you believe that we attribute human personality traits to God? Philosopher Karl Marx and psychoanalyst Sigmund Freud believed that we create God in our own image. What do you think?

The Vedic Period

India's Vedic period takes its name from the ancient series of sacred texts called Vedas (sacred knowledge). The Vedas recorded Aryan ideas on the nature of humankind, the world, and relations between humans and gods. This vast literary collection contains hymns, chants, and prayers as well as the names and histories of various tribes. Dialogues throughout the collection seek answers to questions people have always wondered about: What exists beyond the gods? What is the relation, if any, between actions and their consequences? What knowledge do humans have of themselves?

The Vedas reveal the Aryans' belief that behind the regularities of nature stands an eternal and immutable law of order and justice. This law renders the world a moral stage on which everything good, bad, or in between is earned and deserved. To realize a good life, we naturally seek to avoid suffering. According to the Vedas, becoming attached to what we do not have and, in fact, can never have causes suffering. It follows that if we can cultivate a spirit of non-attachment to unavailable objects, our suffering will cease. This concept remains characteristic of Hindu and Buddhist philosophical and religious ideas to the present day.

> **Reflections**
> Have you ever desired a person, object or a job that you could not have? Would non-attachment have made you happier, or did you prefer to suffer?

The Early Vedas

The oldest document in any Indo-European language, and perhaps the oldest religious text in the world, is a collection of hymns and chants called the *Rig-Veda* ('the Veda of stanzas of praise'). Written in early Sanskrit, the Rig-Veda is a collection of hymns composed over several centuries, reaching its final form around 900 BCE. It is one of four Vedas that inform the Hindu religion. The others are: *Sama Veda*, a collection of chants; *Yajur Veda*, hymns for ritual sacrifices; and *Atharva Veda*, a collection of incantations that are used for magical and medicinal purposes. Other traditional collections of ritual and philosophical texts are the Brahmanas, the Aranyakas, and the Upanishads.

Rig-Veda

1. He, O Men, is Indra. Rig-Veda II: 12: 1–5, 13

1. The chief wise god who as soon as born
     surpassed the gods in power;
   Before whose vehemence the two worlds trembled by reason
     of the greatness of his valor; he. O men, is Indra.
2. Who made firm the quaking earth
     who set at rest the agitated mountains;
   Who measures out the air more widely,
     who supported heaven: he, O men, is Indra.
3. Who having slain the serpent released the seven streams.
     Who drove out the cows by the unclosing of Vala,
   Who between two rocks has produced fire,
     Victor in battles: he, O men, is Indra.
4. ... Who has made subject the Dasa colour [the non-Aryan population] and
     has made it disappear;
   Who, like a sinning gambler the stake,
   Has taken possession of the foe: he, O men, is Indra.
5. The terrible one of whom they ask 'where is he,'
     of whom they also say 'he is not';
   He diminishes the possessions of the foe like the stakes of
     gamblers. Believe in him: he, O men, is Indra ...
13. Even Heaven and Earth bow down before him;
     before his vehemence even the mountains are afraid
   Who is known as the Soma-drinker [mysterious drink of the gods],
     holding the bolt in his arm; he, O men, is Indra.

Hymns to Agni, the God of Fire

2. Agni, Be With Us. Rig-Veda I: 1, 7, 8, 9

1. I praise Agni, domestic priest, divine minister of sacrifice,
    Invoker, greatest bestower of wealth ...
7. To thee, dispeller of the night, O Agni, day by day with prayer,
    Bringing thee reverence, we come;
8. Ruler of sacrifices, guard of Law eternal, radiant one,
    Increasing in thine own abode.
9. Be to us easy of approach, even as a father to his son:
    Agni, be with us for our weal.

3. Agni, the Lord of Men Rig-Veda II: 1, 9, 14

1. Thou, Agni, shining in thy glory through the days art brought
    to life from out the waters, from the stone;
    From out the forest trees and herbs that grow on ground, thou,
    sovereign lord of men, art generated pure.
9. Agni, men seek thee as a father with their prayers, win thee, bright-formed,
    to brotherhood with holy act ...
14. By thee, O Agni, all the immortal guileless gods eat with thy
    mouth the oblation that is offered them.
    By thee do mortal men give sweetness to their drink.
    Pure art thou born, the embryo of the plants of earth.

4. New Hymn for Agni. Rig-Veda VII: 4, 8, 10, 13, 15

4. I have begotten this new for Agni, falcon of the sky:
    will he not give us of his wealth?
8. Shine forth at night and morn: through thee with
    fires are we provided well ...
10. Bright, purifier, meet for praise,
    immortal with refulgent glow,
    Agni drives Rakshasas [demons] away.
13. Agni preserve us from distress:
    consume our enemies, O God,
    Eternal, with thy hottest flames
15. Do thou preserve us ... from sorrow,
    from the wicked man,
    Infallible! By day and night.

3. Hymn to Varuna, the All-knowing God. Rig-Veda 1: 3, 7, 9–11

3. To gain thy mercy, Varuna, with hymns we bind thy heart,
    as binds
    The charioteer his tethered horse ...
7. He knows the path of birds that fly through heaven, and
    sovereign of the sea,
    He knows the ships that are thereon ...
9. He knows the pathway of the wind, the spreading, high and
    mighty wind;

He knows the gods who dwell above.

10. Varuna, true to holy law, sits down among his people; he,
    most wise, sits there to govern all.

11. From thence perceiving he beholds all wondrous things, both
    what hath been,
    And what hereafter will be done.

6. Who Can Say How Creation Happened? Rig-Veda X: 129: 1–7

1. Then even nothingness was not, nor existence.
    There was no air then, nor the heavens beyond it.
   What covered it? Where was it? In whose keeping?
    Was there then a cosmic water, in depths unfathomed?

2. Then there were neither death nor immortality,
    nor was there then the torch of night and day.
   The One breathed windlessly and self-sustaining.
    There was that One then, and there was no other.

3. At first there was only darkness wrapped in darkness.
    All this was only unillumined water.
   That One which came to be, enclosed in nothing,
    arose at last, born of the power of heat.

4. In the beginning desire descended on it –
    that was the primal seed, born of the mind.
   The sages who have searched their hearts with wisdom
    know that which is, is kin to that which is not.

5. And they have stretched their cord across the void,
    and know what was above, and what below,
   Seminal powers made fertile mighty forces.
    Below was strength, and over it was impulse.

6. But, after all, who knows, and who can say
    whence it all came, and how creation happened?
   The gods themselves are later than creation,
    so who knows truly whence it has arisen?

7. Whence all creation had its origin,
    he, whether he fashioned it or whether he did not,
   he, who surveys it all from highest heaven,
    he knows – or maybe even he does not know.

7. King Varuna is There. Atharva-Veda IV: 16: 1–5

1. The great guardian among these (gods) sees as if from anear. He that thinketh he is moving stealthily – all this the gods know.

2. If a man stands, walks, or sneaks about, if he goes slinking away, if he goes into his hiding-place; if two persons sit together and scheme, King Varuna is there as a third, and knows it.

3. Both this earth here belongs to King Varuna, and also yonder broad sky whose boundaries are far away. Moreover these two oceans are the loins of Varuna; yea, he is hidden in this small (drop of) water.

4. He that should flee beyond the heaven far away would not be free from King

Varuna. His spies [stars] come hither from heaven, with a thousand eyes do they watch over the earth.

5. King Varuna sees through all that is between heaven and earth and all that is beyond. He has counted the winkings of men's eyes. As a (winning) gamester puts down his dice, thus does he establish these (laws).

The Vedic Caste System (*Varna*)

About 500 BCE, the caste system had become firmly established, although the Rig-Veda had earlier implied the beginnings of the caste system by describing the four groups of people. These four groups were: (1) *Brahmins,* or priests, who have divine knowledge. Born with an intuitive grasp of high moral values, they were the religious and educational teachers in society. (2) *Kshatriyas,* born with the ability to organize, were military leaders or administrators. Their duty was to protect the people and administer a just and good government. (3) Born with business savvy, the *Vaisyas,* or merchants, provided for the community's economic needs. (4) The *Shudras* had little ability to concentrate for long periods of time and so needed supervision. They worked mainly as laborers, cultivating the land and serving the three upper castes.

The three upper castes were called 'twice born' and the lower shudra caste the 'once born.' Members of each group had specific duties that they must obey. In time, the Brahmins became the highest group, serving as mediators between the gods and humans at sacrificial rituals. They received donations for their priestly functions and enjoyed important privileges, such as exemption from taxes.

Later in the Vedic Age, outcastes or 'untouchables' were added to the original four castes. They had to live outside the cities and perform duties no one else wanted, such as cremating corpses and cleaning latrines. From this basic five-tier arrangement other groups or sub-groups developed. Various prohibitions against mixing castes in marriage, dining, drinking, and so on became fixed and many remain to some degree in Hindu culture today, although modern India's constitution removed 'untouchables' from the caste system.

Traditionally, one's caste determines what one eats, and the higher the caste the more restricted its diet. An orthodox Brahmin, for example, will eat grain cooked in water only if the cook is another high-caste Brahmin. The caste system affects not only food but also drinking, marrying, and all kinds of fraternizing.

Reflections

Do you agree with classical Hinduism that by our very nature each of us is best suited to a particular lifestyle? Is there a method similar to the Hindus for defining people's position in your society?

---

8. Creation of the Caste System. Rig-Veda X: 90: 1–3, 6, 8–14
(*Here these social divisions are given a transcendent sanction.*)

1. A thousand heads had Purusha, a thousand eyes, a thousand feet.
   He covered earth on every side, and spread ten fingers' breadth beyond.

2. This Purusha is all that yet hath been and all that is to be;
   The Lord of Immortality which waxes greater still by food.
3. So mighty is his greatness; yea, greater than this is Purusha.
   All creatures are one-fourth of him, three-fourths eternal life in heaven ...
6. When gods prepared the sacrifice with Purusha as their offering,
   Its oil was spring, the holy gift was autumn; summer was the wood ...
8. From that great general sacrifice the dripping fat was gathered up.
   He formed the creatures of air, and animals both wild and tame.
9. From that great general sacrifice ... hymns were born;
   Therefrom the metres were produced ...
10. From it were horses born, from it all creatures with two rows of teeth;
    From it were generated kine, from it the goats and sheep were born.
11. When they divided Purusha how many portions did they make?
    What do they call his mouth, his arms? What do they call his thighs
       and feet?
12. The Brahman [Brahmin, priestly caste] was his mouth, of both his arms
       was the Rajanya [Kshatriya] made.
    His thighs became the Vaishya, from his feet the Shudra was produced.
13. The moon was gendered from his mind, and from his eye the sun
       had birth;
    Indra and Agni from his mouth were born, and Vayu from his breath.
14. Forth from his navel came mid-air; the sky was fashioned from his head.
    Earth from his feet, and from his ear the regions. Thus they formed
       the worlds.

9. Duties of the Four Castes. Early Vedas
Brahmins, Kshatriyas, Vaishyas, and Shudras are the four castes. The first three
of these are called twice-born. They must perform with mantras [sacred words
or chants] the whole number of ceremonies, which begin with impregnation and
end with the ceremony of burning the dead body. Their duties are as follows. A
Brahmin teaches the Veda. A Kshatriya has constant practice in arms. A Vaishya
tends cattle. A Shudra serves the twice-born. All the twice-born are to sacrifice
and study the Veda. Their modes of livelihood are as follows. A Brahmin sacrifices
for others and receives alms. A Kshatriya protects the world. A Vaishya engages
in farming, keeps cows, trades, lends money at interest, and grows seeds. A
Shudra engages in all branches of crafts. In times of distress, each caste may
follow the occupation of that below it in rank. Duties common to all castes
are patience, truthfulness, restraint, purity, liberality, self-control, not to kill,
obedience toward one's gurus [teachers], visiting places of pilgrimage, sympathy,
straightforwardness, freedom from covetousness, reverence toward gods and
Brahmins, and freedom from anger.

Stages of Life (Laws of Manu)

According to the laws of caste, there are four stages of life called the Laws of Manu
that were written between 300 BCE and 300 CE. The first stage of life is the *student*
or ages ranging from about 8 through about 20 years old. Male children of the
three upper castes are initiated into the Hindu faith by the ritual of the 'sacred

thread' that could be compared to baptism in Christianity or bar mitzvah for Jews. A priest places a triple-stranded thread over the left shoulder and under the right arm of the youth. The boy then leaves home, carefully taking the first step with his right foot, and goes to live in the house of a guru. Here the student will learn the scriptures and other subjects that are appropriate to his caste. During this period in his life, the young man must remain celibate and pay close attention to his guru.

The second stage of Hindu life begins with *marriage* and includes the period when the individual's interests focus on family, vocation, and community. At this stage, one seeks to take good care of the family and become successful in the world.

The third stage is *retirement*, when the individual renounces the world, withdraws from social obligations, and goes into the forest to discover Atman/ Brahman.

In the fourth stage, the individual breaks free from all ties of time and place and lives the life of an *ascetic*. Taking no thought of the future and looking with indifference to the present, he or she lives the last stage of life 'identified with the eternal Self.'

In today's society few Hindus practice the Four Stages of Life. The fourth stage, especially, is seldom experienced. Instead, most Hindus practice the task of bettering humanity by social action, seeking to improve the world rather than renounce it.

10. Student Stage. Laws of Manu 2: 69–70

Having performed the rite of initiation, the teacher must first instruct the pupil in the rules of personal purification, conduct, fire-worship, and twilight devotions. A student who is about to begin the study of the Veda shall receive instruction after he has sipped water according to the sacred law ... has put on clean clothing, and has brought his sexual organs under due control. At the beginning and at the end of a lesson in the Veda he must always clasp both the feet of his teacher ... The teacher, always unwearied, must say to him who is about to begin studying, 'Recite!' He shall stop when the teacher says: 'Let stoppage take place!' Let him always pronounce the syllable 'Om' at the beginning and at the end of a lesson in the Veda. Unless the syllable 'Om' precedes, the lesson will slip away from him, and unless it follows it will fade away ...

11. Householder Stage. Laws of Manu 3: 4–10

With the permission of his teacher, having bathed and performed according to the rule the ritual for returning home, a twice-born man shall marry a wife of equal caste who is endowed with auspicious bodily marks ... In connecting himself with a wife, let him carefully avoid the ten following types of families ... He must avoid a family that neglects the sacred rites, one in which no male children are born, one in which the Veda is not studied, one that has thick hair on the body, those that are subject to hemorrhoids, tuberculosis, weakness of digestion, epilepsy, or white and black leprosy. Let him not marry a young woman with reddish hair, nor one who has a redundant body part, nor one who is sickly, nor one either with no hair on the body or too much hair. Let him not marry one who is too talkative or has red eyes. Let him not marry one named after a constellation, a tree, or a river, nor one bearing the name of a low caste, or of a mountain, nor one named after a bird, a snake, or a slave, nor one whose name inspires terror. Let him wed a female free from bodily defects and who has an agreeable name. She must have the graceful gait of a swan or of an elephant, moderate hair on the body and on the head, small teeth, and soft limbs.

12. Stage of Retirement. Laws of Manu 6: 1–4
A twice-born Snataka, who has lived according to the law of householders, taking a firm resolution and keeping his organs in subjection, may dwell in the forest. He must duly observe the rules given below. When a householder sees his skin wrinkled, and his hair white, and the sons of his sons, then he may depart to the forest. Abandoning all food raised by cultivation, and all his belongings, he may depart into the forest. He may either commit his wife to his sons or be accompanied by her. Taking with him the sacred fire and the implements required for domestic sacrifices, he may go forth from the village into the forest and reside there, controlling his senses.

13. Ascetic Stage. Laws of Manu 6: 33–34
Having passed the third part of his natural term of life in the forest, a man may live as an ascetic during the fourth part of his existence. First he must abandon all attachment to worldly objects. He who offers sacrifices and subdues his senses, busies himself with giving alms and offerings of food, and becoming an ascetic gains bliss after death.

Reflections
Most religions and cultures recognize the importance of certain stages in life. What, if any, stages in life hold significance for you?

The Upanishads

Gradually, a totally new kind of religious and philosophical thinking sought fresh spiritual answers to questions about the origin and meaning of life and the universe. These questions were addressed in a series of thoughtful commentaries on the Vedas called the Upanishads, which means 'to sit at the feet of a master.' Students sat at the feet of a guru (teacher) to learn the truth of human nature and the world. Most of the commentaries were composed between 900 and 600 BCE by a group of religious thinkers that included some of the most enlightened philosophers and sages the world has ever known. Dissatisfied with the outwardly ritualistic kind of religion described in the earlier Vedas these philosophers wrestled with concepts of personal salvation and release from bondage to the physical world.

The new approach to religion expressed in the Upanishads soon gave rise to several movements whose devotees shared many ideas in common. These concepts included *reincarnation* – the rebirth of the soul into new lives; *karma* – the law of action and reaction, or whatever one sows one also reaps; and *moksha* – the state of final freedom and release. Strong believers in nonviolence, these devotees refused to participate in the ritual sacrifice of animals and practiced vegetarianism. By the sixth century BCE, asceticism or the practice of extreme self-deprivation, was considered the highest form of religious life in India, and it still is in Jainism and in some systems of Hinduism today.

Four elements: (1) the sense of mysticism; (2) the necessity for self-denial and self-discipline; (3) the acceptance of responsibility for one's collective deeds; and (4) the possibility of achieving eventual release from the bonds of the physical world by experiencing the true Self, were particularly influential in the development of Hinduism. The Hindu religion became the major civilizing force in Southeast Asia from the second to the ninth centuries CE and the dominant religion of India up to the present day.

The Self (*Atman*)

The Upanishads ask, 'What am I, in my deepest existence? I may appear to be a physical body, but is that what I really am? Is the 'I' that thinks the self to be a physical body also physical? Isn't the 'I' more properly the Self (Spirit/God) than the body?' The philosophers of the Upanishads concluded that no such thing exists as a personal 'I.' What we think is 'I' is actually the individual personality, or ego, which may appear real now but is actually transitory, or changing all the time. The true Self or 'I' is Spirit/God.

Reflections

Do you agree with the Hindus that your soul or spirit is one with the divinity, or do you view God as 'totally other' – separate from you?

---

14. The True Self. Chandogya Upanishad 6: 12–13

OM. There lived once a boy, Svetaketu Aruneya by name. One day his father spoke to him in this way: 'Svetaketu, go and become a student of sacred wisdom. There is no one in our family who has not studied the holy Vedas and who might only be given the name of Brahman [God] by courtesy.'

The boy left at the age of twelve and, having learnt the Vedas, he returned home at the age of twenty-four, very proud of his learning and having a great opinion of himself.

His father, observing this, said to him: 'Svetaketu, my boy, you seem to have a great opinion of yourself, you think you are learned, and you are proud. Have you asked for that knowledge whereby what is not heard is heard, what is not thought is thought, and what is not known is known?'

'What is that knowledge, father?' asked Svetaketu.

'Just as by knowing a lump of clay, my son, all that is clay can be known, since any differences are only words and the reality is clay:

Just as by knowing a piece of gold all that is gold can be known, since any differences are only words and the reality is only gold' ...

Svetaketu said: 'Certainly my honored masters knew not this themselves. If they had known, why would they not have told me? Explain to me, father.'

'So be it, my son. Place this salt in water and come to me tomorrow morning.'

Svetaketu did as he was commanded, and in the morning his father said to him: 'Bring me the salt you put into the water last night.'

Svetaketu looked into the water, but could not find it, for it had dissolved.

His father then said, 'Taste the water from this side. How is it?'

'It is salt.'

'Taste it from the middle. How is it?'

'It is salt.'

'Taste it from that side. How is it?'

'It is salt.'

'Look for the salt and come again to me.'

The son did so, saying: 'I cannot see the salt. I only see the water.'

His father then said: 'In the same way, O my son, you cannot see the Spirit. But in truth he is here. 'An invisible but subtle essence is the Spirit of the whole universe. That is Reality. That is Truth. THOU ART THAT.'

Reflections

Is this scripture verse saying that the Divine Spirit is who we truly are? Or is there another way of looking at 'Thou Art That'?

---

15. The Self in all Beings. Isa Upanishad 1–2, 4, 6–7, 17

Behold the universe in the glory of God: and all that lives and moves on earth. Leaving the transient, find joy in the Eternal: set not your heart on another's possessions…

The Spirit, without moving, is swifter than the mind; the senses cannot reach him: He is ever beyond them. Standing still, he overtakes those who run. To the ocean of his being, the spirit of life leads the streams of action.

… Who sees all beings in his own Self, and his own Self in all beings, loses all fear.

When a sage sees this great Unity and his Self has become all beings, what delusion and what sorrow can ever be near him?

… May life go to immortal life, and the body go to ashes, OM [sacred sound of reality]. Oh my soul, remember past strivings, remember! O my soul, remember past strivings, remember!

16. Brahman (God), the Unknown. Kena Upanishad I: 4–8.

What cannot be spoken with words, but that whereby words are spoken:
Know that alone to be Brahman, the Spirit; and not what people here adore.

What cannot be thought with the mind, but that whereby the mind can think:
Know that alone to be Brahman, this Spirit; and not what people here adore.

What cannot be seen with the eye, but that whereby the eye can see: Know that alone to be Brahman, the Spirit; and not what people here adore.

What cannot be heard with the ear, but that whereby the ear can hear: Know that alone to be Brahman, the Spirit; and not what people here adore.

What cannot be indrawn with breath, but that whereby breath is indrawn: Know that alone to be Brahman, the Spirit; and not what people here adore.

17. Know the Self. Katha Upanishad 3: 3-6.
Know the Atman [True Self] as Lord of a chariot; and the body as the chariot itself. Know that reason is the charioteer; and the mind indeed is the reins.

The horses, they say, are the senses; and their paths are the objects of sense. When the soul becomes one with the mind and the senses he is called 'one who has joys and sorrows'.

He who has not right understanding and whose mind is never steady is not the ruler of his life, like a bad driver with wild horses.

But he who has right understanding and whose mind is ever steady is the ruler of his life, like a good driver with well-trained horses.

18. The Razor's Edge. Katha Upanishad 3: 14-15.
Awake, arise! Strive for the Highest, and be in the Light! Sages say the path is narrow and difficult to tread, narrow as the edge of a razor.

The Atman [true Self] is beyond sound and form, without touch and taste and perfume. It is eternal, unchangeable, and without beginning or end: Indeed above reasoning. When consciousness of the Atman manifests itself, man becomes free from the jaws of death.

19. The Spirit Rules. Katha Upanishad 5: 11-12
As the sun that beholds the world is untouched by earthly impurities, so the Spirit that is in all things is untouched by external sufferings.

There is one Ruler, the Spirit that is in all things, who transforms his own form into many. Only the wise who see him in their souls attain the joy eternal.

20. Brahman Hidden in the Heart. Mundaka Upanishad 2: 1
Radiant in his light, yet invisible in the secret place of the heart, the Spirit is the supreme abode wherein dwells all that moves and breathes and sees. Know him as all that is, and all that is not, the end of love-longing beyond understanding, the highest in all beings.

21. Two Birds on the Same Tree. Mundaka Upanishad 3: Ch. 1: 1-2
There are two birds, two sweet friends, who dwell on the self-same tree. The one eats the fruits thereof, and the other looks on in silence.

The first is the human soul who, resting on that tree, though active, feels sad in his unwisdom. But on beholding the power and glory of the higher Spirit, he becomes free from sorrow.

Karma and Rebirth

According to Hinduism, this is an orderly universe. The planets, stars, and all of nature are guided by law. Karma is the eternal law of cause and effect or action and reaction – what goes around comes around.

Hindus believe there are three types of karma: (1) that operating in the present life; (2) that held over from past lives; and (3) that stored for future lives. Circumstances in the present life depend on the choices we made in a previous life, or previous lives. Choices made in our present life will determine our character and destiny for future lives. Hindus believe that we carry the whole of our past as we now create our future. The day of judgment is here and now. Once we learn our lessons, the old karma ceases and we accumulate new karma. What we sow we also reap. Thus karma signifies universal order. There is no such thing as random chance.

Reflections

Twentieth-century physicist, Albert Einstein, said that God doesn't play dice – there is no chance in the universe. That statement is similar to the Hindu concept of the law of karma. Do you agree with Einstein and the Hindus that nothing happens by chance? Do we always reap what we sow?

According to the rebirth theory, there is a long evolution of the soul during which we experience a gradual self-finding as we grow from our ego-personality into knowledge of the Atman or true Self. Suffering, pain, unhappiness, and misfortune as well as happiness and prosperity are necessary experiences of the 'soul-in-training.' It may not be possible to gain in one lifetime all the knowledge and experience needed to achieve perfection or the highest possible spiritual living. Just as physical bodies, emotions, and ways of thinking change as we mature, so will our personality change with each rebirth. As adults, we remain essentially the same person we were as infants indicating that the real person (the soul or Self) does not change in essence throughout its long evolution.

The rebirth pilgrimage proceeds in accordance with the laws of karma. Everyone must ascend through the many degrees of intelligence. Until we reach moksha (liberation), we must experience life after life in this world. According to the laws of karma and rebirth there are no special privileges or gifts to smooth the way and no miracles: everything happens according to karmic law. Each of us is currently at the stage of our physical, emotional, mental, and moral achievements. We all are exactly where we belong in the universal scheme of things. Reincarnation, insists Hinduism, gives everyone the opportunity to try and try again, with the assurance that each sincere effort will benefit the soul.

22. Who Knows God Becomes God. Mundaka Upanishad 2: 2, 8–9.

A man whose mind wanders among desires, and is longing for objects of desire, goes again to life and death according to his desires [karma]. But he who possess the End of all longing, and whose self has found fulfillment, even in his life his desires will fade away ...

As rivers flowing into the ocean find their final peace and their name and form disappear, even so the wise become free from name and form and enter into the radiance of the Supreme Spirit who is greater than all greatness.

In truth who knows God becomes God.

23. The Rebirth of the Soul. Svetesvatara Upanishad 5: 11–13

The soul is born and unfolds in a body, with dreams and desires and the food of life. And then it is reborn in new bodies, in accordance with its former works.

The Quality of the soul determines its future body: earthly or airy, heavy or light. Its thoughts and its actions can lead it to freedom, or lead it to bondage, in life after life.

But there is the God of forms Infinite, and when a man knows God he is free from all bondage …

He is an incorporeal Spirit, but he can be seen by a heart which is pure … He is God, the God of love, and when a man knows him then he leaves behind his bodies of transmigration [rebirth].

24. Liberation (Moksha) Maitri Upanishad 6: 24

If men thought of God as much as they think of the world, who would not attain liberation?

The mind should be kept in the heart as long as it has not reached the Highest End. This is wisdom, and this is liberation. Everything else is only words.

Words cannot describe the joy of the soul whose impurities are cleansed in deep contemplation – who is one with his Atman, his own Spirit. Only those who feel this joy know what it is.

Mind is indeed the source of bondage and also the source of liberation. To be bound to things of this world: this is bondage. To be free from them: this is liberation.

25. All Beings Come From Joy, Unto Joy They All Return. Taittiriya Upanishad 3: 1–6

Once Bhrigu Baruni went to his father Varuna and said: 'Father, explain to me the mystery of Brahman.'

Then his father spoke to him of the food of the earth, of the breath of life, of the one who sees, of the one who hears, of the mind that knows, and of the one who speaks. And he further said to him, 'Seek to know him from whom all beings have come, by whom they all live, and unto whom they all return. He is Brahman.'

So Bhrigu went and practiced *tapas*, spiritual prayer.

Then he thought that Brahman was the food of the earth …

Then he thought that Brahman was mind …

Then he thought that Brahman was reason …

Then he saw that Brahman is joy: for FROM JOY ALL BEINGS HAVE COME, BY JOY THEY ALL LIVE, AND UNTO JOY THEY ALL RETURN.

The Bhagavad Gita

The *Mahabharata,* an epic of more than 100,000 verses, is the longest poem in the world – thirty times longer than Milton's *Paradise Lost.* A small portion (700 verses) of the *Mahabharata* called the *Bhagavad Gita* (Bah'-guh-vuh Gee'tah), or the Lord's Song, probably dates from the fourth or fifth century BCE, and is often called the Hindu Bible.

The scene of the Bhagavad Gita is a battlefield where a fight is about to occur between the good princes and their evil cousins, whose illegal rule of the kingdom has become more and more corrupt. More than a good battle story, the Gita is also an allegory of the cosmic struggle between good and evil and of the spiritual struggle in which the prince Arjuna (representing humankind in general) is engaged with his own ego, the very obstacle to living the spiritual life. In the Gita we find the great spiritual struggle of a human soul.

The Bhagavad Gita is a dialogue between Prince Arjuna and Lord Krishna, who, as a direct incarnation of the Vishnu aspect (the savior of humans) of Brahman, manifests himself whenever the forces of evil threaten to destroy human values. But as Krishna prepares to enter the fray on the side of the good princes, Arjuna sees his relatives, friends, and childhood comrades facing him on the battlefield and is unwilling to fight against them. Succumbing to grief and despair, he throws down his weapons.

Reflections

If you, like Arjuna, were preparing to fight for the good of your country and saw your friends and relatives on the enemy's side, what would you do?

---

26. Arjuna's Distress. Bhagavad Gita 1: 34–39

ARJUNA

34. Facing us in the field of battle are teachers, fathers and sons; grandsons, grandfathers, wives' brothers; mothers' brothers and fathers of wives.
35. These I do not wish to slay, even if I myself am slain. Not even for the kingdom of the three worlds: how much less for a kingdom of the earth!
36. If we kill these evil men, evil shall fall upon us: what joy in their death could we have, O Janardana, mover of souls?
37. I cannot therefore kill my own kinsmen, the sons of king Dhrita-rashtra, the brother of my own father. What happiness could we ever enjoy, if we killed our own kinsmen in battle?
38. Even if they, with minds overcome by greed, see no evil in the destruction of a family, see no sin in the treachery to friends;
39. Shall we not, who see the evil of destruction, shall we not refrain from this terrible deed?

27. Krishna's Response: Throw off this Discouragement! Bhagavad Gita 2: 2–3, 11–13, 19, 22, 27, 31

KRISHNA

2. Whence this lifeless dejection, Arjuna, in this hour, the hour of trial? Strong men know not despair, Arjuna, for this wins neither heaven nor earth.
3. Fall not into degrading weakness, for this becomes not a man who is a man. Throw off this ignoble discouragement, and arise like a fire that burns all before it.
11. Thy tears are for those beyond tears; and are thy words of wisdom? The wise grieve not for those who live; and they grieve not for those who die – for life and death shall pass away.
12. Because we all have been for all time: I, and thou, and those kings of men. And we all shall be for all time, we all for ever and ever.
13. As the Spirit of our mortal body wanders on in childhood, and youth and old age, the Spirit wanders on to a new body: of this the sage has no doubts.
19. If any man thinks he slays, and if another thinks he is slain, neither knows the ways of truth. The Eternal in man cannot kill; the Eternal in man cannot die.
22. As a man leaves an old garment and puts on one that is new, the Spirit leaves his mortal body and then puts on one that is new.
27. For all things born in truth must die, and out of death in truth comes life. Face to face with what must be, cease thou from sorrow.
31. Think thou also of thy duty and do not waver. There is no greater good for a warrior than to fight in a righteous war.

Realizing that Arjuna is still perplexed, Lord Krishna explains how Arjuna can lift himself from his worldly nature to his higher spiritual nature by practicing *yoga*. Yoga means 'to yoke' the mind to God. A person who practices yoga is a 'yogi.' In the highest state, meditating yogis silence all their senses: they do not hear or see or taste, or feel, or smell. Beyond good and evil, time and space, they are one with the divinity. Ultimately yoga leads to liberation of the five senses. First, however, the personal self (ego) must be brought under control by performing every action as an offering to God. The yoga of action, called *karma yoga* is one of the core teachings of the Bhagavad Gita.

28. Karma Yoga. Bhagavad Gita 2: 47–48, 50

KRISHNA

47. Set thy heart upon thy work, but never on its reward. Work not for a reward; but never cease to do thy work.
48. Do thy work in the peace of Yoga and, free from selfish desires, be not moved in success or in failure. Yoga is evenness of mind – a peace that is ever the same.
50. In this wisdom a man goes beyond what is well done and what is not well done. Go thou therefore to wisdom. Yoga is wisdom in work.

> **Reflections**
> Could you, like the karma yogis, look only at your motives and never to the result of your actions: or do you try to control the consequences of your acts?

29. Action is Greater Than Inaction. Bhagavad Gita 3: 3–5, 8, 19

3. In this world there are two roads of perfection, as I told thee before, O Prince without sin: Jnana Yoga, the path of wisdom of the Sankhyas, and Karma Yoga, the path of action of the Yogis.
4. Not by refraining from action does man attain freedom from action. Not by mere renunciation does he attain supreme perfection.
5. For not even for a moment can a man be without action. Helplessly are all driven to action by the forces of Nature.
8. Action is greater than Inaction: perform therefore thy task in life. Even the life of the body could not be if there were no action.
19. In liberty from the bonds of attachment, do thou therefore the work to be done; for the man whose work is pure attains indeed the Supreme.

30. Harmony in Yoga. Bhagavad Gita 4: 41–42; 5: 10, 12
KRISHNA

41. He who makes pure his works by Yoga, who watches over his soul, and who, and who by wisdom destroys his doubts, is free from the bondage of selfish work.
42. Kill therefore with the sword of wisdom the doubt born of ignorance that lies in thy heart. Be one in self-harmony, in Yoga, and arise, great warrior, arise.

31. Offer All Works to God. Bhagavad Gita 5: 10, 12

10. Offer all thy works to God, throw off selfish bonds, and do thy work …
12. This man of harmony surrenders the reward of his work and thus attains final peace: the man of disharmony, urged by desire, is attached to his reward and remains in bondage.

32. Krishna Explains the Fruits of Meditation. Bhagavad Gita 6: 27, 29–30, 32
KRISHNA:

27. … joy supreme comes to the Yogi whose heart is still, whose passions are peace, who is pure from sin, who is one with Brahman, with God.
29. He sees himself in the heart of all beings and he sees all beings in his heart. This is the vision of the Yogi of harmony, a vision which is ever one.
30. And when he sees me in all and he sees all in me, then I never leave him and he never leaves me.
32. And he is the greatest Yogi he whose vision is ever one: when the pleasure and pain of others is his own pleasure and pain.

Chapter 11 is the essence of the Gita's teaching. Arjuna asks Lord Krishna, who has been his charioteer in human form, to reveal himself as He really is. Krishna grants his request. As the vision unfolds, Arjuna sees beautiful light – all things in

God and God in all things, and he begins a hymn of praise. As the vision becomes more intense, Arjuna sees the light of God become a fire that burns to consume all things, as if at the end of time. God's radiance is both a great light and a burning fire. Terrified, Arjuna wants to know the identity of this awesome God.

Finally, the vision is too much for Arjuna and he wishes to see once again the human face of God. Krishna grants his wish and returns to human form.

33. Krishna Reveals His Divine Form. Bhagavad Gita 11: 5–8, 10–11, 13–14. 16–19

KRISHNA:

5. By hundreds and then by thousands, behold, Arjuna, my manifold celestial forms of innumerable shapes and colours.
6. Behold the gods of the sun, and those of fire and light; the gods of storm and lightning, and the two luminous charioteers of heaven. Behold, descendant of Bharata, marvels never seen before.
7. See now the whole universe with all things that move and move not, and whatever thy soul may yearn to see. See it all as One in me.
8. But thou never canst see me with these thy mortal eyes: I will give thee divine sight. Behold my wonder and glory.
10. *And Arjuna saw in that form countless visions of wonder: eyes from innumerable faces, numerous celestial ornaments, numberless heavenly weapons;*
11. *Celestial garlands and vestures, forms anointed with heavenly perfumes. The Infinite Divinity was facing all sides, all marvels in him containing.*
13. *And Arjuna saw in that radiance the whole universe in its variety, standing in a vast unity in the body of the God of gods.*
14. *Trembling with awe and wonder, Arjuna bowed his head, and joining his hands in adoration he thus spoke to his God.*

ARJUNA

16. All around I behold thy infinity: the power of thy innumerable arms, the visions from thy innumerable eyes, the words from thy innumerable mouths, and the fire of life of thy innumerable bodies. Nowhere I see a beginning or middle or end of thee, O God of all, Form Infinite!
17. I see the splendour of an infinite beauty which illumines the whole universe. It is thee! With thy crown and scepter and circle. How difficult thou art to see! But I see thee: as fire, as the sun, blinding, incomprehensible.
18. Thou art the Imperishable, the highest End of knowledge, the support of this vast universe. Thou, the everlasting ruler of the law of righteousness, the Spirit who is and who was at the beginning.
19. I see thee without beginning, middle, or end; I behold thy infinite power, the power of thy innumerable arms. I see thine eyes as the sun and the moon. And I see thy face as a sacred fire that gives light and life to the whole universe in the splendour of a vast offering.

34. Krishna Shows Arjuna His Terrifying Form. Bhagavad Gita 11: 23, 28–30, 32–33, 35, 36–38, 45, 49, 51–55

ARJUNA:

23. But the worlds also behold thy fearful mighty form, with many mouths and eyes, with many bellies, thighs and feet, frightening with terrible teeth: they tremble in fear, and I also tremble.

28. As roaring torrents of waters rush forward into the ocean, so do these heroes of our mortal world rush into thy flaming mouths.

29. And as moths swiftly rushing enter a burning flame and die, so all these men rush to thy fire, rush fast to their own destruction.

30. The flames of thy mouths devour all the worlds. Thy glory fills the whole universe. But how terrible thy splendours burn!

KRISHNA

32. I am all-powerful Time which destroys all things, and I have come here to slay these men. Even if thou dost not fight, all the warriors facing thee shall die.

33. Arise therefore! Win thy glory, conquer thine enemies, and enjoy thy kingdom. Through the fate of their Karma I have doomed them to die: be thou merely the means of my work.

35. *When Arjuna heard the words of Krishna he folded his hands trembling; and with a faltering voice, and bowing in adoration, he spoke.*

ARJUNA

36. It is right, O God, that peoples sing thy praises, and that they are glad and rejoice in thee. All evil spirits fly away in fear; but the hosts of the saints bow down before thee.

37. How could they not bow down in love and adoration, before thee, God of gods, Spirit Supreme? Thou creator of Brahma, the god of creation, thou infinite, eternal, refuge of the world! Thou who art all that is, and all that is not, and all that is Beyond.

38. Thou God from the beginning, God in man since man was. Thou Treasure supreme of this vast universe. Thou the One to be known and the Knower, the final resting place. Thou infinite Presence in whom all things are.

45. In a vision I have seen what no man has seen before: I rejoice in exultation, and yet my heart trembles with fear. Have mercy upon me, Lord of gods, Refuge of the whole universe: show me again thine own human form.

KRISHNA

49. Thou hast seen the tremendous form of my greatness, but fear not, and be not bewildered. Free from fear and with a glad heart see my friendly form again.

ARJUNA

51. When I see thy gentle human face, Krishna, I return to my own nature, and my heart has peace.

KRISHNA

52. Thou hast seen now face to face my form divine so hard to see: for even the gods in heaven ever long to see what thou hast seen.
53. Not by the Vedas, or an austere life, or gifts to the poor, or ritual offerings can I be seen as thou hast seen me.
54. Only by love can men see me, and know me, and come unto me.
55. He who works for me, who loves me, whose End Supreme I am, free from attachment to all things, and with love for all creation, he in truth comes unto me.

35. Dear to God. Bhagavad Gita 12: 1, 13–20

ARJUNA

1. Those who in oneness worship thee as God immanent in all; and those who worship the Transcendent, the imperishable – Of these, who are the best Yogis?

KRISHNA

13. The man who has a good will for all, who is friendly and has compassion; who has no thoughts of 'I' or 'mine', whose peace is the same in pleasures and sorrows, and who is forgiving;
14. This Yogi of union, ever full of my joy, whose soul is in harmony and whose determination is strong; whose mind and inner vision are set on me – this man loves me, and he is dear to me.
15. He whose peace is not shaken by others, and before whom other people find peace, beyond excitement and anger and fear – he is dear to me.
16. He who is free from vain expectations, who is pure, who is wise and knows what to do, who in inner peace watches both sides, who shakes not, who works for God and not for himself – this man loves me, and he is dear to me.
17. He who feels neither excitement nor repulsion, who complains not and lusts not for things; who is beyond good and evil, and who has love – he is dear to me.
18. The man whose love is the same for his enemies or his friends, whose soul is the same in honour or disgrace, who is beyond heat or cold or pleasure or pain, who is free from the chains of attachments;
19. Who is balanced in blame and in praise, whose soul is silent, who is happy with whatever he has, whose home is not in this world, and who has love – this man is dear to me.
20. But even dearer to me are those who have faith and love, and who have me as their End Supreme: those who hear my words of Truth, and who come to the waters of Everlasting Life.

36. Clear Vision. Bhagavad Gita 15: 19–20

KRISHNA

19. He who with a clear vision sees me as the Spirit Supreme he knows all there is to be known, and he adores me with all his soul.
20. I have revealed to thee the most secret doctrine, Arjuna. He who sees it has seen light, and his task in this world is done.

37. Thy Will Be Done. Bhagavad Gita 18: 63–66, 73, 78

KRISHNA

63. I have given thee words of vision and wisdom more secret than hidden mysteries. Ponder them in the silence of thy soul, and then in freedom do thy will.

64. Hear again my Word supreme, the deepest secret of silence. Because I love thee well, I will speak to thee words of salvation.

65. Give thy mind to me, and give me thy heart, and thy sacrifice, and thy adoration. This is my Word of promise: thou shalt in truth come to me, for thou art dear to me.

66. Leave all things behind, and come to me for thy salvation. I will make thee free from the bondage of sins. Fear no more.

ARJUNA

73. By thy grace I remember my Light and now gone is my delusion. My doubts are no more, my faith is firm; and now I can say 'Thy will be done'.

78. *Wherever is Krishna, the End of Yoga, wherever is Arjuna who masters the bow, there is beauty and victory, and joy and all righteousness. This is my faith.*

Summary

The earliest civilized inhabitants of India lived in the Indus River region. They respected the earth, worshipped a mother goddess, and believed in an afterlife. In approximately 2000 BCE, Aryan invaders entered India and dominated the history of northern India for 2,000 years until 500 CE. They had a philosophical turn of mind, devoting thought to the mysteries of the origin of the universe.

The Vedic period takes its name from a series of ancient texts called the Vedas. The Vedas recorded the Aryan ideas on the nature of humankind, the world, and relations between humans and gods. The oldest religious text in the world is the *Rig-Veda*, which was written in the early Sanskrit language. Four Vedas inform the Hindu religion.

According to the Vedas, the caste system and the Laws of Manu illustrate how a Hindu fits into family, society, and occupation. The caste system (*Varna*) is composed of four groups: (1) *Brahmins*, or priests, have divine knowledge; (2) *kshatriyas*, military leaders or administrators, are born with the ability to organize; (3) *vaisyas*, or merchants, provide for the economic needs of the community; and (4) *shudras*, or laborers, serve the three upper castes. The Laws of Manu includes Four Stages of Life: (1) *student*; (2) *marriage*; (3) *retirement*; and (4) *ascetic*.

The Upanishads are commentaries on the Vedas composed between 900 and 600 BCE. The Upanishads ask, 'What am I, in my deepest experience?' Their subjects include explanations of God (Brahman) and the soul (Atman). The Upanishads explain the world as fleeting and illusory and include Hinduism's tenets of karma (the law of action and reaction) and reincarnation (the pilgrimage of the soul from life to life).

Included in the *Mahabharata,* the longest poem in the world is the holiest Hindu text of the *Bhagavad Gita* (the Lord's Song). Its scene is a battlefield where a fight is about to occur between the good princes and their evil cousins. The Gita is an allegory of the cosmic struggle between good and evil, and of the spiritual struggle in which Prince Arjuna (Everyman) is engaged with his own ego, the very obstacle to living the spiritual life. The Bhagavad Gita is a dialogue between Prince Arjuna and Lord Krishna – the savior of humankind. It includes an explanation of the yoga paths: Jnana Yoga (knowledge), Bhakti Yoga (love or devotion), Karma Yoga (service), and Raja Yoga (mental discipline).

Hindu India Today

Various invasions beginning with the Aryans, have affected the development of Indian religion and culture. Alexander the Great's invasion of northern India brought a strong and lasting Hellenistic and Persian influence to the area. In approximately 500 BCE, Jainism and Buddhism entered India. During the 700s CE, Arab Muslims invaded the Sind region of India in the lower Indus River valley. In 1000 CE, Turkish Muslims conquered the Sind and the Punjab and later established a sultanate in Delhi. In the fifteenth century Nanak founded the Sikh religious movement.

Until the eighteenth century, much of northern India was under Muslim control, but the Hindus did not assimilate Muslim religious and cultural tradition. In 1763, India fell under British control and remained a colony of the British Empire until 1947, when Mahatma Gandhi and his followers were ultimately successful in achieving India's independence. To Gandhi's despair, in 1947, Muslims officially separated from Hindu India to form the independent Muslim republic of Pakistan. Since then, Muslim–Hindu animosities continue to be the source of seemingly irreconcilable and increasingly violent conflicts and confrontations from small villages and towns to big cities and border regions.

At the beginning of the twenty-first century, in India's cities as well as villages, Hinduism remains the religion followed by the majority of people. What unite Hindus are scriptures such as the Vedas, Upanishads, and the Bhagavad-Gita, the practice of yoga, and their belief in the divinity in all things. Whatever diversity they encounter among themselves converges in the universal will to come closer to God by whatever path or means possible. No way is excluded, and no way is preferred as long as the destination gets nearer all the time.

In the West, Hindu's earliest impact resulted from the translations of the Upanishads and the Bhagavad-Gita into Latin, German, French, and English. Hindu beliefs in yoga, reincarnation, karma, and the ultimate unity of all things have influenced and continue to influence poets, artists, writers, musicians, philosophers, and scientists throughout the world.

Timeline

c. 2500 BCE	Harappa Civilization in Indus Valley.
c. 2000 BCE	Aryan migration into Indus River Valley; Aryan domination of Harappa Culture.
c. 1550 to 1000 BCE	The Vedic Period: Rig-Veda, Sama-Veda, Yajur-Veda, Atharva-Veda.
c. 900 to 600 BCE	Composition of the Upanishads.
c. 600 to 500 BCE	Caste system firmly established.
c. 600 to 500 BCE	Buddhism and Jainism entered India.
c. 500 BCE to 400 CE	Composition of the Mahabharata and Bhagavad-Gita.
c. 300 BCE to 300 CE	Laws of Manu (Four Stages of Life).
700 CE	Muslims invaded the Sind region of the lower Indus Valley.
1200 CE	Muslim capital established at Delhi.
1469 to 1539 CE	Guru Nanak founded the Sikh religion.
1763 CE	India fell under British rule.
1947 CE	Mahatma Gandhi and his followers achieved India's freedom.

Study Questions

1. What was the Harappa's contribution to Indian culture and religion?
2. Discuss the influence the Aryans had on northern India.
3. What is the oldest document in any Indo-European language?
4. Explain the significance of the Vedas to Hinduism.
5. According to the Vedas what is the relation, if any, between actions and their consequences?
6. Present the main features of Vedic religion: its worldview and its gods. How does it set the stage for the development of later Hindu philosophy and religion?
7. Interpret the fundamental meaning of the Hindu caste system.
8. Explain the meaning of the Laws of Manu (the Four Stages of Life).
9. What is the significance of the Upanishads?
10. What is the importance of cultivating a spirit of non-attachment?
11. Explain the importance of Atman (the Self).
12. What is karma and how does it operate?
13. Briefly explain the Hindu concept of reincarnation.
14. The Bhagavad Gita is a portion of what epic poem?
15. If Hinduism is a religion of non-violence, why does Lord Krishna counsel Arjuna to fight, kill the opposing warriors, and win the battle?
16. Describe the yoga paths found in the Bhagavad Gita.

Suggested Reading

1. Arnold, Sir Edwin, trans. (1957), *The Song Celestial: Bhagavad Gita*. Bombay, India: Jaico Publishing House.
2. Aurobindo, Sri (1965), *The Life Divine*. Third edition. New York: India Library Society.
3. Basham, A.L. (1959), *The Wonder That Was India*. New York: Grove.
4. Bryant, Edwin F., trans. (2003), *Krishna: The Beautiful Legend of God*. New York: Penguin Books.
5. Eck, Diana (1985), *Darsan: Seeing the Divine Image in India*. Pennsylvania: Anima Books.
6. Eliade, Mircea (1973), *Yoga: Immortality and Freedom*. Princeton: Princeton University Press.
7. Fischer, Louis, ed. (1983), *The Essential Gandhi*. New York: Random House.
8. Follmi, Danielle and Follmi, Olivier (2004), *Wisdom: 365 Thoughts from Indian Masters*. New York: Harry N. Abrams, Inc.
9. Harvey, Andrew (1992), *Hidden Journey: A Spiritual Awakening*. New York: Arkana/Penguin.
10. Herman, A.L. (1976), *An Introduction to Indian Thought*. New Jersey: Prentice-Hall, Inc.
11. Radhakrishnan, Sarvepalli and Moore, Charles A., eds. (1971), *A Sourcebook in Indian Philosophy*. Fourth edition. New Jersey: Princeton University Press.

Sources

The Vedas

1. Rig-Veda II: 12: 1–3, 5, 13. A.A. Macdonell, trans. (1917), *A Vedic Reader for Students*. Oxford: Claredon Press, pp. 45–54; quoted in M. Eliade, ed., *Essential Sacred Writings from Around the World*. San Francisco: Harper & Row, 1967; p. 36.
2. Rig-Veda I: 1, 7, 8, 9. R.T.H Griffith (Benares: 1889–1891), *The Hymns of the Rig-Veda* 1–111. All selections from R.T.H. Griffith are quoted in Eliade, ed., *Essential Sacred Writings*; pp. 280–282.
3. Rig-Veda II: 1, 9, 14. R.T.H. Griffith (1889–1891), *The Hymns of the Rig-Veda* 1–111.
4. Rig-Veda VII. R.T.H. Griffith (1889–1891), *The Hymns of the Rig-Veda* 1–111.
5. Rig-Veda I: 125; 3, 7, 9–11. Griffith, *The Hymns of the Rig-Veda*, pp. 42–43; quoted in Eliade, ed., *Essential Sacred Writings*, p. 31.
6. Rig-Veda X: 129; 1–7. A.L. Basham (1954), *The Wonder That Was India*. London, pp. 247–248, quoted in Eliade, ed., *Essential Sacred Writings*, pp. 227–228.
7. Atharva-Veda IV: 16; 2–5. Maurice Bloomfield, trans. (1897), *Hymns of the Atharva-Veda*, in *Sacred Books of the East*, XLII. Oxford, pp. 88–89.
8. Rig-Veda X: 90; 1–3, 6, 8–14, Griffith (1892), *The Hymns of the Rig-Veda*. Benares, pp. 289–293; quoted in Eliade, ed., *Essential Sacred Writings*, pp. 227–228.
9. Julius Jolly, trans. (1880), *The Institutes of Vishnu, Sacred Books of the East*. Vol. 7: 1–10. Oxford University Press.
10. G. Buhles, trans. (1886), *The Laws of Manu, Sacred Books of the East*. Vol. 25. 2. 69–70, 3. 1–4, 6. 1–4, 6. 33–34. Oxford University Press.
11. Buhles, trans., *The Laws of Manu*. Vol. 25. 3: 4–10.
12. Buhles, trans., *The Laws of Manu*. Vol. 25. 6: 1–4.
13. Buhles, trans., *The Laws of Manu*. Vol. 25. 6: 33–38.

The Upanishads

All selections are quoted from Juan Mascaro, ed. and trans. (1975), *The Upanishads*. London: Penguin. Page numbers listed below after the semicolon refer to this text.

14. Chandogya Upanishad 6: 12–13; pp. 116–118.
15. Isa Upanishad: 1–2, 4, 6, 15; pp. 49–50.
16. Kena Upanishad I: 4–8; p. 51.
17. Katha Upanishad 3: 3–6; p. 60.
18. Katha Upanishad 3: 14–15; p. 61.
19. Katha Upanishad 5: 10–11; p. 64.
20. Mundaka Upanishad 2: 2; 2; p. 78.
21. Mundaka Upanishad 3: 1; 1–2; p. 80.
22. Mundaka Upanishad 2: 2, 8–9; p. 81.
23. Svetesvatara Upanishad 5: 11–13; p. 94.
24. Maitri Upanishad 6: 24; pp. 103–104.
25. Taittiriya Upanishad 3: 1–6; pp. 110–111.

Bhagavad Gita

All selections are quoted from Juan Mascaro, trans. (1973), *The Bhagavad Gita*. Middlesex: Penguin. Page numbers listed below after the semi colon refer to this text.

26. Bhagavad Gita 1: 34–39; p. 46
27. Bhagavad Gita 2: 2–3, 11–13, 19, 22, 27, 31; pp. 48–51
28. Bhagavad Gita 2: 47–48, 50; p. 52
29. Bhagavad Gita 3: 3–5, 8, 19; pp. 56–57.
30. Bhagavad Gita 4: 41–42; pp. 64–65.
31. Bhagavad Gita 5: 10, 12; p. 67.
32. Bhagavad Gita 6: 27, 29–30, 32; pp. 71–72.
33. Bhagavad Gita 11: 5–8, 10, 11, 13–14, 16–19; pp. 89–91.
34. Bhagavad Gita 11: 23, 28–30, 32–33, 36–38, 45, 49, 51–55; pp. 91–94.
35. Bhagavad Gita 12: 1, 13–20; pp. 96–98.
36. Bhagavad Gita 15: 19–20; p. 108.
37. Bhagavad Gita 18: 63–66, 73, 78; pp. 121–122.

Buddhist Wisdom

Wheel of the Law
*The circle symbolizes the completeness of
the Dharma. The eight spokes represent the
Eightfold Path leading to enlightenment.*

Religion of Compassion

Unlike Hinduism, which had no one particular founder, Buddhism originated from the enlightened teachings of one man, Siddhartha Gautama (c. 563–483 BCE) who came to be called the Buddha or 'Awakened One.' Buddhism is now one of the world's major religions. As a missionary religion, it has spread from India throughout Asia and the Western world. There are approximately 600 to 700 million Buddhists in the world today.

Many people question whether Buddhism is really a religion, because it is not based on a belief in God and does not have an official sacred scripture, dogma, or central authority. Buddhism, however, gives humankind a goal for life that transcends the physical world, and it espouses certain truths about life and the universe. The Buddha also set forth methods for living ethically and attaining *nirvana* (inner peace and bliss).

Like Socrates, the great Greek ethical philosopher, and Jesus Christ, the founder of Christianity, the Buddha wrote nothing. From his disciples we have collections of his findings after he reached enlightenment and the methods he suggested for attaining truth. Perhaps the main core of the Buddha's teaching is compassion. 'Always think compassion,' he said, 'That is all you need to know.' He preached a religion devoid of authority and challenged everyone to seek truth for themselves: 'Be lamps unto yourselves.'

The Buddha taught a religion that avoided speculation. When people asked him whether the world is eternal or not eternal, finite or infinite, whether the soul is the same as the body, whether the Buddha exists after death or does not exist after death, the Buddha maintained a 'noble silence.' Why? He did not want to promote greed for theological views in which groups would form that insisted their way was the right way and another group's way the wrong way.

One of the Buddha's most profound teachings is that the spiritual life does not depend on whether the world is eternal or finite, whether the body and soul are distinct, or whether the Buddha exists after death. What matters is *how* one lives one's life.

Reflections

Do you agree with the Buddha that spiritual life does not depend on dogma or doctrine, but rather on how we live our lives?

Buddhism is one of the few religions that can adapt in many different cultures. It has never demanded sole allegiance from people, and it can coexist with other religious traditions without replacing them. The Buddha's teachings will enhance rather than oppose most religions in the world, because his is a method of spiritual living. He did not claim to be a god or a prophet. When the people asked the Buddha who he was – a god, an angel, or a saint? He answered, 'I am awake.'

'I am awake' is the essence of Buddhism: the meaning of the word *Buddha* derives from the Sanskrit root *budh*, to wake up.

The Life of Siddhartha Gautama

Siddhartha Gautama was born in an ancient kingdom at the foot of the Himalayas in northeast India (now Nepal). His father was an Indian king of the Sakya clan and, like Arjuna, a member of the Hindu warrior caste. Before his birth, Siddhartha's mother dreamed that a white elephant touched her side with his trunk and it melted like a cloudy vapor into her womb. Dream readers predicted she would give birth to a child who would become either a king or a Buddha.

Legend relates that the dream readers warned the king, 'If the child is to be a king, there are four sights he must never see':

1. An old man
2. A sick man
3. A dead man
4. A holy monk

'If he sees these four sights,' said the dream readers, 'he will become a holy Buddha.'

At his birth, they named him Siddhartha Gautama. His mother died seven days after he was born and his aunt cared for him until he married in his late teens. Siddhartha was brought up in great luxury and comfort. The king provided him with the finest intellectual and physical training, and with rich entertainment. But even at the fun-loving festivals, family and friends often found the boy seated cross-legged, absorbed in meditation.

Reflections
Why do you think these particular four sights would turn Siddhartha from kingship to a spiritual path? Have these four sights had any effect on your life?

To keep him from seeing the four sights that would prompt him to take the solitary spiritual path, the king confined his son to the palace grounds. But Siddhartha's curiosity to view the world 'outside the palace gates' took him into the city. First he saw, to his dismay, a decrepit old man leaning on a stick. Next he saw a sick man suffering in pain. Third, a corpse surrounded by mourners passed near him. The fourth sight was a monk in a yellow robe carrying a begging bowl. These four sights struck Siddhartha with the force of revelation – all human beings are subject to suffering. Siddhartha must find the solution to the problem of human suffering. To do so, he would have to renounce his princely life and become a wandering monk.

Before Siddhartha left home, his wife Yasodhara gave birth to a son. Tempted to stay home with his family, Siddhartha named the infant Rahula, which means hindrance (to his leaving). One night, while his wife and child slept, Siddhartha bade them a silent goodbye and left the palace. Out in the forest, he cut off his hair, removed his princely dress, and put on a monk's robe. His life as a wandering ascetic had begun.

First he studied under two famous Hindu priests. Later in the company of five ascetics, he practiced fasting and self-mortification. Legends recount how he sat on a couch of thorns and ate only a few grains of rice each day. After six years, he reached a point where he could touch his backbone through his stomach. He became so ill that when he stood up, he fainted. During his illness, Siddhartha came to the conclusion that the strict regimen of fasting and self-mortification was not the path to enlightenment for him. To renew his health, he started eating and drinking properly again. Outraged by what they considered his surrender to self-indulgence, the five ascetics left him in disgust.

While sitting beneath the famous Bodhi Tree, the future Buddha swore he would stay there until he found the secret to life. For forty days and nights Siddhartha struggled with temptations. Evil demons approached and tempted him to abandon his virtuous but hopeless quest, because his family needed him. One demon in the form of a god informed him that his cousin had imprisoned his father and taken his wife. But the future Buddha sat unmoved. The demons sent beautiful girls to seduce him, but Siddhartha ignored them. When a host of demons attacked him with their deadly swords, he touched the ground with the fingers of his right hand. His contact with the earth produced a volcanic thundering that frightened the demons away.

Reflections
When evil or unkind thoughts enter your mind, how do you drive them away?

Just before dawn, a golden light flooded Siddhartha's being. The dark forces vanished as the ocean of truth poured into his mind and heart. In a state of pure bliss, he beheld past, present, and future as one. The mysterious secrets of birth and death and the passing into new lives opened before him. He experienced the eternal laws of the universe. The essence of spiritual knowledge was his. Prince Siddhartha was now the Buddha – one perfect in enlightenment!

According to legend, he lifted his eyes to the heavens and spoke triumphantly of his attainment: 'Bliss is within reach of all whom set their faces to the heights in true endeavor.' And he added, 'Enlightenment is not the dewdrop lost in the ocean, but the ocean drawn into the dewdrop.'

During the stages of his enlightenment, the Buddha saw himself and all life as a process, an ever-moving stream of becoming and extinction, and within this ever-moving flow of energies, he recognized as delusion the idea of the existence of an individual self or soul. He realized that what we take for the 'self' is actually a composite of various aggregates and psychophysical reactions with no true center.

This insight gave the Buddha a deep sense of freedom. It delivered him from all egoistic drives motivated by greed, hate, and delusion. After forty days and nights of meditation on his discovery, the Buddha journeyed to Banaras where he met the five ascetics.

When the five ascetics saw him coming, they decided to turn their backs on the former prince who practiced self-indulgence. But as he drew closer, his face shining with what he had seen and understood, they found themselves preparing a place for him and then sat at his feet. The Buddha preached to them his first discourse. When he finished, the five ascetics became his first disciples and founding members of the *Sangha*, or monastic order. The Buddha now devoted his time preaching his new wisdom. He traveled to his former home and shared the truth with his family. His father, stepmother, and wife converted, and they were followed by many others. His own son became a monk.

Forty-five years the Buddha taught. His appeal was to the individual, that each should look within for enlightenment. At age eighty, after eating a meal at Chunda the blacksmith's house, the Buddha became ill and soon died. His death is known as *Parinirvana* – the final blowing-out.

Branches of Buddhism

After his death, the Buddhist religion divided into two main branches: Hinayana (also called Theravada) and Mahayana. Both called themselves *yanas*, meaning rafts or ferries, because both disciplines carry people across life's seas to the shores of enlightenment. Adherents of the Mahayana branch, which is based on the principle of compassion, considered themselves to constitute 'Buddhism for the people' and thus the larger of the two rafts, 'the great vehicle.' The Hinayana branch insisted on individual effort: 'Be lamps unto yourselves; work out your salvation with diligence.' This group considered Buddhism a full-time job; thus its adherents would have to give up the worldly life and become monks or nuns. Because Hinayana was more demanding and appealed to fewer people, it was called the 'little raft.'

Hinayanists have preferred to call their Buddhism Theravada ('the way of the elders'). This tradition is found in the southern Asia countries of Sri Lanka,

Thailand, Burma, Cambodia, and Laos. Mahayana ('the great vehicle') is found in Asia's northern and eastern regions. Tibetan Buddhism, a variation on Mahayana, is followed in Tibet, Mongolia, Sikkim, Bhutan, and northwestern China, whereas a variety of Buddhist traditions are followed in China, Japan, Korea, and Vietnam.

Tibetan Buddhism is famous for its *Book of the Dead,* which gives instructions to the dying; Zen Buddhism is famous for its disciplined meditation and koans; Pure Land Buddhism teaches that all will eventually be reborn in the Pure Land; and devotees of Nichiren Buddhism repeat the mantra of the *Lotus Sutra* many times a day.

Buddhist Scriptures

Like Jesus, the Buddha wrote nothing. Unlike Jesus, however, there is no book of sacred scripture for all Buddhists. The Buddha's teachings were memorized and recited, but not written down for several centuries. The scriptures that guide followers of Theravada Buddhism are known as the *Pali Canon* and were written around the first century BCE. The Pali Canon is divided into three sections known as the *Tripitaka*, meaning 'three baskets.' The scriptures of the Mahayana Buddhists are similar to the Pali Canon, but teach distinctively Mahayana ideas. Among the Mahayana scriptures are the *Lotus Sutra*, the *Pure Land Sutras*, the *Heart Sutra*, and the *Perfection of Wisdom Sutras*.

The Buddha's Teachings

The Four Noble Truths and the Eightfold Path: From the Buddha's First Sermon, 'Setting the Wheel of Truth.'

1. The Four Noble Truths. Samyutta Nikaya 56. 11

Suffering, as a noble truth, is this: Birth is suffering, ageing is suffering, sickness is suffering, death is suffering, sorrow and pain … and despair are suffering, association with the loathed is suffering, dissociation from the loved is suffering, not to get what one wants is suffering – in short suffering is the five [groups] of clinging's objects.*

Thus *the origin of suffering*, as a noble truth, is this: It is the craving that produces renewal of being, accompanied by enjoyment and lust – in other words, craving for sensual desires, craving for being, craving for non-being.

Cessation of suffering, as a noble truth, is this: It is remainderless fading and ceasing … letting go and rejecting, of that same craving.

The way leading to the cessation of suffering, as a noble truth is this: It is simply *the eightfold noble path* [of] *right view, right intention, right speech, right action, right livelihood, right effort, right mindfulness, right concentration.*

---

* The 'groups of clinging's objects' are the five *skandhas* (body, feelings, perceptions, dispositions, and consciousness) that make up a human individual.

> **Reflections**
> Are you free of guilt, anxiety, stress, fear, and pain? Or do you agree with the Buddha that life is frustrating and uncertain – full of suffering?

2. The Middle Way. Samyutta Nikaya 56. 11

Monks, these two extremes ought not to be cultivated by one gone-forth from the home-life. What are the two? There is ... indulgence ... in the objects of sensual desire, which is inferior, low, vulgar, ignoble, and leads to no good; and there is devotion to self-torment, which is painful, ignoble, and leads to no good.

The middle way ... avoids both these extremes; it gives vision, it gives knowledge, and it leads to peace, to direct acquaintance to nibbana [nirvana]. And what is that middle way? It is simply the noble eightfold path ...

3. The Noble Eightfold Path. Samyutta Nikaya V. 8

The Lord said, 'What, monks, is the Noble Eightfold Way? It is namely right view, right intention, right speech, right action, right livelihood, right effort, right mindfulness, right concentration.

'And what, monks, is the right view? The knowledge of pain, knowledge of the cause of pain, knowledge of the cessation of pain, and knowledge of the way that leads to the cessation of pain ... That, monks is called right view.

'And what is right speech? Refraining from falsehood, from malicious speech, from harsh speech, from frivolous speech ... That, monks is called right speech.

'And what is right action? Refraining from taking life, from taking what is not given, from sexual intercourse ... That monks, is called right action.

'And what is right livelihood? Here a noble disciple abandoning a false mode of livelihood gets his living by right livelihood ... That, monks is called right livelihood.

'And what is right effort? Here a monk ... applies and exerts his mind; with the dispelling of bad and evil thoughts ... increasing, enlarging, developing and filling [his mind] up of good thoughts ... That monks, is called right effort.

'And what is right mindfulness? Here ... a monk abides contemplating, ardent, thoughtful, and mindful, dispelling his longing and dejection towards the world ... That, monks is called right mindfulness.

'And what is right concentration? Here (1) a monk free from passions and evil thoughts attains and abides in the first trance of joy and pleasure, which is accompanied by reasoning and investigation ... (2) With the ceasing of reasoning and investigation, in a state of internal serenity ... he attains and abides in the second trance. (3) With equanimity and indifference towards joy he abides mindful and self-possessed ... 'Dwelling with equanimity, mindful and happy,' attains and abides in the third trance. (4) Dispelling pleasure and pain ... he attains and abides in the fourth trance ... with the purity of mindfulness and equanimity: that monks, is called right concentration.'

The Skandhas and the Chain of Causation

Essential to understanding the Buddha's teachings is the concept of *anicea* (the impermanence of everything). Believing that all remains in a state of process or constant flux – the chain of causation – the Buddha denied the existence of a personal individual soul or self that is reborn from one life to the next.

According to the Buddha, we are composed of five *skandhas*: (1) body; (2) feelings; (3) perceptions; (4) dispositions; and (5) consciousness. When these five skandhas come together in birth, they interact in a way that makes us think of ourselves as separate personalities. Material elements make up the body. Feelings include sensations – both the pleasant and the unpleasant. Perceptions include sight, hearing, touch, taste, and smell. Dispositions are part of human sense perceptions and strong emotions such as fear, hatred, and love. Higher states of consciousness occur in the realm of thoughts, ideas, and virtue.

What we call the personality or individual self is the combination of the skandhas. Each individual is a unique combination of skandhas with distinctive characteristics and potential. Most people want the five skandhas to be the true self, but the Buddha asks us to 'wake up' from the delusion of possessing an eternal and individual personality, because as long as we harbor this desire, we will suffer. Only by 'letting go' can we experience nirvana – the goal of the Buddha's teachings.

4. The Five Skandhas and the Chain of Causation. Buddhacarita 16: 28, 30, 35, 40

[28] The body is composed of the five skandhas, and produced from the five elements. It is all empty and without soul, and arises from the action of the chain of causation. This chain of causation is the cause of coming into existence, and the cessation of this chain is the cause of the state of cessation.

[30] … Whoever has his mind indifferent and is empty of all desire for any further form of existence, let him abolish causation. When these effects of the chain of causation are ended one by one, he at last, being free from all stain and substratum, will pass into a blissful Nirvana.

[35] 'Listen, all of you, for your own happiness, with your minds free from stain. I will declare to you step by step this chain of causation. The idea of ignorance is what gives the root to the huge poison-tree of mundane existence with its trunk of pain. The impressions are caused by this, which produce [the acts of] the body, voice, and mind. Consciousness arises from these impressions, which produces the five senses and the mind.

[40] … 'Attachment to continued existence,' … sets itself in action towards pleasure and the rest. From attachment springs continued existence, which is sensual, possessing form, or formless. From existence arises birth through a returning to various wombs. On birth is dependent the series of old age, death, sorrow and the like. By putting a stop to ignorance and what follows from it, all these cease successively. This is the chain of causation, which has many turns, whose sphere of action is created by ignorance … He who knows it thoroughly reaches at last to absolute thinness. Then he becomes blissfully extinct.

Karma and Rebirth

As a stone thrown into a pool disturbs the still water, so disharmony in one's life, imbalance of one's actions (ignorance), brings *karma* into action. Selfishness, for example, not only disturbs the individual's own life, but sends karmic ripples all around. Thus karma is the force or energy created by one's thoughts, words, and deeds.

Basic to Buddhism is that every cause, including the illusion of being an individual self, has a corresponding effect. From life to life we bring together another set of five skandhas. Each of our lives depends on our previous thoughts and actions. We shape our own destiny. Present likes and dislikes, abilities, and interests are results of patterns set up in past lives. In this life we are creating patterns for future lives. Attitudes of kindness, morality, and compassion follow us from one life to the next. If we die with envy and greed in our heart, then the skandhas that have fashioned them carry that attitude into the next life. Current thoughts and actions prepare future karma. Hardships now are a result of our past actions and thoughts. Karmic burdens can be lifted by following the Eightfold Path.

Reflections
If we are a composite of skandhas that will one day come apart, how can Buddhists talk of karma and reincarnation? What is there to reincarnate?

---

5. Karma is Will. Anguttara Nikaya 6: 63
It is volition [will] that I call 'karma.' Having willed, one [then] acts by body, speech, and mind.

6. Karmic Deeds. Anguttara Nikaya 10: 206
All beings are the owners of their deeds (karma), the heirs of their deeds, their deeds are the womb from which they sprang … Whatever deeds they do − good or evil − of such they will be the heirs.

7. The Cause of Rebirth. Majjhima-Nikaya 43
Truly, because beings, obstructed by ignorance and ensnared by craving, seek ever fresh delight, fresh rebirth continually comes to be.

8. Greed, hatred and Delusion. Anguttara Nikaya 3: 33

And the action ... that is done out of greed, hatred and delusion ... wherever this action ripens there one experiences the fruits of this action, be it in this life, or the next life, or in some future life.

9. The Round of Rebirths. Samyutta Nikaya 15: 3

Which do you think is more: the flood of tears, which weeping and wailing you have shed upon this long way – hurrying and hastening through this round of rebirths, united with the undesired, separated from the desired – this, or the waters of the four oceans?

Long have you suffered the death of father and mother, of sons, daughters, brothers and sisters. And whilst you were thus suffering, you have indeed shed more tears upon this long way than there is water in the four oceans.

No-Self (*Anatta*)

The Buddha discovered that nothing in the world is constant, not even ideas. One may like to think his or her individuality is everlasting, but according to the Buddha, what an individual calls the 'self' is only a process. As long as anyone holds the view that there is a personal, individual self that continues after death, enlightenment is not possible. Attachment to such thinking is the cause of rebirth.

Is there some kind of self beyond the personal ego? Buddhists would answer 'yes and no.' The self is absolute subjectivity. No one can view it from the outside and no one can view it from the inside. The self is a center that is everywhere and a circumference that is nowhere. Because the self is not an object, no one can study or identify it. Thus, Buddhists label the doctrine of no permanent personal self as *anatta*.

Reflections

If there is no personal, individual self, what do you think would constitute the nature of an enlightened person?

According to the Buddha, enlightenment has to do with *awareness*. When you hear music, for instance, your awareness is not separate from the music. The music becomes an object only when you separate yourself from the music you hear. The moment you question the source of the music or the name of the composition, you establish duality. The self as a subject can only be known when you turn it into an object, thereby separating it from the whole. Buddhists say there is no self as object, only whatever is arising moment to moment. When self as absolute subjectivity knows itself as nothing, as *emptiness* or *pure awareness*, then it can no longer be called self. Awareness of everything as it is – is no longer identifiable as any one thing.

10. *Anatta* or No-self: Samyutta Nikaya 22. 95

Suppose a person who was not blind beheld the many bubbles on the Ganges [River] as they drove along ... After he had carefully watched them and examined them they would appear to him empty, unreal and unsubstantial. In exactly the same way does the student of the Buddha behold all corporeal phenomena, sensations, perceptions, moods, and thoughts ... He watches them, examines them carefully, and, after carefully examining them, they appear to him empty, void and without a self.

Law of Dependent Origination

During his enlightenment, the Buddha discovered the law of Dependent Origination, whereby one condition arises out of another, which in turn arises out of prior conditions in a *twelve-link chain of causes.* Each link is based on the principle of Cause and Effect which determines one's condition. According to the Buddha, until an individual understands the cause of suffering and the way to end suffering, that individual will continue to be trapped in a cycle of birth and death.

The twelve links of the Chain of Dependent Origination give a detailed description of the cause of suffering and rebirth: (1) ignorance; (2) karmic actions; (3) consciousness; (4) body and mind; (5) the senses; (6) sense impressions; (7) feelings; (8) craving; (9) clinging; (10) becoming; (11) rebirth; (12) old age and death. (It helps to view the Chain of Dependent Origination as a circular rather than a linear process.)

11. The Twelve Links. Vinaya Pitaka 1: 1

Conditioned by ignorance are the karma-formations; conditioned by the karma-formations is consciousness; conditioned by consciousness is mind-and-body; conditioned by mind-and-body are the six sense fields; conditioned by the six sense-fields is sense-impression; conditioned by sense-impression is feeling; conditioned by feeling is craving; conditioned by craving is grasping; conditioned by grasping is becoming; conditioned by becoming is birth; conditioned by birth there come into being ageing and dying, grief, sorrow, suffering, lamentation and despair. This is the origin of the whole mass of suffering.

12. The Parable of the Oil Lamp. Samyutta-Nikaya 11: 86

He dwelt at Savatthi. 'In one, monks, who abides reflecting on the enjoyment of things that fetter, craving increases. With craving as a cause there is grasping. With grasping as a cause there is becoming the desire to be. With the desire to be as a cause there is rebirth. With rebirth as a cause old age and death, grief, lamentation, pain, dejection, and despair arise. Even so is the cause of this whole mass of pain.

'Just as, monks, on account of oil and on account of a wick an oil lamp would burn, and a man from time to time were to pour oil thereon and trim the wick, even so, monks, an oil lamp with that nutriment, that fuel, would burn for a long time.

'Even so, monks, in one who abides reflecting on the enjoyment of things that fetter, craving increases ... 'Even so is the cause of this whole mass of pain.

'In one, monks, who reflects on the wretchedness of things that fetter, craving ceases. With the cessation of craving grasping ceases ... Even so is the cessation of this whole mass of pain.

'Just as, monks, on account of oil and on account of a wick an oil lamp would burn, and a man from time to time were not to pour oil thereon and not to trim the wick, even so, monks, an oil lamp with the exhaustion of the original fuel and being without nutriment through being unfed with any more would become extinct.

'Even so, monks, in one who abides reflecting on the wretchedness of things that fetter, craving ceases. With the ceasing of craving grasping ceases. With the ceasing of grasping the desire to be ceases. With the ceasing of the desire to be rebirth ceases. With the ceasing of rebirth old age and death, grief, lamentation, pain, dejection, and despair cease. Even so is the cessation of this whole mass of pain.'

Compassion and Loving-Kindness

The Buddhist way of life includes extending compassion and loving-kindness to all beings without exception. This practice includes people whom you like, consider neutral, and even those who do you harm. To express good will to all is very challenging because it is natural to dislike or feel angry towards those that do you harm. After his enlightenment, the Buddha realized that all creatures are trapped in the cycle of birth and death and the suffering that comes with that. The Buddha's teachings, therefore, have their source in his feeling of compassion and the necessity for loving-kindness to all.

13. The Mind of Compassion and Loving-Kindness. Majjhima Nikaya 21: Kakacupama Sutra 1: 126–127, 129

'Monks, there are these five courses of speech that others may use when they address you: their speech may by timely or untimely, true or untrue, gentle or harsh, connected with good or with harm, spoken with a mind of loving-kindness or in a mood of hate ... Herein, monks, you should train thus: "Our minds will remain unaffected, and we shall utter no bitter words; we shall abide compassionate for their welfare, with a mind of loving-kindness, never in a mood of hate ... We shall abide pervading that person with a mind imbued with loving-kindness, and starting with that person, we shall abide pervading the all-encompassing world with a mind imbued with loving-kindness, abundant, exalted, immeasurable, without hostility, and without ill will."

'Monks, even if bandits were to sever you savagely limb by limb with a two-handled saw, he who gave rise to a mind of hate toward them would not be carrying out my teaching. Herein, monks, you should train thus: "Our minds will remain unaffected, and we shall utter no bitter words; we shall abide compassionate for their welfare, with a mind of loving-kindness, never in a mood of hate. We shall abide pervading them with a mind imbued with loving-kindness; and starting with them, we shall abide pervading the all-encompassing world with a mind imbued with loving-kindness, abundant, exalted, immeasurable, without hostility, and without ill will." That is how you should train, monks ...'

Nirvana (*Nibbana*)

The Buddha fulfilled life's goal – the realization of *nirvana*. The word nirvana or *nibbana* means 'to blow out,' or 'to extinguish' selfish craving and desire. Nirvana is the highest realm of the human spirit and cannot be described in words. Trying to characterize nirvana is like trying to explain the ocean to a cat. You can only say what it is not: 'No, the ocean isn't dry land.' 'No, you can't walk on it.' 'No, you can't think an oceanic thought.' Yet, nirvana lacks nothing.

The nirvanic experience includes 'seeing' everything in the universe as a series of interrelationships. The universe neither starts nor stops anywhere. In it everything continually rises and falls, moves in and out of each other. Nothing is stable except the totality itself.

Those few beings that reach nirvana find peace with themselves and the world. The experience removes self-dissatisfaction and fills one with unlimited compassion for others. When disciples asked the Buddha to describe nirvana, he said nirvana is not only indescribable, but also incomprehensible, inconceivable, and unutterable. Then he added that bliss is nirvana. Bliss is the state of freedom from future rebirth, old age, and death. Nirvana is peace and happiness, the absence of suffering.

Reflections

Although not many of us have realized the state of nirvana, can you recall periods of peace or bliss when you were not concerned with desires, fame or success?

---

14. Nirvana is Peace. Anguttara Nikaya 5: 322

This is Peace, this is the excellent, namely the calm of all the impulses, the casting out of all 'basis,' the extinction of craving, dispassion, stopping, Nirvana.

15. End of Karma. Anguttara Nikaya 3: 32

This truly, is Peace, this is the Highest, namely the end of all karma formations, the forsaking of every substratum of rebirth, the fading away of craving, detachment ...

16. Extinction of the Three Poisons. Samyutta Nikaya 38: 1

The extinction of greed, the extinction of hate, the extinction of delusion: this indeed is called Nibanna.

17. End of Ageing and Dying. Sutta Nipata 1093–1094

For those who in mid-stream stay, in great peril in the flood ... do I proclaim the Isle ... of No-beyond. Nirvana do I call it – the utter extinction of ageing and dying.

18. The End of Suffering. Udana 80

There [nirvana], monks, I say, there is neither coming nor going nor staying nor passing away nor arising. Without support or mobility or basis is it. This is indeed the end of suffering.

That which is Selfless, hard it is to see;
Not easy is it to perceive the Truth.
But who has ended craving utterly
Has naught to cling to, he alone can see.

Theravada (Hinayana) Buddhism

According to the Theravada Buddhists, the Buddha was a man – an extraordinary man who discovered the way of salvation but nevertheless human. Buddhas are those few who discover the truth about life for themselves. Such humans are rare because most people depend on a teacher to show them the way. Although the Buddha has passed beyond reach, he laid out a path for others to follow. The goal of the path is to reach nirvana, which is something each person must achieve individually. To attain nirvana, one should renounce worldly pursuits and join the homeless state of a monk or nun. An individual who has achieved enlightenment is known as an *arhat* ('a slayer of the foe'). An arhat is the perfected disciple or saint, who proceeds unswervingly toward nirvana through individual effort alone.

As previously mentioned, the scriptures used by Theravada Buddhists are known as the Pali Canon, written about the first century BCE. The Pali Canon has three sections called the Tripitaka (or 'three baskets'): the *vinaya,* or monastic discipline; the *sutra,* or teachings of the Buddha; and the *abhidhamma,* or systematic philosophy that correlated Buddha's teachings with meditation. One sutra alone, the *Majjhima Nikaya* is 1,100 pages long. Together the three baskets could fill a bookcase.

Theravada Buddhism stresses the Sangha, the order of monks and nuns. Monks in the Sangha are known as *bhikkus* and nuns as *bhikkunis*. As well as striving toward enlightenment, Theravada monks must preserve and spread the *dharma* (the Buddhist teaching) by word and example. The monks shave their heads, dress in simple robes, own only a few material items, eat no solid foods after noon, practice celibacy, and depend on the laity for their food, clothing, and medical supplies. Early every morning they set forth with begging bowls, and the lay people consider it good karma to feed them. In return, the monks offer the lay people spiritual guidance.

Bhikkunis (or Buddhist nuns), however, did not receive much support from the lay people. Thus, the order of fully ordained nuns disappeared in Theravada countries about one thousand years ago. Today some women are attempting to revive the ordained orders of nuns in Theravada countries such as Sri Lanka, but again, they have received little assistance from society.

Reflections

In Theravada Buddhism, the interrelationship between monks and laity is extremely important. In what ways might your community react to their church leaders begging food daily in return for spiritual guidance? Could passing the collection plate be a similar practice?

19. The Arhat. Samyutta Nikaya 38: 1

And for a disciple thus freed, in whose heart dwells peace, there is nothing to be added to what has been done, and naught more remains for him to do. Just as a rock of one solid mass remains unshaken by the wind, even so … neither the desired nor the undesired can cause such a one to waver. Steadfast is his mind, gained is deliverance.

20. The Bhikkhu. Dhammapada 368, 376

The bhikkhu who abides in loving-kindness, who is pleased with the Buddha's teaching, attains to that state of peace and happiness, the stilling of conditioned things, Nibbana.

Let him be cordial in all his ways and refined in conduct; filled thereby with joy, he will make an end of ill.

21. The Three Jewels Formula: Basic Buddhist Act of Piety. Traditional

I take refuge in the Buddha.
I take refuge in the Dharma (teaching).
I take refuge in the Sangha (brotherhood of monks)

Mahayana Buddhism

Theravada Buddhists live by the motto, 'Be lamps unto yourselves; work out your salvation with diligence.' Mahayana Buddhists agree that it is up to the individual to attain enlightenment, but compassion is more important than self-attainment. To gain enlightenment for oneself and leave all other people behind is a contradiction in terms. Mahayanists believe that human beings are more social than individual and that compassion is the highest attribute one can have. Thus, Mahayana Buddhism includes lay people: even its priests usually marry and serve the laity. The ideal for the Mahayana is the *bodhisattva*, or 'the being of enlightenment.' The bodhisattva is one who, having reached the shores of nirvana, voluntarily renounces that heavenly bliss to remain in *samsara* (the cycle of rebirth) to help others.

Unlike the Theravadists, Mahayana Buddhists consider Gautama the Buddha as a savior and thus refer to him as 'Lord Buddha.' The Mahayana school also departs from the Theravadists by including metaphysics in its belief system. Like the Hindu and Christian Trinity, they refer to the *Trikaya*, or three forms of Buddha: *Dharmakaya* (the Buddha nature or truth body), *Sambhogakaya* (glorious celestial transfigured body), and *Nirmanakaya* (earthly manifestations of a historical person such as the Buddha).

Reflections
As a Buddhist, which would appeal to you – the Buddha as an enlightened man or Lord Buddha as a savior?

22. The Infinite Compassion of the Bodhisattva. Santideva's Siksasamuccaya 280–281

A Bodhisattva resolves: I take upon myself the burden of all suffering ... I do not turn or run away, do not tremble, am not terrified ... do not turn back or despond.

And why? ... I have made the vow to save all beings ... The whole world of living beings I must rescue, from the terrors of birth-and-death, from the jungle of false views ... My endeavors do not merely aim at my own deliverance ... I must rescue all these beings from the stream of Samsara ... And I must not cheat beings out of my store of merit. I am resolved to abide in each single state of woe for numberless aeons; and so I will help all beings to freedom, in all the states of woe that may be found in any world system whatsoever.

And why? Because it is surely better that I alone should be in pain than that all these beings should fall into states of woe.

Emptiness (Shunyata)

Nagarjuna (c. 300 CE) was one of the great thinkers in the history of Buddhism who helped formulate the concept of *shunyata* (or emptiness). He also discovered the Mahayana scriptures known as the *Prajnaparamita Sutras*. According to the Mahayana Buddhists, the essence of enlightenment is the Buddha Nature. Because nothing can be said to describe the Buddha Nature, they refer to it by using such non-names as 'emptiness' or 'suchness.' Empty of what? The Buddha Nature is empty of any views through the eyes of ignorance (*samsara*).

Humans and the world of nature are both processes of the Wheel of Becoming. Nothing in the universe has a separate, essential being that is independent of other things: all things exist only relatively and interdependently. Space and time, always related to and dependent on each other, are also relative to the 'becoming process.'

Reflections

If one were to ask a practicing Buddhist, what can one cling to in this ever-changing world, the Buddhist would reply – nothing. Why?

23. The Heart Sutra

Avalokita, the holy Lord and Bodhisattva, was moving in the deep course of the wisdom that has gone beyond. He looked down from on high, he beheld but five [skandhas]. And he saw that in their own-being they were empty.

Here, O Sariputra, form is emptiness and the very emptiness is form, emptiness does not differ from form, form does not differ from emptiness; whatever is form, that is emptiness, whatever is emptiness, that is form.

Here, O Sariputra, all dharmas are marked with emptiness; they are not produced or stopped, not defiled or immaculate, not deficient or complete.

Therefore, O Sariputra, in emptiness there is no form, nor feeling, nor perception, nor impulse, nor consciousness; no eye, ear, nose, tongue, body, mind; no forms, sounds, smells, tastes, touchables or objects of mind; no sight-organ element, and so forth, until we come to: no mind-consciousness-element; there is no ignorance, no extinction of ignorance, and so forth, until we come to: there is no decay and death, no extinction of decay and death; there is no suffering, no origination, no stopping, no path; there is no cognition, no attainment, and no non-attainment.

Therefore, O Sariputra, it is because of his indifference to any kind of personal attainment that a Bodhisattva ... dwells without thought-coverings ... and in the end he attains to Nirvana.

Therefore, one should know the Prajnaparamita [Perfection of Wisdom] as the great mantra [sound or word, or a series of these], the mantra of great knowledge, the utmost mantra, the unequalled mantra, allayer of all suffering, in truth — for what could go wrong?

... The [mantra] ... runs like this:

Gone, Gone, Gone Beyond, Gone Altogether Beyond, O What an Awakening! All Hail!

This completes the Heart of Perfect Wisdom.

Branches of Mahayana Buddhism

Tibetan Buddhism

Before the introduction of Buddhism into Tibet, their native religion was known as *Bon*, a primal religion that included shamanistic rituals involving animal sacrifices, and magical incantations to control demonic powers. In the seventh century CE, Songtsan-Gampo, the new king of Tibet, made Buddhism the national religion. At first, native priests fought this new religion, but a Buddhist monk named Padmasambhava reconciled the two religions, and so Tibetan Buddhism was born.

Tibetan Buddhism has a vast collection of scriptures, including esoteric scriptures, or tantras, that describe the powerful rituals. These are called the *Vajrayana* ('Diamond Vessel' or 'Thunderbolt Vessel').

The Dalai Lama

One of the more important aspects of Tibetan Buddhism is the belief that certain Dalai Lamas are reincarnations of earlier Dalai Lamas, who in turn are considered emanations of Buddhas and bodhisattvas. Each Dalai Lama, the spiritual leader of Tibetan Buddhists, is considered an emanation of *Avalokiteshvara*, the heavenly bodhisattva of compassion. When a Dalai Lama dies, a delegation of monks consults an oracle to find the Dalai Lama's place of rebirth. Once they have found the place and identified the boy they think may be the Dalai Lama's new incarnation, the monks take objects that belonged to the previous Dalai Lama and mix them with similar objects. The boy who recognizes the objects as his and selects *only* those used by the previous Dalai Lama proves his identity. It is a tedious task that may take from months to years of testing before the monks agree they have found the reincarnated Dalai Lama.

The *Tibetan Book of the Dead*

Tibetan Buddhism is famous for its *Tibetan Book of the Dead*, which explains the intermediate states between one life and the next; these are known as the *Bardo* (or transition). The *Tibetan Book of the Dead* offers instructions to the dying person. According to the text, individuals can divide the whole of their existence into four bardos: (1) life; (2) dying and death; (3) after-death; and (4) rebirth.

24. Instructions to the Dying Person. *Tibetan Book of the Dead*

O nobly-born, that which is called death hath now come. Thou art departing from this world, but thou art not the only one; [death] cometh to all. Do not cling, in fondness and weakness, to this life. Even though thou clingest out of weakness, thou hast not the power to remain here. Thou wilt gain nothing more than wandering in this *Samsara*. Be not attached [to this world]; be not weak. Remember the Precious Trinity.

O nobly-born, whatever fear and terror may come to thee … forget not these words; and, bearing their meaning at heart, go forwards: in them lieth the vital secret of recognition:

Alas! When the Uncertain Experiencing of Reality is dawning upon me here,

With every thought of fear or terror or awe for all [apparitional appearances] set aside,

May I recognize whatever [visions] appear, as the reflections of mine own consciousness:

May I know them to be of the nature of apparitions in the Bardo:

When at this all-important moment [of opportunity] of achieving a great end.

May I not fear the bands of Peaceful and Wrathful [Deities], mine own thought-forms.

Repeat thou these [verses] clearly, and remembering their significance as thou repeatest them, go forwards, [O nobly-born]. Thereby, whatever visions of awe or terror appear, recognition is certain; and forget not this vital secret art lying therein.

25. Everything is Buddha

… As is Nirvana, so is Samsara.
Do not think there is any distinction.

Do not sit at home, do not go to the forest,
But recognize mind wherever you are.
When one abides in complete and perfect enlightenment,
Where is Samsara and where is Nirvana?

Do not err in this matter of self and other.
Everything is Buddha without exception …

Zen Buddhism

Once, while the Buddha was sitting in meditation, a disciple brought him a golden flower and asked him to preach the secret of his doctrine. The Buddha took the flower, held it aloft and looked at it in silence. His doctrine, he indicated, lay not in words but in profound contemplation. From this came Zen Buddhism which depends not on books, preaching, or discussion, but upon years of disciplined meditation that at last brings forth a flash of enlightenment. Even simple acts, such as tea drinking, gardening, and the enjoyment of nature, according to Zen, contain the mystery of life and have religious significance.

Zen Buddhists believe the Buddha Nature is inside everyone, and with proper meditation a person can wake up to his or her Buddha Nature. This self-realization is called *satori*.

Zen (or Ch'an, which means meditation) developed mainly in China, Korea, and Japan. The most austere of the Zen Buddhist methods, *zazen*, stresses sitting in meditation and reflecting on a *koan*, which is a riddle or puzzling story with no logical answer. For example, 'What did your face look like before you were born?' Its purpose is to stop the mind in its tracks and teach the student of the riddle that logic and reason have their limitations. Thus, a koan cuts through mental constructs that hinder the realization of truth.

Reflections

What do Zen Buddhists mean when they teach that there is a supreme and wonderful truth, words cannot reach it and words cannot teach it?

---

26. Zen Koan: The Dog

A monk once asked Master Joshu, 'Has a dog the Buddha Nature or not?' Joshu said, 'Mu!'

27. Zen Koan: Wash Your Bowls

Once a monk made a request of [Master] Joshu: 'I have just entered the monastery,' he said, 'please give me instructions, Master.' Joshu said: 'Have you had your breakfast?' 'Yes I have,' replied the monk. 'Then,' said Joshu, 'wash your bowls.' The monk had an insight.

28. Zen Koan: The Oak Tree

A monk asked Joshu, 'What is the meaning of the Patriach's coming from the West?' Joshu answered, 'The oak tree in the front garden.'

29. Zen Koan: Three Pounds of Flax

A monk asked Master Tozan, 'What is the Buddha?' Tozan said, 'Three pounds of flax.'

30. Zen Koan: Why Practice?

Ummon said, 'Look! This world is vast and wide. Why do you put on your priest's robe at the sound of the bell?'

31. Zen Koan: Shit-Stick

A monk asked Ummon, 'What is Buddha?' Ummon said: 'A shit-stick!'

Zen Stories

32. A Cup of Tea

Nan-in, a Japanese master during the Meiji era (1868–1912), received a university professor who came to inquire about Zen.

Nan-in served tea. He poured his visitor's cup full, and then kept on pouring.

The professor watched the overflow until he no longer could restrain himself. 'It is overfull. No more will go in!'

'Like this cup,' Nan-in said, 'you are full of your own opinions and speculations. How can I show you Zen unless you first empty your cup?'

33. Muddy Road

Tanzan and Ekido were once traveling together down a muddy road. A heavy rain was still falling.

Coming around a bend, they met a lovely girl in a silk kimono and sash, unable to cross the intersection.

'Come on, girl,' said Tanzan at once. Lifting her in his arms, he carried her over the mud.

Ekido did not speak again until that night when they reached a lodging temple. Then he no longer could restrain himself. 'We monks don't go near females,' he told Tanzan, 'especially not young and lovely ones. It is dangerous. Why did you do that?

'I left the girl there,' said Tanzan. 'Are you still carrying her?'

Pure Land Buddhism

Pure Land offers the broadest version of Buddhism. It first gained popularity when other forms of Buddhism were restricted to monks and disciplined meditators. The Pure Land form gives hope to ordinary people and is the most popular among the working class, especially in China and Japan. Pure Land Buddhists believe that somewhere there is a pure land where all humans will eventually be reborn through the compassion of *Amitabha* (or Amida) Buddha. They believe that faith in Amitabha Buddha, and repetition of his name, will lead to eventual rebirth in his world, where life is more conducive to the attainment of nirvana. Daily repetition and recitation at the moment of death of the phrase, 'I rely on Amitabha Buddha' will ensure an individual's rebirth in the Pure Land.

Reflections

Do you see similarities between Pure Land and Christianity with Amitabha Buddha replacing Jesus Christ as the savior?

34. The Pure Land of Amitabha, the Buddha. Sukhavativyuha: Chapters 15–18
... The world system of the Lord Amitabha is rich and prosperous, comfortable, fertile, delightful. And in this world system ... there are no hells, no animals, no ghosts, no Asuras and none of the unauspicious places of rebirth ...

And that world system ... emits many fragrant odors, it is rich in a great variety of flowers and fruits, adorned with jewel trees, which are frequented by flocks of various birds with sweet voices ... And these jewel trees ... have various colours, many colours, many hundreds of thousands of colours.

On all sides it is surrounded with golden nets, and all round covered with lotus flowers made of all the precious things. Some of the lotus flowers are half a mile in circumference, others up to ten miles. And from each jewel lotus issues thirty-six hundred thousand kotis of rays. And at the end of each ray there issue thirty-six hundred thousand kotis of Buddhas, with golden-colored bodies, who bear the thirty-two marks of the superman ...

And many kinds of rivers flow along in this world system, up to fifty miles broad and twelve miles deep ... their water is fragrant with manifold agreeable odours ...

And ... both the banks of those great rivers are lined with variously scented jewel trees ... And those rivers flow along with golden sand at the bottom. And all the wishes those beings may think of, they all will be fulfilled, as long as they are rightful.

And ... everyone hears the pleasant sound he wishes to hear, i.e., he hears of the Buddha, the Dharma, the Sangha ... And, hearing this one gains ... joyfulness ... dispassion, calm ... and brings abut the state of mind which leads to the accomplishment of enlightenment ...

And that ... is the reason why this world-system is called the 'Happy Land' ...

Nichiren Buddhism

In the thirteenth century, a Japanese monk who called himself Nichiren felt the need to reform Buddhism and Japanese society. He thought the Pure Land and other schools of Buddhism were focusing too heavily on their own enlightenment and the afterlife, rather than on helping society. His teaching was based on one Mahayana scripture, the *Lotus Sutra*, a large compilation of parables, verses, and descriptions of the Lord Buddha. Nichiren was particularly interested in the bodhisattva and the conviction that each person is potentially a Buddha. He taught that the Buddha, who appeared to be born on earth and pass away, had been enlightened since the beginning of time and still actively works for the salvation of all beings.

Devout followers of Nichiren Buddhism repeat the mantra of the Lotus Sutra many times a day: *namo myoho regye kyo,* which means, 'Praise to the mystic law of the Lotus Sutra.' They believe that recitation of the mantra will connect them with the spiritual power of the universe.

35. Nichiren on Faith in the Buddha and the Lotus Sutra
When you fall into an abyss and someone has lowered a rope to pull you out, should you hesitate to grasp the rope because you doubt the power of the helper?

Has not the Buddha declared, 'I alone am the protector and savior'? There is the power! Is it not taught that faith is the only entrance? There is the rope! ... Our hearts ache and our sleeves are wet [with tears], until we see face to face the tender figure of the One, who says to us, 'I am thy Father.' ... Should any season be passed without thinking of the compassionate promise, 'Constantly I am thinking of you'? Should any month or day be spent without revering the teaching that there is none who cannot attain Buddhahood? ... Devote yourself wholeheartedly to the 'Adoration to the Lotus of the Perfect Truth,' and utter it yourself as well as admonish others to do the same. Such is your task in this human life.

The Dhammapada

The Dhammapada, usually translated as 'Scripture Verses,' may be the most readable Buddhist text for the general practitioner. Drawn from many parts of the Pali Canon, the Dhammapada is a collection of some four hundred moral sayings attributed to the Buddha, and is among the classics of the world's ethical literature.

36. Twin Verses. The Dhammapada, Ch. 1
All that we are is the result of what we have thought: it is founded on our thoughts, it is made up of our thoughts. If a man speaks or acts with an evil thought, pain follows him, as the wheel follows the foot of the ox that draws the carriage.

All that we are is the result of what we have thought: it is founded on our thoughts, it is made up of our thoughts. If a man speaks or acts with a pure thought, happiness follows him, like a shadow that never leaves him.

> 'He abused me, he beat me, he defeated me, he robbed me' – in those who harbor such thoughts hatred will never cease.
> 'He abused me, he beat me, he defeated me, he robbed me' – in those who do not harbor such thoughts hatred will cease.
> For hatred does not cease by hatred at any time; hatred ceases by love – this is an old rule.

The virtuous man delights in this world, and he delights in the next; he delights in both. He delights and rejoices when he sees the purity of his own work.

The evildoer suffers in this world, and he suffers in the next; he suffers in both. He suffers when he thinks of the evil he has done; he suffers more when going on the evil path.

37. On Earnestness. The Dhammapada. Ch. II
Fools follow after vanity. The wise man keeps earnestness as his best jewel.

Follow not after vanity, not after the enjoyment of love and lust! He who is earnest and meditative obtains ample joy.

38. Taming the Mind. The Dhammapada, Ch. III

As a fletcher makes straight his arrow, a wise man makes straight his trembling and unsteady thought, which is difficult to guard, difficult to hold back.

It is good to tame the mind, which is difficult to hold in and flighty, rushing wherever it lists; a tamed mind brings happiness.

39. The Fool. The Dhammapada, Ch. V

If a traveler does not meet with one who is his better, or his equal, let him firmly keep to his solitary journey; there is no companionship with a fool.

Fools of poor understanding have themselves for their greatest enemies, for they do evil deeds which bear bitter fruits.

40. The Wise Man. The Dhammapada, Ch. VI

Do not have evildoers for friends, do not have low people for friends: have virtuous people for friends, have for friends the best of men.

As a solid rock is not shaken by the wind, wise people falter not midst blame and praise.

Well-makers lead the water wherever they like; fletchers bend the arrow; carpenters bend a log of wood; wise people fashion themselves.

41. Anger. The Dhammapada, Ch. XVII

He who holds back rising anger like a rolling chariot, him I call a real driver; other people are but holding the reins.

Let a man overcome anger by love, let him overcome evil by good; let him overcome the greedy by liberality, the liar by truth!

42. Good People. The Dhammapada, Ch. XXI

Good people shine from afar, like the snowy mountains; bad people are not seen, like arrows shot by night.

A man full of faith, if endowed with virtue and glory, is respected, whatever place he may close.

Summary

The Buddhist religion originated from the enlightened teachings of the Buddha – the word Buddha means 'Awakened One.' The Buddha preached a religion devoid of authority and speculation. What matters, he said, is how we live our lives.

The Buddha was born Siddhartha Gautama, the son of a king. He left all his princely possessions, however, to seek truth. After his enlightenment, he taught unselfishly for forty-five years. To Buddhists, his teachings are *dharma* or law. Essential to understanding the Buddha's teachings is the concept of *anicca*, the impermanence of everything. All things are in a state of flux; there is no personal soul. Human beings are composed of five *skandhas*: (1) body; (2) feelings; (3) perceptions; (4) dispositions; and (5) consciousness.

The skandhas act as a chain of cause and effect that the Buddha called the Wheel of Becoming. He summed up the Wheel of Becoming in the Four Noble

Truths and the Eightfold Path. Central to the Buddha's teachings is the Middle Way – the path between two extremes.

Like Hinduism, the Buddha taught the twin law of karma and rebirth. Karma is the force of energy created by human thoughts, words, and deeds. Individual lives are the result of thoughts and actions in previous lives. Human beings shape their own destiny. Nirvana is freedom from karma and rebirth. It is freedom from suffering. The word nirvana means 'to blow out' or 'to extinguish' selfish craving and desire. Nirvana is the highest realm of the human spirit and cannot be described by words.

The Buddha taught *anatta*, or no-self. Because there is no-self as an object, there is only what is arising moment to moment. When the self as absolute subjectivity knows itself as nothing – emptiness or pure awareness – it can no longer be called self.

The Buddhist religion is divided into two main branches: Hinayana (also called Theravada) and Mahayana. The scriptures that guide followers of Theravada Buddhism are known as the *Pali Canon* and were written around the first century BCE. The Pali Canon is divided into three sections known as the *Tripitaka*, meaning 'Three Baskets.' The scriptures of the Mahayana Buddhists are similar to the Pali Canon, but teach distinctively Mahayana ideas. Among the Mahayana scriptures are the *Lotus Sutra*, the *Pure Land Sutras*, the *Heart Sutra*, and the *Perfection of Wisdom Sutras*.

The major branches of Mahayana Buddhism include: Tibetan Buddhism, famous for its *Book of the Dead*, which gives instructions to the dying; Zen Buddhism, which is famous for its disciplines meditation and koans; Pure Land Buddhism, which teaches that all will eventually be reborn in the Pure Land; and Nichiren Buddhism, whose devotees repeat the mantra of the Lotus Sutra many times a day.

The Dhammapada may be the most readable Buddhist text. Drawn from the Pali Canon, The Dhammapada is a collection of some four hundred moral sayings attributed to the Buddha.

Buddhism Today

Emperor Ashoka (r. 273–232 BCE) was a devout Buddhist who sent missionaries to foreign lands to spread the faith. During his reign, Buddhism became the state religion of India. However, orthodox Brahmins rebelled against Buddhism and by the seventh century, Hinduism had been reestablished as India's state religion.

Today, Theravada Buddhism flourishes in Sri Lanka and Thailand. Various forms of Mahayana Buddhism are practiced in Japan and South Korea. When communism overtook China, Buddhism declined, and when China invaded Tibet, the Dalai Lama and practicing Buddhists fled to India and other countries to keep their religion alive.

Buddhism has moved into the hearts and minds of the contemporary Western world. Because it is not bound to any particular culture or society, race or ethnic group, religions and individuals of many cultures embrace Buddhism's methods. The Four Noble Truths and the Eightfold Path, for example, are used by many religions as part of their spiritual exercises. Rather than emphasizing external dogmas and theories, Buddhism stresses the importance of verifying truth through one's own experience.

One of the characteristic developments of Buddhism is its emphasis on kindness and compassion as essential aspects of wisdom. Since its beginning, Buddhism has always been a religion of non-violence. According to the Buddhist dharma, people should treat each other and animals with kindness and compassion. Today many Buddhists are social activists, who protest against oppression, animal cruelty, war, and environmental destruction. Buddhists believe that the world's problems can only be solved by looking to the underlying cause – the lack of universal compassion in the human heart.

In science, there is a striking parallel between the Buddha's own experience of the Wheel of Becoming and that of modern physics. During his enlightenment, the Buddha experienced the unity and interrelation of all things and events. Modern quantum theory also reveals an essential interconnectedness of the universe. Quantum theory shows that the world cannot be decomposed into independently existing units. From this point of view, science does not objectively explain nature but is part of the interplay between nature and humankind. The external world and the internal world are interwoven.

Timeline

c. 563 BCE	Birth of Siddhartha Gautama, the historical Buddha.
c. 534 BCE	Gautama goes outside the palace gates for first time and sees the four sights – an old man, a sick man, a dead man, and a holy monk.
c. 528 BCE	Gautama attains enlightenment – travels to Deer Park to begin teaching.
c. 483 BCE	Death of the Buddha.
c. 250 BCE	King Ashoka (272 to 231 BCE) converts to Buddhism. Sends out missionaries.
first century BCE	Entire scriptural canon of Theravada School committed to writing on palm leaves.
200 BCE to 220 CE	Rise of Mahayana Buddhism. Composition of *Lotus Sutra* and other Mahayana Buddhist scriptures. Buddhism enters China and Central Asia.
third century CE	Buddhism expands to Burma, Cambodia, Laos, Vietnam, and Indonesia.
520 CE	Introduction of Buddhism to Japan. Bodhidharma: founder of Zen Buddhism.
sixth century CE	Buddhism becomes state religion of Japan.
seventh century CE	Buddhism adopted in Tibet.
1133 to 1212 CE	Honen establishes Pure Land Buddhism in Japan.
1222 CE	Nichiren founds school of Japanese Buddhism named after him.

thirteenth century CE	Dogen (1200–1253) founds Zen school of Japanese Buddhism.
1391 to 1474 CE	First Dalai Lama of Tibet.
1935 CE	Birth of Tenzin Gyatso, the fourteenth Dalai Lama of Tibet.
1951 CE	Chinese occupation of Tibet.
1959 CE	Dalai Lama flees Tibet to India. Tibetan Buddhism spreads to Western countries.
1989 CE	Dalai Lama receivs Nobel Peace Prize.

Study Questions

1. Explain the meaning of the term 'Buddha.'
2. Why do some theologians question whether Buddhism is really a religion?
3. What did the Buddha have in common with Socrates and Jesus?
4. What were the four sights that Siddhartha Gautama could never see if he were to become king?
5. What famous tree was the Buddha sitting under when he reached enlightenment?
6. Who were the founding members of the Sangha?
7. Explain the importance of the Four Noble Truths and the Eightfold Path.
8. Explain the Buddhist teaching: the Middle Way.
9. Discuss the skandhas and how they function.
10. How can a person who is a current collection of skandhas reap karma from a previous collection of skandhas?
11. Discuss the major differences between Theravada and Mahayana Buddhism.
12. What school of Buddhism is traditionally associated with the doctrine of the *Trikaya*?
13. Explain the difference between an arhat and a bodhisattva.
14. What are the four major branches of Mahayana Buddhism?
15. Of what use is the *Tibetan Book of the Dead*?
16. What is the importance of the koan in Zen Buddhism?
17. Who is Amitabha Buddha?
18. What mantra do the Nichiren Buddhists use daily?
19. Why is *The Dhammapada* considered among the classics of the world's ethical literature?

Suggested Reading

1. Armstrong, Karen (2001), *Buddha*. New York: Viking/Penguin.
2. deBary, William Theodore, ed. (1972), *The Buddhist Tradition in India, China, & Japan*. New York: Random House.
3. Fremantle, Francesca, and Trungpa, Chogyam (1975), *The Tibetan Book of the Dead*. Boston and London: Shambhala Publications.
4. Friedman, Lenore (1987), *Meetings With Remarkable Women: Buddhist Teachers in America*. Boston and London: Shambhala Publications.
5. Khyentse, Dzongsar Jamyang (2008), *What Makes You Not a Buddhist*. Boston: Shambhala Publications.

6. Middleton, Ruth (2008), *Alexandra David-Neel: Portrait of an Adventurer*. Boston: Shambhala Publications.
7. Nanamoli, Bhikkhu (1992), *The Life of the Buddha*. Sri Lanka: Buddhist Publication Society.
8. Roshi, Suzuki (2004), *Zen Mind, Beginner's Mind*. Boston: Shambhala Publications.
9. Suzuki, D.T. (1970), *The Field of Zen*. New York: Harper & Row Publishers.

Sources

1. Samyutta Nikaya 56.11, Nanamoli Thera, trans. (1972), *Three Cardinal Discourses of the Buddha*. Kandy, Sri Lanka: Buddhist Publication Society, pp. 7–8.
2. Samyutta Nikaya 56.11, Thera, trans. *Three Cardinal Discourses*, p. 6.
3. Samyutta-Nikaya, V.8, E.J. Thomas, trans. (1935), *Early Buddhist Scriptures*. London, pp. 94–96.
4. Buddhacarita 16. 28, 30, 35, 40, E.B. Cowell, trans. (1894), *Buddhist Mahayana Texts: Sacred Books of the East* Vol. 49. Oxford: Oxford University Press, pp. 174–180.
5. Anguttara Nikaya 6. 63, in Nyanatiloka Mahathera, ed. and trans. (1981), *The Word of the Buddha*. Kandy, Sri Lanka: Buddhist Publication Society, pp. 89–90.
6. Anguttara Nikaya 10. 206, in Nyanatloka, ed. and trans., *Word of the Buddha*, p. 19.
7. Majjhima-Nikaya 43, in Nyanatiloka, ed. and trans., *Word of the Buddha*, p. 44.
8. Anguttara Nikaya 3. 33, in Nyanatiloka, ed. and trans., *Word of the Buddha*, p. 44.
9. Samyutta Nikaya 15.3, in Nyanatiloka, ed. and trans., *Word of the Buddha*, pp. 14–15.
10. Samyutta Nikaya 22. 95, in Nyanatiloka, ed. and trans., *Word of the Buddha*, p. 12.
11. Vinaya Pitaka 1.1, Edward Conze et al. (1964), *Word of the Buddha*. New York: Harper & Row, p. 67.
12. Samyutta-Nikaya 11, 86, E.J. Thomas, trans. (1935), *Early Buddhist Scriptures*. London, pp. 122–123.
13. Kakacupama Sutra I, 126–127, 129; quoted in Bhikkhu Bodhi, ed. (2005), *In the Buddha's Words: An Anthology of Discourses from the Pali Canon*. Boston: Wisdom Publications, pp. 278–279.
14. Anguttara Nikaya V.322; F.L. Woodward and E. M. Hare, trans. (1951), *Gradual Sayings*, 5 vols. London: Pali Text Society, p. 65.
15. Anguttara Nikaya 3. 32, Nyanatiloka, ed. and trans., *Word of the Buddha*, p. 24.
16. Samyutta Nikaya 38.1, Nyanatiloka, ed. and trans., *Word of the Buddha*, p. 24.
17. Sutta Nipata 10. 93–94, Conze, et al., *Buddhist Texts*, pp. 92–93.
18. Udama 80, David Maurice, ed. (1962), *The Lion's Roar: An Anthology of the Buddha's Teachings Selected from the Pali Canon*. London: Rider & Co., p. 48.
19. Samyutta Nikaya 38.1, Nyanatiloka, ed. and trans., *Word of the Buddha*, p. 24.
20. Dhammapada 368, 376, Narada Maha Thera, trans. (1972), *The Dhammapada*, Colombo, Sri Lanka: Vajirarama, pp. 161–162.
21. Traditional
22. Santideva's Siksasamuccaya 280–281, Conze et al. *Buddhist Texts*, pp. 131–132.
23. Conze, *Buddhist Scriptures*, pp. 164–167.
24. W.Y. Evans-Wentz, trans. and ed. (1957), *The Tibetan Book of the Dead*. Oxford: Third edition, pp. 101–104.
25. Conze et al., *Buddhist Texts*, p. 238.
26. Zenkei Shibayama (1974), *Zen Comments on the Mumonkan*. New York: New American Library, p. 19.

27. Shibayana, *Zen Comments*, p. 94.

28. Shibayana, *Zen Comments*, p. 265.

29. Shibayana, *Zen Comments*, p. 139.

30. Shibayana, *Zen Comments*, p. 125.

31. Sjobayana, *Zen Comments*, p. 160.

32. Paul Reps (1981), *Zen Flesh, Zen Bones.* New York: Doubleday & Company, Inc., p. 5.

33. Reps, *Zen Flesh, Zen Bones*, p.18.

34. Sukhavativyuha, Ch. 15–17, 18, Conze et al, *Buddhist Texts*, pp. 202–206.

35. W.T. de Bary, ed. (1958), *Sources of Japanese Tradition.* New York: Columbia University Press, p. 217.

36. Clarence H. Hamilton, ed. (1952), *Buddhism: Selections from Buddhist Literature.* New York: The Bobbs-Merrill Co., Inc., pp. 64–65.

37. Hamilton, ed., *Buddhism*, p. 66.

38. Hamilton, ed., *Buddhism*, p. 67.

39. Hamilton, ed., *Buddhism*, pp. 69–70.

40. Hamilton, ed., *Buddhism*, p. 71.

41. Hamilton, ed., *Buddhism*, p. 82.

42. Hamilton, ed., *Buddhism*, p. 88.

4 Jain and Sikh Wisdom

The Jain Symbol of Ahimsa
Ahimsa refers to non-violence.

The Sikh Symbol Ek Onkar
Ek Onkar means 'God is One.'

Two Religions Arising in India

Although neither has ever been the state religion of India, both Jainism and Sikhism have been and remain the religion of choice in large segments of the population. Jainism is an ancient religion, while Sikhism is comparatively young. Both religions have connections with Hinduism, including beliefs in rebirth and karma. Both rose in protest, however, against Hinduism's rituals and polytheism. For the Jains, no one particular God or Supreme Being creates the universe or plays any part in the universal scheme of things. Impersonal universal laws control everything in nature. The Jains accept the many gods of Hinduism, but they believe the gods need liberation, which they can attain only while they are in human form. For the Sikhs, on the other hand, there is only one God, called the True One, which is reminiscent of Allah (God) in the Muslim faith.

Like the Hindus, both Jains and Sikhs have a similar concept of exalted beings – called 'Ford-makers' for the Jains and 'Gurus' for the Sikhs – that incarnate from age to age. Both Jainism and Sikhism, however, rejected the authority of the Hindu Vedas, the domination of priests, and the concept of caste.

> **Reflections**
> Do you agree with the Jains that universal laws control everything in nature? Or do you, like the Sikhs, believe that one God is in control?

Jainism

Jainism is often called the 'religion of conquerors,' because of its emphasis on achieving *moksha* (liberation) through rigorous ascetic practices. The Jains self-imposed privation is extremely harsh: they subject the body to excessive cold and heat and they fast on a regular basis. According to traditional Jains, death by fast is an eminently worthy, in fact a supreme accomplishment, that was first achieved by Mahavira, the religions' founder.

Similar to the Hindu belief in exalted beings, the Jains believe twenty-four Ford-makers (*tirthankaras*)* have reached perfection and shown the way to others through the ages. Ford-makers are given this name because their teaching provides the ford by which souls can cross to salvation. A Ford-maker, however, is not a 'bridge builder,' because each individual must cross the river by going *through* the water by him or herself. Mahavira, the founder of the religion now known as Jainism, is the twenty-fourth and most recent Ford-maker.

Mahavira's Life

Born to a noble family, Mahavira (c. 599–527 BCE) was given the name Nataputta Vardhamana meaning 'increasing,' because after his birth his family's wealth kept increasing. Nataputta Vardhamana later earned the name Mahavira (great hero), whose followers believe the universe has no beginning or end but passes through endless cycles of rising and falling levels of civilization. When the cycle reaches a state of decline, a Ford-maker appears to guide humans away from evil to the good life. Mahavira is the Ford-maker of the present age.

Mahavira married and had a daughter, but at age thirty, he plucked out his hair (as a symbol of his renunciation), gave up his family and withdrew from society. He joined the religious Order of Nirgranthas, whose adherents wore clothes, but after a year, Mahavira removed his clothes and remained naked for the rest of his life. For six years, he traveled around with a fellow ascetic named Gosala, also of the Nirgrantha Order, but they parted over a philosophical dispute. Gosala believed that karma was absolute destiny and humans have no power over their own destiny. Mahavira took the position that humans are free to overcome karma by their own efforts.

> **Reflections**
> Do we control our own destiny? For example, do you control how hard you study and thus what grades you earn? Or is our destiny in the hands of a higher source? When someone dies unexpectedly, we often hear: 'It was God's will.' How free are we?

For twelve years Mahavira wandered through the kingdoms of the Ganges River valley, enduring terrible hardships, often fasting for days on end. Even when attacked by men or wild animals, he remained calm and continued to meditate.

---

* A *ford* is a place in a river or stream where people can cross through the water to the other side.

1. Mahavira's Enlightenment. Akaranga Sutra 2. 24, 25.

... During the thirteenth year in the second month of summer ... on its tenth day ... on the bank of the river Rigupalika, not far from an old temple, in the field of the householder Samaga, under a Sal tree ... in a squatting position with joined heels exposing himself to the heat of the sun, after fasting two and a half days without drinking water, being engaged in deep meditation, reached the highest knowledge and intuition, called Kevala [Nirvana], which is infinite, supreme, unobstructed, unimpeded, complete, and full.

When the Venerable Ascetic Mahavira had become an Arhat ... he was a Kevalin [enlightened being], omniscient and comprehending all objects. He knew all conditions of the world, of gods, men, and demons: whence they come, whither they go, whether they are born as men or animals or become gods or hell-beings. [He knew] the ideas, the thoughts of their minds, the food, doings, desires, the open and secret deeds of all the living beings in the whole world. He, the Arhat, for whom there is no secret, knew and saw all conditions of all living beings in the world, what they thought, spoke, or did at any moment.

After his enlightenment, Mahavira accepted but reinterpreted the Hindu concepts of karma, reincarnation, and moksha (liberation). The Jains' ultimate goal is to stop karma and rid oneself of all karma accumulated over lifetimes, thus achieving liberation. To this end Jains practice a life of asceticism as well as confession, penance, the diligent acquisition of knowledge, and meditation. As in Buddhism, we are in charge of our own lives: no supreme creator God intercedes.

Gathering many followers about him, Mahavira became a well-known teacher in the kingdoms around the Ganges River. Some of the kings in the area gave aid to both Mahavira and his contemporary, the Buddha. Like the Buddha, Mahavira sought to make religion a personal experience and a part of daily life. Unlike the Buddha, who taught the path of moderation, the 'Middle Way,' Mahavira lived in extreme austerity. Both Mahavira and the Buddha opposed ritual, especially the animal sacrifices of Hinduism, and both rejected the caste system. Recall that the Hindus had four ranked social classes: At the top were the priests or Brahmins, followed by the warrior or administrator caste, then the merchants and farmers; at the bottom were the laborers and servants. Outside this hierarchical social system were the untouchables, whose mere approach was thought to pollute the higher classes.

The function of the Brahmins was to ensure the correct performance of ritual sacrifices through which embodied souls could gain liberation from further rebirth. Mahavira preached that birth and sacrifice had no relevancy for salvation; the only way to gain salvation was to perform severe acts of bodily asceticism. He begged his food, but ate only leftovers from a meal of some other person. To discipline his naked body, he sought out the coldest spots in the winter and the hottest places in the summer. Whenever angry people sent their dogs after him, Mahavira allowed the animals to attack.

Mahavira is said to have ended his days at age seventy-two by starving himself to death in a Jain monastery. Thus, after living a long life of virtue and detachment, Jainism allows one to end life out of consideration for others. Gentle methods of ending one's life, such as walking into an ocean or lake, are esteemed. Self-starvation is the 'holy death' that Jains prepare for over the years by practicing fasting. Self-starvation consists of taking liquids but no food and is considered the highest expression of nonattachment and freedom.

Reflections

Is starvation a form of euthanasia? Do you think starvation could be a valid, even noble way to die?

According to Jain tradition, Mahavira earned the title 'conqueror' because he heroically conquered the forces of life. Free from karma, he also gained final liberation from further rebirth.

2. Conquering the Self. Uttaradhyayana Sutra 9. 34–36

Though a man should conquer thousands and thousands of valiant foes, greater will be his victory if he conquers nobody but himself.

Fight with yourself; why fight with external foes? He who conquers himself through himself will obtain happiness …

Difficult to conquer is oneself; but when that is conquered, everything is conquered.

Jain Scriptures

Mahavira established a following of 36,000 nuns and 14,000 monks, who were supported by a lay community of nearly 500,000 men and women. After his death, many wealthy rulers and lay people supported Jainism, and by 50 BCE, the religion had spread into India's southern and western regions. Because Mahavira wrote down nothing, and because his disciples led the ascetic life without possessions (including paper and writing utensils), his teachings were transmitted orally from teacher to student. Through the years, however, the spoken language of the day changed, and gradually the teachings were lost to all but a few learned monks. When at last a council committed the teachings to writing, many of the Jain monks disagreed with the council's interpretations and a major split occurred. The two sects became the Shvetambaras and the Digambaras.

Neither the Shvetambara nor Digambara monks recognize the authenticity of the other group's scriptures.

The scriptures of the Shvetambara sect consist of forty-five works divided into six canons: *Angas* (limbs), *Chedasutras* (discipline), *Culikasutras* (appendixes), *Mulasutras* (basic texts), *Prakirnakas* (mixed texts), and *Upangas* (sub-Angas). The Angas are the oldest part of the canon and contain the *Acarangasutra* (Life of Mahavira, and laws for monks and nuns). The second Angas called the *Sutrakritanaga,* contains the major Jain teachings. According to the Jains, the *Uttaradhyayana Sutra* contains the last teachings of Mahavira. The Shvetambara sect believes the Angas to be the teachings of Mahavira, even though these scriptures did not reach their final written form until two hundred years after his death.

The Digambara sect accepts the *Purvas* (foundation) scriptures, the *Prakaranas* scripture that includes the *Aradhana* (accomplishment), the *Mulacara* (on conduct), the *Pravancanasara* (teaching) and the *Samayasara* (on doctrine). They also accept certain commentaries on scriptures. Both Jain sects treat Umasvamin's work on Jaina philosophy, the *Tattvarthadhigama Sutra* (Book for Attaining the Meaning of Principles), as an important contribution to Jainism. For centuries these sacred texts written in highly specialized language, were objects of veneration rather than texts to be read by the lay person. The situation changed in the nineteenth century, however, when published editions of the sacred texts made them available to the public.

Some of the popular literature for lay believers teaches the truths of Jainism through folk tales and amusing stories.

Reflections

In all religions, major splits seem to occur. How do you know which group of adherents to believe? Or does it matter if people interpret their Holy Scriptures in different ways?

The Digambara Order (Sky-clad)

The Digambara monks wear no clothes to symbolize their non-attachment to material goods. Considering their physical bodies as part of the natural environment, they live simply and face weather conditions in a stoic fashion. The monks' only possessions are a small broom of feathers dropped by peacocks or other birds and a gourd for drinking water.

The two orders also disagree on the status of women. Digambaras believe that women lack the willpower needed to attain liberation and thus are not suited for monastic life. Women may become monks in their next life if they have the good fortune to be born as men. They also reject that Mahavira was ever married.

The Shvetambara Order (White-clad)

Most members of the Shvetambara order live in northeastern, northwestern, and western India. The group's name means 'white-clad' or 'clothed in white.' These monks believe that dressing in white robes will not prevent them from attaining liberation. Like the Digambaras, the Shvetambara monks and nuns carry small brooms to brush away any living creature, because one of their vows is not to harm any form of life, including tiny insects. They accept that Mahavira was married and left home to seek enlightenment.

The Shvetambara order softens strict asceticism and allows women to enter monastic life. Although they believe that the nineteenth Ford-maker was a woman, Shvetambarans consider the status of nuns less than that of monks. Even the most senior nun is held to be junior to the most recently initiated monk.

> **Reflections**
> Like the Jains, do you believe we should revere all forms of life? How do you feel about killing ants and flies? Or killing cattle for their meat? Should we pick flowers, or allow them to live?

Jain Teachings

Worldview

Although Jains worship *Jinas* (Ford-makers such as Mahavira) and several gods, Jains do not believe in a creator God or Supreme Being. The universe has no beginning or end, but passes through endless cycles of rising and falling levels of civilization. The cycles respond to inherent universal laws of evolution and degeneration, of birth, death, and rebirth. The ultimate human goal is to follow a path that leads to the final deliverance, that is, to the final release of the soul from further karma and rebirth.

Recall that the Jains believe, according to universal law, there would arise twenty-four Jinas ('conquerors' or Ford-makers), who will attain complete enlightenment or liberation and can teach the truth for others to follow. Mahavira is the Jina of the present age. It is proper to worship the Jinas – not as 'gods' who hear our prayers and save us – but as conquerors and Ford-makers whose souls enjoy the bliss of liberation. The word Jain means a follower of a Jina, one who endured the road to final deliverance.

3. **The Road to Final Deliverance. Uttaradhyayana Sutra 28. 1, 10, 25, 30.**

   Learn the true road leading to final deliverance, which the Jinas have taught. It depends on four causes and is characterized by right knowledge and faith. Right knowledge, Faith, Conduct, and Austerities; this is the road taught by the Jinas who possess the best knowledge. Right knowledge, faith conduct, and austerities – beings who follow this road will obtain beatitude.

   Knowledge is fivefold: (1) Sruta, knowledge derived from the sacred books; (2) perception; (3) supernatural knowledge; (4) knowledge of the thoughts of other people; (5) Kevala, the highest, unlimited knowledge.

   Substance is the substrate of qualities; the qualities are inherent in one substance; but the characteristic of developments is that they inhere in either substances or qualities. Dharma (good), Adharma (evil), space, time, matter, and souls are the six kinds of substances. They make up this world, as has been taught by the Jinas who possess the best knowledge. Dharma, Adharma, and space are each one substance only; but time, matter, and souls are an infinite number of substances. The characteristic of Dharma is motion, that of Adharma immobility, and that of space, which contains all other substances, is to make room (for everything).

   [10] The characteristic of time is duration, that of soul the realization of 'knowledge, faith, happiness, and misery.' The characteristic of Soul is knowledge, faith, conduct, austerities, energy, and realization of its developments. The

characteristic of matter is sound, darkness, luster, light, shade, sunshine, color, taste, smell, and touch. The characteristic of development is singleness, separateness, number, form, conjunction, and disjunction.

The nine truths are: (1) Soul; (2) the inanimate things; (3) the binding of the soul by Karma; (4) merit; (5) demerit; (6) that which causes the soul to be affected by sins; (7) the prevention of asrava by watchfulness; (8) the annihilation of Karma; (9) final deliverance. He who truly believes the true teaching of the fundamental truths possesses righteousness.

He who obtains righteousness by the study of the Sutras, either Angas or other works, believes by the study of Sutras. He who by correctly comprehending one truth arrives at the comprehension of more – just as a drop of oil expands on the surface of water – believes by suggestion. He who truly knows the sacred lore, namely the eleven Angas, the Prakirnas, and the Drishtivada, believes by the comprehension of the sacred lore. He who understands the true nature of all substances by means of all proofs and nayas [logical arguments], believes by a complete course of study.

[25] He who sincerely performs all duties implied by right knowledge, faith, and conduct, by asceticism and discipline, and by all Samitis [rules] and Guptis [discipline] believes by religious exercise.

[30] He who holds no wrong doctrines though he is not versed in the sacred doctrines nor acquainted with other systems, believes by brief exposition. He who believes in the truth of the realities, the Sutras, and conduct, as it has been explained by the Jinas, believes by the Law.

Without faith there is no knowledge, without knowledge there is no virtuous conduct, without virtues there is no deliverance, and without deliverance there is no perfection.

The Soul

In contrast to Buddhists, who deny the existence of a soul, Jains believe everything has a soul – human beings, animals, plants, and even stones. They also believe that all souls are essentially equal, confined to this universe of motion, rest, and space, where they are categorized according to the number of sense organs they possess. That number ranges from one, or those souls that have only the sense of touch (the four material elements and plants) to those with five senses (birds, mammals, and humans). The higher animals, humans, and gods have minds with varying degrees of rationality.

According to the Jains, the human soul is originally pure, and though clouded by evil actions, it can be cleansed by pure behavior. Because violence to other souls is especially evil, Mahavira and his monks carried whisks to brush aside insects without harming them and wore masks over their noses and mouths to keep from breathing in and thus inadvertently killing an insect.

Reflections
Do you believe with the Jains that everything has soul?

Ahimsa (Non-violence)

The Jain religion is notable for its practice of *ahimsa* (or non-violence). Jains not only refrain from harming human life, but also take great care to prevent unnecessary harm to animals and plants. Even a drop of water contains thousands of living organisms, all of them wanting to live. We humans have no right to supremacy: all things deserve to live their lives as best they can. Jains are strict vegetarians and treat everything with respect. They have built hospitals to care for injured and mistreated animals. If they see animals for sale in a marketplace to be killed as meat, they buy the animals and raise them. Even to pick a flower is to injure a living being.

Because Jains vow not to harm any living thing, they must avoid some occupations such as those that involve taking life or making profit from the slaughter of living things. Jain adherents avoid such occupations as the military, butchering, fishing, extermination, leatherworking, manufacturing arms, selling intoxicants, and farming. They tend to enter commercial professions such as banking, accounting, clerical work, education, medicine, law, and publishing. In these fields, their reputation for honesty and morality is well known and appreciated. Jains have made notable contributions to the public welfare by establishing libraries, public dispensaries, and schools. Ahimsa extends also to speaking and thinking. Our abusive words and negative thoughts can injure others psychologically.

> **Reflections**
> One of the Ten Commandments in the Western religious traditions is 'Thou shalt not kill.' Could this commandment have the same meaning as the 'ahimsa' vow of the Jains?

4. Sutrakritanga 1. 7. 1–9

These classes of living beings have been declared by the Jinas: earth, water, fire, wind; grass, trees, and plants; and the moving beings, both the egg-bearing and those that bear live offspring, those generated from dirt and those generated in fluids. Know and understand that they all desire happiness. By hurting these beings, people do harm to their own souls, and will repeatedly be born as one of them.

Every being born high or low in the scale of the living creation, among movable and immovable beings, will meet with its death. Whatever sins the evildoer commits in every birth, for them, he must die.

In this world or in the next the sinners suffer themselves what they have inflicted on other beings, a hundred times, or suffer other punishment. Living in the Samsara [ignorance] they always acquire new Karma, and suffer for their misdeeds.

Some leave their mother and father to live as Sramanas, but they use fire. The prophet [Mahavira] says, 'People are wicked who kill beings for the sake of their own pleasure.' He who lights a fire kills living beings; he who extinguishes it kills the fire. Therefore a wise man who well considers the Law should light no fire. Earth contains life, and water contains life; jumping or flying insects fall in the fire;

dirt-born vermin and beings live in wood. All these beings are burned by lighting a fire.

Plants are beings possessed of natural development. Their bodies require nourishment, and they all have their individual life. Reckless men who cut them down for their own pleasure destroy many living beings. By destroying plants, when young or grown up, a careless man does harm to his own soul. The prophet says, 'People are wicked who destroy plants for their own pleasure.'

The Twelve Vows

Jainism prescribes twelve vows for lay people to follow:

1. Ahimsa (non-violence). Never knowingly take the life of any creature. Never engage in butchering, fishing, brewing, or any occupations that take life.
2. Always tell the truth.
3. Do not steal, or take what is not given.
4. Never be unchaste. Always be faithful to wife or husband. Always be pure in thought and deed.
5. Check greed by limiting wealth and giving away excess.
6. Avoid temptation to sin or to gain unnecessary pleasures.
7. Live a simple life.
8. Be on guard against evils that can be avoided.
9. Schedule periods of meditation.
10. Observe periods of self-denial.
11. Spend some days as a monk or nun.
12. Give alms, especially in support of ascetics.

Of these twelve vows, ahimsa is the most important.

> **Reflections**
> Do you find a resemblance between the twelve Jain vows for lay people and the Buddha's Eightfold Path? With which teaching are you more at ease?

Karma (*Karman*)

According to Hinduism and Buddhism, the condition of our current life depends on the karma we gained in our past life, and our future life will depend on the karma we created in our present life. Recall that the meaning of karma is 'action and reaction.' Basically, both the Hindu and Buddhist traditions believe that pure thoughts and actions lead to a worthy rebirth, and impure thoughts and actions lead to a disagreeable rebirth. Mahavira, on the other hand, taught that all karma is unfavorable. Karma means the soul is bound to the material world.

For the Jains, karma is material and made of subtle matter called 'karma-matter.' When the soul has vices such as anger, pride, greed, desires or passions, karma sticks to the soul like glue. The more karma that sticks, the heavier the soul becomes leading it to bondage in matter. If it is full of karma-matter, it sinks into the lower states of existence. If it has only a little karma-matter in it, the soul will be light enough to rise, perhaps into the heavens and find embodiment in a god. The lightest of souls may rise higher still and reach liberation.

5. The Jain Conception of Karman (Karma). Sutrakritanga 1, 2, 1

(Rishabha said to his sons):

Acquire perfect knowledge of the Law! Why do you not study it? It is difficult to obtain instruction in it after this life. The days (that are gone by) will never return, nor is it easy a second time to obtain human birth.

See, young and old men, even children in the mother's womb die. As a hawk catches a quail, so (life) will end when its time is spent.

(A man) may suffer for the sake of his parents; he will not easily obtain happiness after this life. A pious man should consider these causes of danger and cease to act.

For in this world living beings suffer individually for their deeds for the deed they have done themselves, they obtain (punishment), and will not get over it before they have felt it.

… Not withstanding their pleasures and relations, all men must suffer in due time the fruit of their works; as a cocoa-nut detaching itself from its stalk (falls down), so (life) will end when its time is spent.

Even a very learned or virtuous man, or a Brahmana or an ascetic, will be severely punished for his deed when he is given to actions of deceit.

See, those (heretics) who search for the knowledge of truth, but who do not cross the Samsara, talk only about the highest good (without teaching it).

How will you understand what is near you and what is beyond? In the meanwhile you suffer for your deeds.

He who walks about naked and lean, he who eats only once after a month, if he is filled with deceit, will be born an endless number of times.

Man, cease from sins! For the life of men will come to an end. Men who are drowned (in lust, as it were), and addicted to pleasure will, for want of control, be deluded.

Exert and control yourself! For it is not easy to walk on ways where there are minutely small animals. Follow the commandments which the Arhats have well proclaimed.

… It is not myself alone who suffers, all creatures in the world suffer; this a wise man should consider, and he should patiently bear (such calamities) as befall him, without giving way to his passions.

… Some people are (foolishly) attached to others, and are thereby deluded; the unrighteous make them adopt unrighteousness, and they exult in their wickedness.

Therefore a worthy and wise man should be careful, ceasing from sin and being entirely happy. The virtuous heroes of faith (have chosen) the great road, the right and certain path to perfection.

He who has entered the road leading to the destruction (of Karman), who controls his mind, speech, and body, who has given up his possessions and relations and all undertakings, should walk about subduing his senses.

The Five Great Vows

To reach liberation or what the Jains call 'final deliverance,' one must be a human being and live the life of an ascetic monk or nun. Initiation into the life of a monk includes pulling one's hair out by the roots to show indifference to pain. Monks and nuns follow the following steps leading to the path of liberation:

1. Faith in the twenty-four Tirthankaras (Jinas or Ford-makers).
2. Study the teachings of the Tirthankaras.
3. Practice right conduct: the control of thoughts, words, actions, emotions, and sensations.

Because all actions lead to the soul's bondage, the only way to attain liberation is to cease from action so that no fresh karma can stick to the soul. For the Jains, following Mahavira's life of renunciation provides the best way to collect less karma. For the ascetic monks and nuns, such a life includes the Five Great Vows:

6. Five Great Vows. Akaranga Sutra 2. 15. i–v

The Venerable Ascetic Mahavira, endowed with the highest knowledge and intuition, taught the five great vows, with their clauses …

The first great vow, Sir, runs thus: I renounce all killing of living beings, whether tiny or large, whether movable or immovable. I myself shall not kill living beings nor cause others to do it, nor consent to it. As long as I live, I confess and blame, repent and exempt myself of these sins, in the threefold way, in mind, speech and body …

The second great vow runs thus: I renounce all vices of lying speech arising from anger or greed or fear or mirth. I shall neither myself speak lies, nor cause others to speak lies, nor consent to the speaking of lies by others. I confess and blame, repent and exempt myself of these sins in the threefold way, in mind, speech, and body …

The third great vow runs thus: I renounce all taking of anything not given, either in a village or a town or a wood, either of little or much, of small or great, of living or lifeless things. I shall neither take myself what is not given, nor cause others to take it, nor consent to their taking it. As long as I live, I confess and blame, repent and exempt myself of these sins in the threefold way, in mind, speech and body …

The fourth great vow runs thus: I renounce all sexual pleasures, either with gods or men or animals. I shall not give way to sensuality, nor cause others to give way to it, nor consent to their giving way. As long as I live, I confess and blame, repent and exempt myself …

The fifth great vow runs thus: I renounce all attachments, whether little or much, small or great, living or lifeless. I myself shall not form such attachments, nor cause others to do so, nor consent to their doing so. As long as I live, I confess and blame, repent and exempt myself.

> **Reflections**
> Which of the 'Five Great Vows' would be the most difficult for you to follow at this particular stage in your life?

To stop karma-matter from clinging to their souls, Jain monks and nuns must meditate on the Jain truths, practice asceticism (including long fasts), keep themselves inwardly and outwardly pure, and practice serenity, unselfishness, and perfect conduct.

Because so few souls reach liberation most will be reborn in an earthly body life after life. The souls who do attain liberation – freedom from karma-matter – will shed their physical bodies and ascend to a blissful state. The liberated souls lose their personal individuality and acquire a spiritual quality of omniscience. Because of their conquest of karma, these souls are called *jinas* (conquerors). Thus Jainism, the religion of conquerors, involves a heroic journey of self-liberation. No god or Supreme Being plays a part in the Jain system: its major emphasis is on self-disciplined morality.

Sikhism

Founded in the fifteenth century by Guru Nanak, Sikhism is the youngest of the religions originating in India. Sikhism took root in an area of the Punjab, the land of the five rivers, an area that spans modern-day northern Pakistan and northwestern India. For four centuries Hindus and Muslims lived side by side in the Punjab in anxious tension. Sikhism drew from both Hinduism and Islam while developing an individuality of its own. The word *Sikh* means 'disciple' and the Sikhs are the disciples of ten gurus, beginning with Guru Nanak and ending with Guru Gobind Singh (d. 1708 CE).

Nanak's teachings marked a distinct shift away from Hindu and Jain theology and devotional practice. Unlike the Hindus, who believe the universe has approximately 330,000,000 gods, and the Jains, who believe there is no one supreme god, only universal law, Sikhism, like Islam, believes in one formless creator God. According to Nanak, God is not accessible through rituals and ceremonies, but through hard work, adoring the divine name, and sharing the fruits of one's labors.

> **Reflections**
> Do you agree with the Sikhs that God is not accessible through rituals and ceremonies? Are rituals and ceremonies important to your own belief system?

At first, Sikhism was a pacifist reform movement, but under Guru Hargobind (1606–1644 CE), the religion became increasingly militant. This major change marked the integration of political and spiritual affairs within the Sikh community.

Life of Guru Nanak

Nanak (1469–1539 CE) was born in the village of Talwandi, an area of the Punjab now in Pakistan. His father was an accountant and both his mother and father were Hindus. As a member of the kshatriya caste (administrators and warriors), Nanak received an excellent education. A precocious student in all subjects, he excelled in literature, especially poetry. He spent his boyhood years taking the family cattle to pasture and in the company of spiritual teachers. He especially enjoyed conversation with spiritual teachers.

At age thirteen Nanak married and became the father of two sons. For a while Nanak worked in an accounting office where he met a Muslim minstrel named Mardana. Together they wrote and sang hymns to the Creator. Even today part of the Sikhs sacred hymnology includes these early hymns.

At age twenty-nine Nanak experienced a mystical awakening that was the turning point of his life. While bathing in a river, he disappeared from view and his friends were afraid he had drowned. However, according to the *Janamsakhis* ('life stories'), while under water Nanak was called by God and given a mission to repeat God's name and 'cause others to do likewise.' When he reappeared from the river waters Nanak announced to his friends: 'There is no Hindu. There is no Muslim.'

From that time, he abandoned worldly pursuits and set out with his companion and friend, the minstrel Mardana, who wrote and sang sacred hymns with Nanak. They visited holy places and spend much of their time discussing spiritual problems with ascetics and holy men. Undaunted by the hostility of religious authorities and public ridicule, Nanak sang and preached and made a few converts along the way.

One story from his travels illustrates the virtues of hard work and integrity. Nanak often visited the house of a carpenter named Lalo. Once while he was staying with his friend Lalo, a rich man of the village named Bhago, held a feast and summoned everyone to attend. Guru Nanak refused to go. When Bhago personally went to Lalo's house to insist on Nanak's presence at the feast, Nanak agreed to attend. But before leaving, Nanak put some food from Lalo's house in his pocket. At the feast, Nanak held up both hands. In one hand he held food from Bhago's house and in the other hand he held food from Lalo's house. When he squeezed his hands, blood came from Bhago's food and milk trickled from Lalo's food. Asked the significance of such an act, Guru Nanak explained that the difference in the food illustrated the honesty of Lalo in contrast to Bhago, who exploited others to gain wealth.

While in Hardwar during one of his journeys, Nanak watched pilgrims throw handfuls of water to the rising sun as an offering to their ancestors in heaven. Nanak cupped some water in his hands and threw it toward the earth. When questioned, he said, 'If you can send water to your dead ancestors in heaven, surely I can send it to my fields in the Punjab.' True or false, this story demonstrates Nanak's notion that because God was everywhere, ritual was pointless

Reflections
Do you agree with Nanak that because God is everywhere, ritual is unnecessary?

By the time Nanak and his friend returned home, they were too old to take any more strenuous journeys. But soon after they settled down at Kartapur, Mardana became ill and died. Nanak appointed a disciple named Angad, to be his successor and continued to instruct Hindus and Muslims who came to him. Many became his disciples or *sisyas,* from which the Punjabi word Sikh is derived.

At age sixty-nine, when Nanak's death was approaching, both Hindu and Muslim Sikhs tried to claim his body. The Hindus wanted to cremate him as a Hindu, and the Muslims wanted to bury him as a Muslim. When they referred the argument to Nanak, he told the Hindus to place flowers on his right and the Muslims to place flowers on his left. Those whose flowers were found fresh in the morning could dispose of his body any way they wished. Then he covered himself with a sheet. The next morning when his followers lifted the sheet, his body was gone and the flowers on both sides were in bloom. Since then Sikhs have cremated their dead just like the Hindus.

Reflections
How do you feel about cremation as opposed to burial?

The Ten Gurus

Just before he died, Guru Nanak appointed his disciple Guru Angad (1539–1552) as his successor. Usually the word guru means 'teacher,' but to Sikhs, the word signifies 'leader.' After Nanak's death, Guru Angad began the compilation of the *Granith Sahib,* Sikh scripture, based on what he had learned from Nanak. He also included some of his own devotional passages.

The third guru, Guru Amar Das (1552–1574) continued the teachings of Nanak, founded the town of Goindwal, and established a Sikh common kitchen for all. Muslim Emperor Akbar once ate a meal in the guru's kitchen to stress the importance of equality. The fourth guru, Guru Ram Das (1574–1581), Amar Das's son-in-law, founded the city of Amritsar and moved the spiritual center of Sikhism from Goindwal to Amritsar, the current site of the Golden Temple, which was built on land granted by the Emperor Akbar. One of Guru Ram Das's most important contributions was the compilation of the *Adi Granth* (Granith Sahib). His writings include hymns of Nanak and other gurus, verses by Hindu *bhakti* (devotional) yogis, one thousand of Kabir's verses, and verses of Muslim Sufi mystics.

By the time of the fifth guru, Guru Arjan (1581–1606), Sikhism had established a strong foothold in Punjab's central districts. The spread of Sikhism did not go unnoticed by Emperor Jehangir, a Muslim, who sent troops to halt its growth. During battle, Guru Arjan was captured and given the choice of accepting Islam or dying by torture. He chose the latter and was tortured to death in 1606. Guru Arjan was the Sikhs' first guru martyr.

Until the martyrdom of Guru Arjan, the Sikhs had been a pacifistic reform movement. Their new militancy began with the sixth guru, Guru Hargobind (1606–1644), who built the Lohgarh fortress at Amritsar. He wore two swords to symbolize the integration of spiritual and temporal authority. The seventh and eight gurus – Guru Har Rai (1630–1661) and Guru Hari Kishen (1656–1664) – were both military leaders, although they tried to avoid direct confrontation with Mogul authorities in Delhi. The ninth guru, Guru Tegh Bahadur (1621–1675) the youngest son of Guru Hargobind, founded many new Sikh centers and aided persecuted Hindus. He was publicly beheaded for the latter actions in 1675.

The tenth guru, Guru Gobind Singh (1668–1707), Guru Tegh Bahadur's son, was a strong military leader. While preparing for a crisis against the Muslims, Guru Gobind Singh stood before an assembly of Sikh men and fiercely demanded a head. The startled Sikhs backed away, but one man volunteered. He and the Guru went into a tent. A blow was heard then the onlookers saw blood seep under the tent. The Guru came out and demanded another head. Another Sikh finally volunteered and the process was repeated three more times. Then the Guru opened the tent to five headless goats and five whole men. The five men earned the title of 'Five Beloved Ones' and were baptized the first members of the *Khalsa* (the Pure), who would fearlessly defend the community.

Reflections
Is there any principle for which you would willingly lay down your life?

All Khalsa members are baptized in a special ceremony and assume a common surname – Singh (Lion) for males and Kaur (Princess) for females. All Singhs swear always to wear the Five 'Ks:'

1. *Kesh:* long uncut hair and beard. A symbol of the lion and its power.
2. *Kacha:* short pants indicating alertness and readiness to fight
3. *Kirpan:* a steel dagger or sword for defense.
4. *Kara:* a steel bracelet symbolizing strength.
5. *Kanga:* a comb to hold the long hair in place.

The Khalsa brotherhood is the main unifying force among Sikhs today. Singhs also vow to avoid tobacco and intoxicants, adultery, and the meat of animals that have not been killed by one stroke of the sword but that have instead bled slowly to death.

When Muslims killed Guru Gobind Singh's small sons, he fled to south India where he also was assassinated. Before he died, he proclaimed that he was the last in the line of Gurus. From that time on, the Adi Granth (Granth Sahib) scripture would be the Guru for all Sikhs, thus bringing to an end the tradition of personal guru leaders.

7. **The Holy Sword. Vichitar Natak, Vol. 5, 1**
   (Guru Gobind Singh addresses God as a sword to destroy his enemies).
   I bow with love and devotion to the Holy Sword.
   Assist me that I may complete this work.
   Thou are the Subduer of countries, the Destroyer of the armies of the wicked, in the battlefield you greatly adorn the brave.

Thine arm is infrangible, Thy brightness resplendent, Thy radiance
   and splendor dazzle like the sun.
Thou bestowest happiness on the good, Thou terrify the evil, Thou scatterest
   sinners, I seek Thy protection.
Hail! Hail to the Creator of the world, the Saviour of creation, my
   Cherisher, hail to Thee, O Sword!
I bow to Him who holdeth the arrow [sword] in His hand; I bow to the
   Fearless One;
I bow to the God of gods who is in the present and the future.
I bow to Scimitar, the two-edged sword, the Falchion, and the Dagger.
   Thou, O God, hast ever one form; Thou art ever unchangeable.
I bow to the Holder of the mace
Who diffused light through the fourteen worlds.
I bow to the Arrow and the Musket,
I bow to the Sword, spotless, fearless, and unbreakable;
I bow to the powerful Mace and Lance
To which nothing is equal.
I bow to Him who holdest the discus,
Who is not made of the elements and who is terrible.
I bow to Him with the strong teeth;
I bow to Him who is supremely powerful,
I bow to the Arrow and the Cannon
Which destroy the enemy.
I bow to the Sword and the Rapier
Which destroy the evil.
I bow to all weapons called Shastar (which may be held).
I bow to all weapons called Astar (which may be hurled or discharged).

Sikh Scripture

In the Sikh temples, the only object of worship is the Granth Sahib or Adi Granth. *Granth* means 'book' and *Sahib* 'holy.' *Adi* means 'first'. Sikhs bow before this sacred book and walk around it: the book is always on their right side. Most of the material in the Adi Granth consists of hymns used by the gurus for religious instructions. In the daily life of devout Sikhs and in all Sikh ceremonies the Adi Granth, which is generally known as the Guru Granth Sahib, is the central authority. The Guru Granth Sahib is divided into three parts: the *Japji*, thirty-nine 'tunes' by Guru Nanak and later gurus, and collected works, including poems and hymns from Hindu, Muslim and Sikh gurus and saints. The Japji, a poem by Guru Nanak tells about God and the joy of union with Him. The opening statement is known as the *Mul Mantra* (the basic teaching).

8. Sikh Morning Prayer. Japji, Intro. 1– III, V.
   (A small portion of the Sikh morning prayers from the Japji)
   There is only one God whose name is true, the creator, devoid of fear and enmity, immortal, unborn, self-existent; by the favor of the Guru.

REPEAT HIS NAME!

The True One was in the beginning; the true
   One was in the primal age.
The True One is now also, O Nanak; the True
   One also [forever] shall be.

I

By thinking I cannot obtain a conception of Him, even though I think hundreds of thousands of times.

Even though I be silent and keep my attention firmly fixed on Him, I cannot preserve silence.

The hunger of the hungry *for God* does not subsideth though they obtain the load of the worlds.

If man should have thousands and hundreds of thousands of devices, even one would not assist him in obtaining God.

How shall *man* become true before God? How shall the veil of falsehood be rent?

By walking, O Nanak, according to the will of the Commander as preordained.

II

By His order bodies are produced; His order cannot be described.

By His order souls are infused into them; by His order greatness is obtained.

By His order men are high or low; by His order they obtained preordained pain or pleasure.

By His order some obtained their reward; by His order others must ever wander in transmigration.

All are subject to His order; none is exempt from it.

He who understandeth God's order, O Nanak, is never guilty of egoism

III

Who can sing His power? Who hath power *to sing it?*
Who can sing His gifts or know His signs?
Who can sing His attributes, His greatness, and His deeds?
Who can sing His knowledge, whose study is arduous?
Who can sing Him, who fashioneth the body and *again* destroyeth it?
Who can sing Him, who takes away life and restoreth it?
Who can sing Him, who appeareth to be far, *but* is known *to be near?*
Who can sing Him, who is *all*-seeing and omnipresent?
In describing Him there would never be an end.
Millions of men give millions upon millions of descriptions of Him, *but they fail to describe Him.*
The Giver giveth; the receiver groweth weary of receiving.
In every age man subsisteth by *His* bounty.
The commander by His order has laid out the way *of the world.*
Nanak, God the unconcerned is happy ...

V

He is not established, nor is He created.

The Pure One existeth by Himself

They who worshipped Him have obtained honour.

Nanak, sing His *praises* who is the Treasury of excellences.

Sing and hear and put His love into your hearts.

Thus shall your sorrows be removed, and you shall be absorbed in Him who is the abode of happiness.

Under the Guru's instruction God's word is *heard*; under the Guru's instruction its knowledge is *acquired*; under the Guru's instruction *man learns that God* is everywhere contained.

Early in the morning at the Golden Temple in Amritsar, a gloved attendant sets the Guru Granth Sahib on a cushion under a canopy for professional readers to recite aloud. At night the holy book is 'put to bed.' Many Sikhs enshrine the book in their homes and read it daily or recite portions of scripture from memory every morning, evening, and before going to bed. The holy book is a constant source of spiritual guidance.

Reflections

Do you have a 'holy book' as a source of spiritual guidance? If so, how does it help you?

The Guru Granth Sahib, a later companion to the Dasam Granth, is a collection of miscellaneous works attributed to Guru Gobind Singh. It offers Sikh ideals and is a valuable source of seventeenth and eighteenth-century Sikh history.

Sikhs believe that, in essence, all religions are one, because there is but one God. Nanak particularly wished to end the animosity between Hindus and Muslims, believing they shared the ultimate, eternal truth. Sikhs do not try to convert people to their own religion, and the Khalsa are specifically directed not to offend adherents of other faiths.

Nanak, however, did not accept the scriptures of either Hindus (the Vedas) or Muslims (the Koran), and the true Sikh uses only the Sikh scripture and follows the teachings of the Sikh gurus.

The Teachings of Guru Nanak

Guru Nanak taught that God transcends the universe and is present in the universe. For Nanak, God is the 'True Name,' a formless yet personal entity, who created the universe and everything in it. God is omnipresent and immanent (always present in everything) as well as omnipotent and transcendent (all-powerful and beyond the universe). God does not appear in the form of a human body, but spiritual union with God is possible during this lifetime through the guru's grace, and by constantly remembering the True One and serving others.

> **Reflections**
>
> Do you, with Guru Nanak, believe that God both transcends the universe and is present in everything?

For the Sikhs, 'Remembering' is a way of deep reflection. The words of Guru Arjan are frequently repeated after the Japji morning prayers.

9. Remembering God. Sukhmani [Peace of Mind] 1–4
(The words of Guru Arjan)

1

Remember, remember God; by remembering Him you shall obtain happiness,
And erase from your hearts trouble and affliction.
Remember the praises of the one all-supporting God.
Numberless persons utter God's various names.
Investigating the Vedas, the Puranas, and the Smritis,
Men have made out the one word which is God's name.
His praises cannot be recounted,
Who treasures *God's name* in his heart even for a moment.
Saith Nanak, save me, *O Lord*, with those who are desirous of one glance of
Thee ....

2

By remembering God man doth not *again* enter the womb;
By remembering God the tortures of Death disappear.
By remembering God death is removed;
By remembering God enemies retreat;
By remembering God no obstacles are met;
By remembering God we are watchful night and day;
By remembering God fear is not felt;
By remembering God sorrow troubleth not …

3

By remembering God we obtain wealth, supernatural power, and the nine
   treasures;
By remembering God we obtain divine knowledge, meditation, and the essence
   of wisdom;
Remembrance of God is the *real* devotion, penance, and worship.
By remembering God the *conception* of duality is dispelled;
By remembering God we obtain the *advantages* of bathing at places of
   pilgrimage;
By remembering God we are honoured at His court;
By remembering God we become reconciled to His will
By remembering God men's *lives* are very profitable;
They whom He has caused to do so remember Him –
Nanak, touch the feet of such persons.

4

To remember God is the most exalted of all duties.
By remembering God many are saved;
By remembering God thirst is quenched;
By remembering God man knoweth all things;
By remembering God there is no fear of death;
By remembering God our desires are fulfilled;
By remembering God mental impurity is removed
And the ambrosial name filleth the heart.
God abideth on the tongue of the saint
Whose most humble slave Nanak is.

The Guru as Guide

Created for communion with God, the soul is the essence of human nature. Those who believe they are separate from God live in spiritual ignorance, which is the cause of evil in the world. They need to be awakened to see or recognize the presence of God in themselves and the world. The soul that loves God is happy. The self-centered (or egoistic) soul that loves only the personal self suffers. Because most people cannot recognize God, they should let the Guru guide them. Only the Guru, through his guidance, can help them attain liberation. The Guru keeps his followers on the path of truth; he is the divine bridge to union with God, or the divine ferryman, who takes devotees across the 'ocean of life.' The Guru is a shade below God, thus he is to be consulted and respected, but not worshipped. Nanak always referred to himself as the slave and servant of God.

10. Importance of the Guru. Gauri Hymn
(A hymn by Guru Amar Das)
Through a Guru a few obtain divine knowledge:
He who knoweth God through the Guru shall be acceptable.
Through the Guru there resulteth divine knowledge and meditation on the True
   One;
Through the Guru the gate of deliverance is attained.
It is only by perfect good fortune the Guru cometh in one's way.
The true become easily absorbed in the True One.
On meeting the Guru the fire of avarice is quenched.
Through the Guru peace dwelleth in the heart.
Through the Guru man becometh pure, spotless, and immaculate.
Through the Guru the Word which uniteth man with God is obtained.
Without the Guru every one wandereth in doubt.
Without the Name great misery is suffered.
He who is pious meditates on the Name.
On beholding the True One, true honour is obtained.
Whom shall we call the giver? The One God.
If He be gracious, the Word by which we meet Him is obtained.
May Nanak meet the beloved Guru, sing the True One's praises,
And becoming true be absorbed in the True One.

Reflections

Nanak taught that human beings are God's supreme creation and rejected the Hindu and Jain doctrine of ahimsa (non-violence). Because humans are the highest creation on earth, we are free to kill and eat animals. Sikhs are among the few East Indians that legitimately eat meat.

Do you believe the doctrine of ahimsa means to refrain from killing animals as well as humans?

Karma and Rebirth

Nanak acknowledged the doctrines of karma and rebirth, but he believed that God controls both karma and rebirth through His supreme will. Evil individuals have accumulated bad karma and are reborn as lower animals until they again reach the opportunity of rebirth in the human state. A person who lives a righteous life but does not meditate on God must spend a period in purgatory (the place for 'purging' oneself of sin) and then take another human birth. Sikhism seeks a mystical union of the soul with God – the only reward worth seeking. Being separated from God (or self-centered) is as severe a punishment as one can endure.

11. Prayer and Praise of God. Bihagra Prayer
(Prayer by Guru Arjan)

Hear my supplication, O my Lord God,

Though I am full of millions of sins, nevertheless I am Thy slave.

O Thou Dispeller of grief, merciful, fascinating, Destroyer of trouble and anxiety,

I seek Thy protection; protect mine honour; Thou art in all things, O spotless One;

Thou hearest and beholdest us; Thou are with us all, O God; Thou art the nearest of all to us.

O Lord, hear Nanak's prayer; save the slave of Thy household.

Thou art ever omnipotent; we are poor and beggars.

O God, save us who are involved in the love of mammon.

Bound by covetousness and worldly love, we have committed various sins.

The Creator is distinct and free from entanglements; man obtaineth the fruits of his acts.

Show us kindness, Thou purifier of sinners; we are weary of wandering through many a womb ...

Thou art great and omnipotent my understanding is feeble

Thou cherishest even the ungrateful: Thou lookest equally on all.

Unfathomable is Thy knowledge, O infinite Creator; I am lowly and know nothing.

Having rejected the gem of *Thy name*, I have amassed kauris [money];

I am a degraded and silly being.

By the commission of sin I have amassed what is very unstable and forsaketh man ...

When I sang God's praises in the association of the saints,

He [Nanak] united me, who had been separated from Him, with Himself ...
My couch, when God accepteth me as His own, is adorned by Him.
Having dismissed anxiety I am no longer anxious, and suffer
    no further pain ...

Reflections

Do you agree with Nanak that the gravest sin is the pride of thinking, 'I am in complete control of my life'?

Salvation

The Sikh's ultimate goal is to achieve *Nirvan*, the state of final salvation that Buddhists call Nirvana. In Nirvan, one is fully absorbed into God or – to put it another way – one's individuality is ultimately overcome in God's being. Some Sikhs believe in a paradise called *Sach Khand*, where souls recognize each other and enjoy eternal bliss.

Sikh Discipline

Guru Nanak taught that love and compassion are the best ways to reach God and receive His grace. Patience, contentment, compassion, honesty, and sincerity constitute right attitude and right conduct, while vices include stealing, murder, lying, greed, slander, selfishness and idolatry. To reach God, one must enter a devotional discipline and persevere in its regular practice until attaining divine harmony. This discipline, as Guru Nanak made clear, has nothing to do with external rituals such as temple rites, mosque worship, pilgrimages, or asceticism. The Sikhs' only ritual is to repeat God's name, which helps to bring them closer to Him.

12. The Power in God's Name. Gauri
(Hymn by Guru Arjan)

There is none beside Him,
In whose power are lords and emperors;
In whose power is the whole world;
Who hath created everything.
Address thy supplication to the true Guru,
That he may arrange all thine affairs.
His court is the most exalted of all;
His name is the prop of all the saints.
The Lord whose glory shines in every heart
Is contained in everything, and filleth *creation*.
By remembering Him the abode of sorrow is demolished;
By remembering Him Death molesteth us not;
By remembering Him what is withered becometh green;
By remembering Him the sinking stone floateth;
Victory be ever to the society of the saints!

God's name is the support of the lives of His servants.
Saith Nanak, hear, O God, my supplication –
By the favour of the saints, grant me to dwell in Thy Name.

Reflections

What do you think of a religion that has no professional priests or ministers? Do lay people need the guidance of some living authority, or are most people capable of participating in a community with the Sikh type of spiritual discipline?

Summary

Jainism

Both Jainism and Sikhism have their roots in India. Jainism is an ancient religion, while Sikhism is comparatively young. Jainism is often called the 'religion of conquerors' because of its emphasis on achieving liberation through disciplined ascetic practices. The Jains believe that through the ages, twenty-four Ford-makers have reached perfection and shown the way to others. Ford-maker Mahavira is the founder of the Jain religion. He lived in extreme austerity and ended his days at age seventy-two by starvation. Self-starvation is the 'holy death' that Jains prepare for over the years by practicing fasting. Mahavira earned the title 'conqueror' because he heroically conquered the forces of life, thus gaining liberation from karma.

Because Mahavira wrote nothing, his teachings were transmitted orally. When a council finally committed his teachings to writing, many Jain monks disagreed with the council's interpretations and a major split occurred. The Digambara monks believed that monks should go naked like Mahavira. The Shvetambara monks wore simple white garments. The monks of neither sect recognize the authenticity of the other's scripture.

Although Jains worship Ford-makers such as Mahavira and several gods, Jainism is an atheistic religion that does not believe in a creator God or Supreme Being. Jains believe the universe has no beginning or end, but passes through countless cycles that respond to impersonal universal laws.

Jains believe everything has a soul and that all souls are equal. Violence to any soul is evil; thus monks carry whisks to brush aside insects without harming them. The Jains practice ahimsa (or non-violence) with all creatures, including plants and animals, so Jains work in professions such as banking, education and law. Of the twelve vows that Jain lay people follow, non-violence is the most important.

Jains believe in the law of karma, although they consider all karma to be bad. The accumulation of karma means the soul is bound to the material world. Living a life of renunciation by practicing asceticism is the only way to attain liberation from karma.

Sikhism

Founded in the fifteenth century by Guru Nanak, Sikhism is the youngest of India's religions. Sikhism drew from both Hinduism and Islam while also developing a character of its own. The word Sikh means disciple, and the Sikhs are the disciples of ten gurus beginning with Guru Nanak.

After his enlightenment, Guru Nanak and a minstrel named Mardana wrote and sang hymns to the Creator while traveling to holy places and preaching Sikh doctrine. At age sixty-nine Guru Nanak died from self-imposed starvation. He taught that there is one God who transcends the world and is contained in everything. God is the 'True Name' or 'True One,' a formless yet personal entity who created the universe and everything in it. Guru Nanak taught that love and compassion are the best ways to reach God and receive His grace.

The Sikhs look to ten gurus as their spiritual leaders: Guru Nanak, Guru Angad, Guru Amar Das, Guru Ram Das, Guru Arjan, Guru Hargobind, Guru Har Rai, Guru Hari Kishen, Guru Tegh Bahadur, and Guru Gobind Singh. Before Guru Gobind Singh died, he announced that the Sikh scripture Granth Sahib (Adi Granth) would be the Guru for all Sikhs, thus bringing an end to the tradition of personal Gurus.

Sikhs believe that, in essence, all religions are one because there is but one God. They do not, however, try to convert people to their own religion. Members of the Khalsa are specifically directed not to offend those of other faiths. Sikhs, nevertheless, do not accept either the ancient Hindu Vedas or the Muslim Koran, following only Sikh scriptures and the teachings of ancient Sikh gurus. The Sikhs' only ritual is to repeat God's name in order to bring them closer to Him. In Sikh temples today, the only object of worship is the Guru Granth Sahib or Adi Granth.

The human soul was created for communion with God. People who believe they are separate from God live in spiritual ignorance and are the cause of evil in the world. The soul that loves God is happy. Sikhs accept the doctrines of karma and rebirth, which are controlled by God's supreme will. Evil persons are reborn as lower animals until they again reach the opportunity of rebirth in the human state. A person who lives a righteous life but does not meditate on God must spend a period in purgatory and then take another human birth. Sikhs seek a mystical union with God.

Jainism Today

An important part of Jain spirituality is pilgrimage to certain holy sites. The most famous pilgrimage sites are Satrunjaya and Mount Girnar in Gujarat, and Mount Abu in Rajasthan. Both sites are large complexes of beautiful Jain temples. These holy places usually have some association with the Ford-makers, so visiting them helps gain religious merit for a future life.

Although only a small portion of India's population is Jain, the religion continues to have significant effects on the cultural and social life of its origin country. Jains have funded public dispensaries, lodgings for the poor and homeless, animal hospitals, schools and libraries. Their reverence for all life does not allow them to engage in agriculture (which requires the use of pesticides). Jains are among India's leading scholars, especially in the fields of religion, philosophy, literature and art; and they have made significant advances in business.

However, in 2005, the Supreme Court of India declined to grant Jains the status of religious minority throughout India, leaving respective states to decide on the minority status of the Jains. In 2006, the Supreme Court ruled that the Jain religion is indisputably not part of the Hindu religion.

Sikhism Today

In recent years, many Sikhs have sought to establish an independent Sikh state in the Punjab area of northwest India. For instance, in 1984, militant Sikhs seized the Golden Temple in Amritsar. Indira Gandhi (1917–1984), Prime Minister of India, ordered troops to remove the Sikh rebels from the Golden Temple. In the ensuing battle hundreds of Sikhs were killed.

Sikhs violently protested the Hindu Prime Minister's invasion of their sacred temple and in 1984 her own Sikh bodyguards assassinated her. The assassination infuriated India's Hindus, who turned on the Sikhs in murderous rage. The Sikhs seized the Golden Temple once more, but again Indian troops removed them. The Sikhs' demand that the Indian government grant them a separate state has so far been refused, and tensions between Hindus and Sikhs remain high. However, in 2004, Manmohan Singh, a Sikh, was sworn in as the first non-Hindu Prime Minister of India.

Approximately twelve million Sikhs now live in the Indian state of Punjab and two million Sikhs outside India. The expansion of the Sikh faith throughout the world has brought new converts and new challenges to the traditional Sikhs of Punjab.

In light of the two million Sikhs outside India, the Sikh community has actively promoted the interests of Sikhs to a global audience. They hope to counter the negative images of a community that is often portrayed only in terms of terrorist activities against Hindus in India. They have established charitable Golden Temple kitchens, social meeting places, and often Golden Temple co-operative health food markets in communities throughout the West.

Timeline
Jainism

c. 599 to 527 BCE	Life of Mahavira, the founder of Jainism.
c. fifth century BCE	Jainism enters India.
c. third century BCE	A Jain community forms in the trading center of Mathura.
fourth–fifth century CE	Umasvati codifies Jain texts in the Tattvartha Sutra. Angas in Prakrit.
fifth century CE	Schism occurs, forming the Svetambara and Digambara sects.
ninth–eleventh century CE	South Indian royalty supports Digambara Jainism.

twenty-first century CE	Many Jains emigrate to East Africa, the United Kingdom and North America.
2005 CE	Supreme Court of India declined Jains status of religious minority in India. Individual states may decide their minority status.
2006 CE	Supreme Court ruled that Jain religion is not part of Hindu religion.

Sikhism

1469–1539 CE	Life of Guru Nanak
1539–1552 CE	Life of Guru Angad. Began compilation of the *Adi Granth* (*Granth Sahib*).
1552–1574 CE	Life of Guru Amar Das.
1574–1581 CE	Life of Guru Ram Das. Compilation of *Adi Granth* (*Granth Sahib*). Established the town of Amritsar.
1581–1606 CE	Life of Guru Arjan Dev. Martyred.
1606–1644 CE	Life of Guru Hargobind. Built Lohgarh fortress at Amritsar.
1621–1675 CE	Life of Guru Tegh Bahadur. Founded many Sikh centers. Established city of Anandpur.
1630–1661 CE	Life of Guru Har Rai. Military leader.
1656–1664 CE	Guru Har Krishan born. Died at age eight.
1668–1707 CE	Life of Guru Gobind Singh. Baptized first members of the Khalsa (The Pure) Confers Guruship to the Guru Granth Sahib Scripture.
1984 CE	India storms Golden Temple. Several hundred Sikhs killed.
2004 CE	Manmohan Singh, a Sikh, is sworn in as the first non-Hindu Prime Minister of India.
2004 CE	400th commemoration year of the Sikh scripture Adi Granth.

Study Questions

1. Which is the older of the two religions: Jainism or Sikhism?
2. Explain the difference between the Jain and the Hindu views of God.
3. Why is Jainism called the 'religion of conquerors'?
4. Explain the significance of a Ford-maker for the Jains.
5. Who was the founder of Jainism?
6. How does the Jain view of karma differ from the Hindu view of karma?
7. Explain the factional split surrounding Jain scripture.
8. What are two major differences between the Digambara and the Shvetambara orders?
9. Why do Jain monks carry whiskbrooms?
10. Explain why Jain monks and nuns must take the Five Great Vows.
11. Which religion – Jainism or Sikhism – is notable for its practice of ahimsa (non-violence)?
12. Explain the difference between the Jain and Sikh views of karma and rebirth.

13. Who was the founder of Sikhism?
14. What is the significance of Guru Nanak's actions in the story of Lalo and Bhago?
15. What is the meaning of the circumstances surrounding Guru Nanak's death?
16. What is the importance of Sikhism's Ten Gurus? Explain the significance of the last Guru.
17. What is the Sikh's only ritual?
18. What are the Five 'Ks'?
19. Why is the Sikh scripture, the Granth Sahib, called Guru Granth Sahib?
20. What do you consider a Sikh's most distinguishing characteristic?

Suggested Reading

Jainism
1. Chitrabhanu, Gurudev Shree (1980), *Twelve Facets of Reality: The Jain Path to Freedom.* New York: Jain Meditation International Center, Dodd, Mead and Company.
2. Dundas, Paul (1993), *The Jains.* London: Routledge.
3. Folkert, Kendall W. (1995), *Scripture and Community: Collected Essays on the Jains.* ed. J.E. Cort. Studies in World Religions Series. Cambridge: Harvard University Center for the Study of World Religions.
4. Jaine, Padmanabh S. (1979), *The Jaina Path of Purification.* Berkeley: University of California Press.
5. Sangave, Vilas A. (1990), *Aspects of Jaina Religion.* New Delhi: Bharatiya Jnanpith.
6. Tobias, Michael 1991), *Life Force: The World of Jainism.* Berkeley, California: Asian Humanities Press.

Sikhism
1. Cole, W. Owen and Sambhi, Piara Singh. (1978), *The Sikhs: Their Religious Beliefs and Practices.* London: Routledge and Kegan Paul.
2. McLeod, W.H. (1976), *Evolution of the Sikh Community.* Oxford: Claredon Press.
3. Singh, Dr. Gopal. (1979), *A History of the Sikh People 1469–1978.* New Delhi: World Sikh University Press.
4. Singh, Khushwant, trans. (1969), *Hymns of Guru Nanak.* New Delhi: Orient Longmans Ltd.
5. Singh, Ralph. *Sikhism: A Distinct, Universal Religion.* Central Square, New York: Gobind Sadan, U.S.A.
5. Singh, Trilochar and others. (1960), *Adi Granth: Selections from the Sacred Writings of the Sikhs.* London: George Allen & Unwin.

Sources

Jainism
1. Akaranga Sutra 2. 24, 25. Jacobi, Hermann, trans. (1884, 1895), *Jaina Sutras: Sacred Books of the East*, vols. 22, 45. Oxford: Claredon Press; reprint (1968), *Jaina Sutras: The Akaranga Sutra, The Kalpa Sutra.* New York: Dover Publications, Inc., pp. 263–64.
2. Uttaradhyayanna Sutra 9. 34–36. Jain, S.A. (1960), trans. *Reality.* Calcutta: Vira Shasan Sangha. My source, Wilson, Andrew. (1995), *World Scripture: A Comparative Anthology of Sacred Texts.* A Project of the International Religious Foundation. New York: Paragon House, p. 522

3. Uttaradhyayanna Sutra 28. 1, 10, 25, 30. Jacobi, Hermann, trans. (1884, 1895), *Jaina Sutras: Sacred Books of the East*. My source, Van Voorst, Robert E. (1997), *Anthology of World Scriptures*, Belmont, CA: Wadsworth Publishing Company, p. 113.

4. Sutrakritanga 1. 7. 1–9. Jacobi, Hermann, trans. (1884, 1895), *Jaina Sutras: Sacred Books of the East*, vol. XLV. Oxford: Claredon Press. My source, Van Voorst, Robert E. *Anthology of World Scripture*, p. 116.

5. Sutrakritanga 1. 2, 1. Jacobi, Hermann, trans. (1884, 1895), *Jaina Sutras*, Part II, in *Sacred Books of the East*, vol. XLV. Oxford: Claredon Press, pp. 249–253.

6. Akaranga Sutra 2. 15, i–v., Jacobi, Hermann. (1968), *Jaina Sutras: The Akaranga Sutra, The Kalpa Sutra*. New York: Dover Publications, Inc., pp. 202–208.

Sikhism

All selections from the Sikh scriptures are taken from Max A. Macauliffe. (1909), *The Sikh Religion: Its Gurus, Sacred Writings and Authors*. Oxford: Oxford University Press. Reprint; six volumes. (2004), Delhi, India: Low Price Publications.

7. Vichitar Natak, Vol. 5, 1, pp. 286–287.

8. Japji I–III, V. Vol. I, pp. 195–199.

9. Gauri Sukhmani, 1, 2, 3, 4. Vol. III, pp. 197–199.

10. Gauri, Vol. III, p. 183.

11. Bihagra Prayer, Vol. III, pp. 347–348.

12. Gauri, Vol. III, p. 141.

5 Chinese Wisdom

The Taoist Symbol Yin -Yang
Yin-Yang represents the harmony of the two cosmic forces in the universe.

Confucianism Water Symbol
Water represents the source of life.

Religion in Early China

China's religious traditions grew from roots planted deep during China's prehistoric period, approximately 3,000 years ago. The Chinese along the Yellow River worshipped their ancestors' spirits as deities. And they felt deep reverence for the mountains, rivers, and earth. Each village built a mound of earth that represented the fertility of the land. In the spring, the villagers performed festivals at this mound to ask the gods to grant them good crops. Each autumn they met at the mound to give thanks for the harvest.

> **Reflections**
> Do the early Chinese religious traditions remind you of specific traditions you have studied so far?

Before Lao-tzu, the founder of Taoism, and the great philosopher Confucius, three dynasties (periods of rule by a royal family) existed. The Hsia Kingdom flourished about 2000 BCE. The emperor of Hsia, believing he descended from the Sky God, called himself the 'Son of Heaven.' In the middle of the city he built an open altar where he could offer sacrifices to the heavenly spirits. His successors called themselves 'sons of heaven.'

The Shang dynasty, 1500–1000 BCE, thrived in the valley of the Yellow River. The people there were excellent farmers and believed that when members of the royal family died, their spirits became superhuman powers. These royal spirits had the power to control the destiny of the people and their crops. Living Shang rulers consulted their ancestral spirits through many types of ritual including animal sacrifices.

The Chou dynasty (c. 1111–700 BCE) that eventually overthrew the Shang treated their conquered subjects with benevolence. They allowed them to continue their accustomed religious rites, and even adopted many Shang ideas and customs. Chou rulers built temples for ancestral worship and preserved the Shangs' written language.

Reflections

Are there differences between how the ancient Chinese felt about their ancestors and how you feel about your ancestors?

The royal Chou family believed in a heaven deity, whom they worshipped as the reigning universal power and ultimate regulator of human affairs. Heaven oversaw human thoughts and actions, particularly those of the temporal ruler, a kind of priest-king whom the Chou believed could rule successfully only with the blessing and under the mandate of heaven. Accordingly, the ancestral cult evolved into an ethical religion, with virtue deemed the chief qualification of a good ruler.

These early beliefs and customs formed the basis for the predominant tenets of Chinese philosophy and religion. Centuries later, the renowned philosopher Confucius cited the humanitarian Chou dynasty as an example of how society should be governed. Confucius also based many of his precepts on Chou ideals, and these continue relevant in many aspects of modern Chinese life.

Yin and Yang

The Chinese people felt close to the earth and were keenly observant of the movements of nature, humans, and the heavens as interacting realities. Based on these concepts, an early school of philosophers defined two opposing principles known as *Yin* (the 'dark side' or 'nature') and *Yang* (the 'light side' or 'spirit'), the interaction of which produced all phenomena of the universe. The Yin principle – fertile, mysterious, secret, and female – predominates in all that is cool, moist, dark, or passive. The Yang principle, seen in the sun and in fire, is male and has to do with all that is hot, dry, bright, or active.

Yin and Yang Symbol
A circle of dark and light representing the complementary
yet opposing forces of the universe

Yin-Yang, which entered into the popular Chinese religion through Taoism, is also a crucial part of Confucian doctrine. To the Chinese, neither principle is superior to the other, the Yin being present in the Yang and the Yang in the Yin, and both existing in balance to produce the 'way of nature'. Heaven is Yang and Earth is Yin. Humans are made up of both heaven and earth. Although males are predominantly Yang and females predominantly Yin, members of each sex reveal characteristics of the other. For example, a log would appear to be Yin, but set afire, it will prove to have Yang qualities in abundance.

> **Reflections**
> Today, many professionals practice *Yin-Yang* in alternative medicine, exercise and nutrition. Do you believe a healthy person must have Yin and Yang in harmony, or does health and sickness depend on our genes?

The Five Classics

The series of literary collections known as the Five Classics produced during the Chou period firmly established the foundations of the rich Chinese culture, religion, and philosophy. Among these important works were:

- *The Book of Songs* or *Book of Odes,* an anthology of three hundred early Chinese poems, which included the hymns of the Chou kings – the first literary expression of Chinese religious feeling.
- *The Book of History,* an early indication of China's concern to record important events.
- *The Book of Rites,* which lists codified behaviors significant in Chou religious ritual.
- *Spring and Autumn Annals,* a compilation of historic events in the late Chou period.
- *I Ching,* a collection of works on divination.

I Ching

The *I Ching* (pronounced E Jing), known in English as the Book of Changes, is probably the oldest of the Chinese classics, predating works of even the earliest sages that have been identified by name. It is a manual of divination based on sixty-four hexagrams arranged around the symbol of Yin-Yang. (A hexagram is a figure comprised of six lines or two trigrams.) At one end of the spectrum is a hexagram of six undivided or unbroken lines, and at the other a hexagram of six divided or broken lines. These and the sixty-two patterns in between include all possible mixtures of six undivided and divided lines.

Trigram ───── ── ──

Trigram ───── ── ──   Hexagram

Unbroken Lines   Broken Lines

By holding thirty yarrow sticks and letting them fall as they will, or by tossing three coins six times, one is led to the hexagram appropriate for guidance in a particular situation. For example, when using coins, one side of the coin (heads) represents the unbroken lines, and the other side (tails) the broken lines. The combination of results produced by the six throws directs one to the only hexagram that matches that particular pattern of broken and unbroken lines. For example:

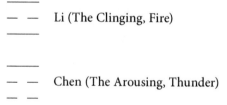

── ──   Li (The Clinging, Fire)

── ──   Chen (The Arousing, Thunder)

Hexagram #21 *Shih Ho/Biting Through*

Each hexagram includes a *judgment*, an *image*, and a brief *statement* or commentary. The person using the I Ching assumes that the hexagram indicated by the fall of the coins or the division of yarrow sticks is the intuition's breakthrough from the unconscious to the conscious mind: the answer was there all along but could not be found without help. The only measure of the validity of the result is the person's opinion that the text of the hexagram is a true rendering of her or his psychic condition.

> **Reflections**
> Have you ever used the *I Ching*? Do you agree that an answer to your nagging problem is actually stored in your intuition, but is somehow blocked? Could a book of divination unblock the answer for you, or is that a foolish idea?

Those who use the *I Ching* do not consider the results it produces mere chance but the meaningful coincidence of events in space and time, which are affected by the person involved. The *I Ching* continues to serve as a guide for Chinese life and to gain increasing scholarly recognition in the West.

Two Religions of China

From the sixth to the third century BCE, learned teachers traveled throughout north central China, establishing schools where they expounded their theories on many subjects. They especially hoped to educate princes, who would then rule according to the philosopher-teacher's ideals.

From the 'Hundred Schools,' as these movements were later called, emerged those of the Taoists and Confucius, whose teachings were to be of profound significance to the religious and ethical experience of China.

While Confucianism was being taught and practiced in the sophisticated courts and capitals of Chou China, Taoism (pronounced 'Dowism') evolved in the countryside among people seeking inner awareness and a kind of spiritual relationship with nature. Unlike Confucianism, which is an activist philosophy concerned with the events of this world and the role of government in enforcing social morality, Taoism is a philosophy of 'quietists,' relying on passivity as a way of life. More mystical than Confucians, Taoists seem more closely related to the shamans of earlier religions than to the aristocratic traditions of the Chou courts.

Taoism

According to tradition, the founder of Taoism was Lao-tzu, meaning 'Old Master,' who was born in approximately 604 BCE. We know little about his early life (it is not certain he was a historic person), but most scholars believe he was keeper of the archives at the Chou court. Legend has it that upon retiring from his position as keeper of the archives, Lao-tzu journeyed to the West on a water buffalo. At the border outpost, the gatekeeper recognized the sage and begged him to stay long enough to write down the main points of his philosophy. Lao-tzu agreed, and in a state of deep absorption, he composed the *Tao Te Ching*, which became the revered book of the Taoists. Then he vanished over the mountain pass, never to be seen again.

Tao Te Ching

A small book of eighty-one chapters of verse, the *Tao Te Ching* (pronounced 'Dow De Jing' and meaning The Way and Its Power) focuses on the harmony of Yin-Yang within the flow of the *Tao* (the way), and on the individual's relationship to society and nature. Taoists emphasize the values of the solitary individual who avoids involvement with the masses in society. They believe that the natural, undisturbed course of nature leads to harmony and perfection and is therefore emulated by the wise person.

> **Reflections**
> Do you agree that the wise person avoids involvement with the masses in society? Or does wisdom come in knowing how to live well in any situation?

Next to the Bible, the Tao Te Ching is the most translated book in the English language. A philosophical work that speaks through metaphors to the intuitive rather than the logical mind, it contains ideas of universal significance that can be understood by persons of widely different cultures. The text provides views about the origins of life, the universe, and everything in the universe. Also within the text is a simple and harmonious guide to living wisely.

Taoist Teachings

The Tao

In common usage, 'tao' means 'way'; thus the term suggests an inner and outer method of conduct, which is to flow with the natural order and live without conflict.

> **Reflections**
> In the fast-paced world of today, is it possible to flow with the natural order and live without conflict and stress? Or does the fast-paced world have little to do with our inner attitude and spirituality?

Tao also means the mystic, powerful 'Way' that is the cosmic force behind all phenomena. Among the concepts of Tao are 'Being' or the 'Nameable,' and 'Nonbeing' or the 'Unnameable.' These two related aspects of Tao grow out of one another and are interdependent.

The Nameable is the law of nature, the harmony between Yin-Yang, the movement of reversal. It is in the nature of things to move to their opposites – as day moves to night, heat ends in cold, or pleasure ends in pain.

'Nonbeing' does not mean nothingness, but emptiness – the absence of perceptible qualities. The Unnameable is not a negative concept of zero, it is positive, because the Nameable comes out of it. Frequently the Unnameable is called the 'uncarved block,' but this is a pointer, not a description, for the Tao is mysterious.

Thus the Nameable depends on the Unnameable for existence, just as things owe their being to the Nameable. Put differently, *Nonbeing needs Being for the manifestation of the Tao in the world, and Being needs Nonbeing to be made manifest.* Tao is the primordial, undivided state underlying both Being and Nonbeing. Tao is the inherent, purposeless, impersonal Cosmic Principle.

1. The Tao: Tao Te Ching: 1, 4, 14, 25, 34, 51

1. The Tao (Way) that can be told of is not the eternal Tao;
    The name that can be named is not the eternal name.
    The Nameless is the origin of Heaven and Earth;
    The Named is the mother of all things.
    Therefore let there always be non-being so we may see their subtlety,
    And let there always be being so we may see their outcome.
    The two are the same.
    But after they are produced, they have different names.
    They both may be called deep and profound.
    Deeper and more profound,
    The door of all subtleties!

4. Tao is empty (like a bowl),
    It may be used but its capacity is never exhausted.
    It is bottomless, perhaps the ancestor of all things.
    It blunts its sharpness,
    It unties its tangle.
    It softens its light
    It becomes one with the dusty world.
    Deep and still, it appears to exist forever.
    I do not know whose son it is.
    It seems to have existed before the Lord.

14. We look at it and do not see it;
        Its name is The Invisible.
    We listen to it and do not hear it;
        Its name is The Inaudible.
    We touch it and do not find it;
        Its name is The Subtle (formless).
    These three cannot be further inquired into,
    And hence merge into one.
    Going up high, it is not bright, and coming down low, it is not dark.
    Infinite and boundless, it cannot be given any name;
    It reverts to nothingness.
    This is called shape without shape,

Form without object.
It is The Vague and Elusive.
Meet it and you will not see its head.
Follow it and you will not see its back.
Hold on to the Tao of old in order to master the things of the present.
From this one may know the primeval beginning [of the universe].
This is called the bond of Tao.

25. There was something undifferentiated and yet complete,
    Which existed before heaven and earth.
    Soundless and formless, it depends on nothing and does not change.
    It operates everywhere and is free from danger.
    It may be considered the mother of the universe.
    I do not know its name; I call it Tao.

34. The Great Tao flows everywhere.
    It may go left or right.
    All things depend on it for life, and it does not turn away from them.
    It accomplishes its task, but does not claim credit for it.
    It clothes and feeds all things but does not claim to be master over them.
    Always without desires, it may be called The Small.
    All things come to it and it does not master them; it may be called The
        Great.

51. Tao produces them (the ten thousand things).
    Virtue fosters them.
    Matter gives them physical form.
    The circumstances and tendencies complete them.
    Therefore the ten thousand things esteem Tao and honor virtue.
    Tao is esteemed and virtue is honored without anyone's order.
    They always come spontaneously.
    Therefore Tao produces them and virtue fosters them.
    They rear them and develop them.
    They give them security and give them peace.
    They nurture them and protect them.
    (Tao) produces them but does not take possession of them.
    It acts, but does not rely on its own ability.
    It leads them but does not master them.
    This is called profound and secret virtue.

Living in Harmony with the Tao

For the Chinese, Tao is the way of nature – the way all of us should follow. Although we cannot conquer nature, we can learn to harmonize our purpose with the way of the Tao. The Tao flows in and through everyone and everything as an impersonal force. It is often compared to a moving body of water progressing endlessly, wearing away the hardest stone, useless to struggle against. To become one with Tao, we must first empty our minds of all thoughts.

2. Living in Harmony: Tao Te Ching: 16, 23, 46, 56, 78

16. Attain complete vacuity [Empty your mind of all thoughts]
    Maintain steadfast quietude.
    All things come into being,
    ... All things flourish,
    But each one returns to its root [source].
    This return to its root [source] means tranquility.
    It is called returning to its destiny.
    To return to destiny is called the eternal (Tao).
    To know the eternal is called enlightenment.
    Not to know the eternal is to act blindly to result in disaster.
    He who knows the eternal is all-embracing.
    ... Being in accord with Tao, he is everlasting,
    And is free from danger throughout his lifetime.

23. Nature says few words.
    For the same reason a whirlwind does not last a whole morning,
    Nor does a rainstorm last a whole day.
    What causes them?
    It is Heaven and Earth (Nature).
    If even Heaven and Earth cannot make them last long,
    How much less can man?
    Therefore he who follows Tao is identified with Tao.

46. When Tao prevails in the world, galloping horses are turned
        back to fertilize (the fields with their dung).
    When Tao does not prevail in the world, war horses
        thrive in the suburbs.
    There is no calamity greater than lavish desires.
    There is no greater disaster than greed.
    He who is contented with contentment is always contented.

56. He who knows does not speak.
    He who speaks does not know.

78. There is nothing softer and weaker than water,
    And yet there is nothing better for attacking hard and strong things.
    For this reason there is no substitute for it.
    All the world knows that the weak overcomes the strong and
        the soft overcomes the hard.
    But none can practice it.

Reflections
Would you consider flowing with the Tao predominately a Yin practice or a Yang practice?

Non-action (*Wu wei*)

A significant part of Taoism is the concept of non-action or letting-be, otherwise called the practice of quietism. Action must flow in harmony with the laws of nature, respecting the cyclical order of change and reversal, or the complementary energies of Yin-Yang. Through the natural course of things, nature accomplishes its purposes of creating, sustaining, or destroying.

Those who refuse to follow the Tao and insist on their own 'way' are doomed to fail, for happiness is only achieved by letting alone, by allowing the Tao free play, by engaging in activities of non-action. Because non-action precludes fighting for or against the course of events, wisdom consists in learning to go with the flow of Tao, calming the desire to assert oneself over others. The wise person acts *without* acting, influencing others without aggression. Legends abound about Taoists who develop mysterious powers so potent that even wild animals will not attack them.

Taoists believe the wise person always seeks good, even returning good for evil. To those who think such a person a fool the Taoist replies that flowing water – the most pliable element of the world – wears down mountains over time.

3. Non-action – Letting-be: Tao Te Ching: 2, 9, 24, 43, 47, 48, 63

2.   … The sage manages affairs without action (*wu-wei*).
And spreads doctrines without words.
All things arise, and he does not turn away from them.
He produces them, but does not take possession of them.
He acts, but does not rely on his own ability.
He accomplishes his task, but does not claim credit for it.
It is precisely because he does not claim credit that his
accomplishment remains with him.

9.   To hold and fill to overflowing
Is not as good as to stop in time.
Sharpen a sword-edge to its very sharpest,
   And the (edge) will not last long.
When gold and jade fill your hall,
   You will not be able to keep them.
To be proud with honor and wealth
   Is to cause one's own downfall.
Withdraw as soon as your work is done.
Such is Heaven's Way.

24.   He who stands on tiptoe is not steady.
He who strides forward does not go.
He who shows himself is not luminous.
He who justifies himself is not prominent.
He who boasts of himself is not given credit.
He who brags does not endure for long.
From the point of view of Tao, these are like remnants of
food and tumors of action,

Which all creatures detest.
Therefore those who possess Tao turn away from them.

43. The softest things in the world overcome the hardest things in the world.
Non-being penetrates that in which there is no space.
Through this I know the advantage of taking no action.
Few in the world can understand teaching without words
and the advantage of taking no action.

47. One may know the world without going out of doors.
One may see the Way of Heaven without looking through the windows.
The further one goes, the less one knows.
Therefore the sage knows without going about,
Understands without seeing,
And accomplishes without any action.

48. The pursuit of learning is to increase day after day.
The pursuit of Tao is to decrease day after day.
It is to decrease and further decrease until one reaches the
point of taking no action.
No action is undertaken, and yet nothing is left undone.

63. Act without action.
Do without ado.

Reflections
Do you think the Taoists would be pacifists or activists under enemy attack? Would you choose to be active or passive in the same situation?

Government

It is not surprising that Taoists, unlike Confucians, believe in governing by inaction. When the state stresses moral rules, for example, citizens begin to act artificially. Although people are innately good, things initiated by the state are impositions that lead them away from their true selves. State intervention causes its citizens to compete with one another, and competition corrupts the goodness in them and leads to strife. Thus a ruler must not interfere with the affairs of his people nor impose policies on them. The ruler must instead, understand the people's feelings and opinions, so the people will feel *they* have accomplished whatever is done.

4. Non-action in Government: Tao Te Ching: 17, 29, 30, 37, 59

17. The best (rulers) are those whose existence is (merely)
known by the people.
The next best are those who are loved and praised.
The next are those who are feared.

And the next are those who are despised.
It is only when one does not have enough faith in others
     that others will have no faith in him.
[The great rulers] value their words highly.
They accomplish their task; they complete their work.
Nevertheless their people say that they simply follow Nature.

29. When one desires to take over the empire and act on it
     (interfere with it),
     I see that he will not succeed.
     The empire is a spiritual thing, and should not be acted on.
     He who acts on it harms it.
     He who holds on to it loses it.
     Among creatures some lead and some follow.
     Some blow hot and some blow cold.
     Some are strong and some are weak.
     Some may break and some may fall.
     Therefore the sage discards the extremes, the extravagant,
        and the excessive.

30. He who assists the ruler with Tao does not dominate the
        world with force.
     The use of force usually brings requital.
     Wherever armies are stationed, briers and thorns grow.
     Great wars are always followed by famines.
     A good (general) achieves his purpose and stops,
     … He achieves his purpose but does not aim to dominate.
     … Which [would be] … contrary to Tao.
     Whatever is contrary to Tao will soon perish.

37. Tao invariably takes no action, and yet there is nothing left undone.
     If kings and barons can keep it, all things will transform spontaneously.
     If, after transformation, they should desire to be active,
     I would restrain them with simplicity, which has no name, is free
        of desires.
   Being free of desires, it is tranquil
   And the world will be at peace of its own accord.

59. To rule people and to serve heaven there is nothing better
        than to be frugal.
     Only by being frugal can one recover quickly.
     To recover quickly means to accumulate virtue heavily.
     By the heavy accumulation of virtue one can overcome everything.
     If one can overcome everything, then he will acquire a capacity
        the limit of which is beyond anyone's knowledge.
     When his capacity is beyond anyone's knowledge, he is fit to rule a state.
     He who possesses the Mother (Tao) of the state will last long.

This means that the roots are deep and the stalks are firm,
which is the way of long life and everlasting existence.

Reflections

Do you agree that competition corrupts the goodness in people and leads to strife?
Or is competition a healthy way of life?

Confucianism

Confucius lived during one of the most intellectually creative periods in the history of China. Yet during the Age of the Philosophers, which identifies this period in Chinese history, China was wracked by political and cultural anarchy. The boundaries between her regions were in a constant state of flux. Under corrupt feudal rulers, qualified to reign only by their noble ancestry, Chinese society suffered general economic and moral deterioration.

Believing political and social relations must be governed by standards of morality, such as loyalty, integrity, dutiful piety, respect for tradition, harmonious family and social relationships, and respect for teachers, Confucius developed and taught the social and ethical system for which he has been revered for over two thousand years. Although he was skeptical of some of the traditional religious practices of his day, he was a devout advocate of dutiful piety and ancestor rites. He felt a sense of mission, which he derived from *T'ien* (Heaven), a power that he regarded as a positive moral force (*te*) and that he relied on during times of personal or political failure.

An old debate as to whether Confucius's social and ethical system amounts to a religion continues to linger. Although he spent more time examining the good life than probing 'the ultimate nature of reality,' his philosophy is in harmony with religious and spiritual patterns of reality. Although, not a prophet in the Western sense or a yogi in the Eastern sense, Confucius was a teacher and reformer whose values have had a crucial influence on the moral, social, and religious life of the Chinese and of people throughout the world.

Reflections

Do you think the teachings of a moral reformer, who follows the 'mandate of heaven' but never speaks of God, should be considered a religion?

Life of Confucius

Confucius (551–479 BCE) was born to aristocratic parents in the northern province of Shantung, China. His family name was Kung, and the name by which we know him is a Latinized version of K'ung Fu-Tzu, or Master Kung.

At age nineteen Confucius married. Soon after, he became a teacher to sons of the nobility. He not only taught them to read and write, but also provided them with a thorough grounding in the rites and liturgy of the Chou royal religion. His teaching manner was cheerful and informal: he had a sense of humor and approved of pleasure in moderation.

Accompanied by a few student disciples, Confucius spent ten or more years traveling through China visiting vassals of the imperial court, regional governors, and powerful warlords, whom he tried to persuade to rule according to his philosophy of government. Sadly, his efforts were doomed to failure. Though he attracted many friends and admirers, Confucius never attained the official recognition and position he sought, possibly because of the uncompromising frankness and sincerity with which he spoke. Profoundly disappointed, Confucius returned to his hometown and resumed teaching there.

Now, however, in an effort to alleviate the monopoly on education enjoyed by the aristocracy – the class to which he belonged and whose sons he had earlier taught – Confucius accepted as students the poorest young men, demanding from them only two qualities: intelligence and willingness to work hard. His own humility was evident in his capacity to listen to his disciples, to compromise, and to admit error.

The three well-known works of Confucius are: *The Analects, The Great Learning*, and *The Doctrine of the Mean*. Student disciples of Confucius recorded his discourses, conversations, and travels in a collection of books called *The Analects* (from the Greek word meaning 'things gathered'). After his death in 479 BCE during the Han dynasty, the Analects were standardized into twenty chapters, each named for an important disciple. The book, the Great Learning, a code of behavior for everyday living, was written by Confucius and his disciple Zing Zi. The Seven Steps in The Great Learning are: (1) the investigations of things; (2) the completion of knowledge; (3) the sincerity of thoughts; (4) the rectifying of the heart; (5) the cultivation of the person; (6) the regulation of the family; and (7) the government of the State. Confucius's moral philosophy and religious thought are expanded in his book, *The Doctrine of the Mean*, which deals with practicing virtue by following the middle way – the way of Heaven and Earth.

Confucius on Himself

5. Analects: Book 2, Wei Chang

The Master said, 'At fifteen, I had my mind bent on learning.

'At thirty, I stood firm.

'At forty, I had no doubts.

'At fifty, I knew the decrees of Heaven.

'At sixty, my ear was an obedient organ for the reception of truth.

'At seventy, I could follow what my heart desired, without transgressing what was right.'

6. Analects: Book 7, Shu R

The Master said, [I am] a transmitter and not a maker, believing in and loving the ancients …

7. Analects: Book 7, Shu R

The Master said, Give me a few more years, so that I may have spent a whole fifty in study, and I believe that after all I should be fairly free from error.

8. Analects: Book 7, Shu R
The Master said, 'I am not one who was born in the possession of knowledge; I am one who is fond of antiquity, and earnest in seeking it there.'

9. Analects: Book 5, Kung-ye Ch'ang
The Master said, 'In a hamlet of ten families, there may be found one honorable and sincere as I am, but not so fond of learning.'

10. Analects: Book 5, Kung-ye Ch'ang
The Master said, 'In letters I am perhaps equal to other men, but the character of the superior man, carrying out in his conduct what he professes, is what I have not yet attained to.'

The Teacher

11. The Sayings of Confucius: Ch. VII, Transmit ...
'To take note of things in silence, to retain curiosity despite much study, never to weary of teaching others: no one surpasses me in these three things.'

12. Analects: Book 7, Shu R
The Master said, 'From the man bringing his bundle of dried flesh for my teaching upwards, I have never refused instruction to any one.'

13. Analects: Book 7, Shu R
The Master said, 'I do not open up the truth to one who is not eager to get knowledge, nor help out any one who is not anxious to explain himself. When I have presented one corner of a subject to any one, and he cannot from it learn the other three, I do not repeat my lesson.'

14. Analects: Book 7, Shu R
The Master said, 'Do you think, my disciples, that I have any concealments? I conceal nothing from you. There is nothing which I do that is not shown to you, my disciples; that is my way.'

15. Book of Rites: 2:11
The Master said, 'As to being a Divine Sage or even a Good Man, far be it from me to make any such claim. As for unwearying effort to learn and unflagging patience in teaching others, those are merits I do not hesitate to claim.'

16. Analects: Book 2, Wei Chang
The Master said, 'If a man keeps cherishing his old knowledge, so as continually to be acquiring new, he may be a teacher of others.'

17. Analects: Book 2, Wei Chang
The Master said, 'Yu, shall I teach you what knowledge is? When you know a thing, to hold that you know it; and when you do not know a thing, to allow that you do not know it; – this is knowledge.'

Reflections

There is a saying: 'The opinionated person is usually without knowledge.' What do you think?

18. Analects: Book 15, Wei Ling Kung

The Master said, 'When a man is not in the habit of saying – "What shall I think of this? What shall I think of this?" I can indeed do nothing with him.'

19. Analects: Book 15, Wei Ling Kung

The Master said, 'In teaching there should be no distinction of classes.'

20. Analects: Book 17, Yang Ho

The Master said, 'Yu, have you heard the six words to which are attached six becloudings?' Yu replied, 'I have not.'

'Sit down, and I will tell them to you.

'There is the love of being benevolent without the love of learning; – the beclouding here leads to a foolish simplicity. There is the love of knowing without the love of learning; – the beclouding here leads to dissipation of mind. There is the love of being sincere without the love of learning; – the beclouding here leads to an injurious disregard of consequences. There is the love of straightforwardness without the love of learning; – the beclouding here leads to rudeness. There is the love of boldness without the love of learning; – the beclouding here leads to insubordination. There is the love of firmness without the love of learning; – the beclouding here leads to extravagant conduct.'

Reflections

Would knowledge of the six 'becloudings' help you become the kind of person you would like to be?

Confucian Ethics

Confucius considered the natural world a good place that provides most things people need so long as they work with nature in accordance with the principles of heaven.

According to the Analects, Confucius repudiated rigid law and punishment, advocating instead the demonstration of virtue based on proper conduct. For instance, we should develop the capacity to deal with others as we would have them deal with us.

Although Confucius advocated the 'Golden Rule,' he disagreed with the Taoist and Christian ideal of returning good for evil. We should, he said, repay kindness with kindness, but repay evil with justice.

> **Reflections**
> Would Confucius sanction capital punishment? What is your position?

Five Cardinal Virtues

Necessary in every aspect of life are the Five Cardinal Virtues: *Jen, Chun tzu, Li Te,* and *Wen.*

1. *Jen* is the ideal relationship between two people that involves a deep feeling of respect for oneself and others. The Jen person is unselfish and looks to all people as brothers and sisters.
2. *Chun tzu* is the 'Superior Man' who treats others with justice and love. In societies that lack Chun tzu war is inevitable.
3. *Li* is the mean (proper balance) between two extremes in moral conduct both within the family and society.
4. *Te* refers to the good government whose leaders follow honest ways. Good rulers inspire loyalty among the people.
5. *Wen* is the art of peace found in the arts, music, and philosophy. Art has the power to guide human beings toward the good.

> **Reflections**
> Do you agree with Confucius that without *Chun tzu*, war is inevitable?

Jen: Respect for Oneself and Others

Confucius said that people, in order to develop their greatest moral potentials, must have and become proper role models. Problems arise when humans promote their own advantage at the expense of others. When people are mean or petty, they forget their responsibilities to family members, friends, and their ruler. They forget, also, that they are both students and teachers of morals. Thus, to live without consideration of others is not only bad for the individual, but is harmful to society, for it sets a bad example.

21. Analects: Book 4, Le Jin
The Master said, 'It is virtuous manners which constitute the excellence of a neighborhood. If a man in selecting a residence does not fix on one where such [manners] prevail, how can he be wise?'

22. Analects: Book 4, Le Jin
The Master said, 'Those who are without virtue cannot abide long either in a condition of poverty and hardship, or in a condition of enjoyment. The virtuous rest in virtue; the wise desire virtue.'

23. Analects: Book 4, Le Jin

The Master said, 'I have not seen a person who loved virtue, or one who hated what was not virtuous. He who loved virtue, would esteem nothing above it. He who hated what is not virtuous, would practice virtue in such a way that he would not allow anything that is not virtuous to approach his person.'

24. Analects: Book 1, Hsio R

The Master said, 'A youth, when at home, should be filial, and abroad, respectful to his elders. He should be earnest and truthful. He should overflow in love to all, and cultivate the friendship of the good. When he has time and opportunity, after the performance of these things, he should employ them in polite studies.'

Chun Tzu: the Superior Man

The superior man feels neither fear nor anxiety, but is always calm and at peace. The inferior man in contrast is typically anxious and worried. The superior man is virtuous. The inferior man lacks integrity. The qualities by which Confucius distinguished the superior from the inferior man are love, compassion, righteousness, virtue, and the achievement of inner harmony.

Reflections

Is Confucius correct that superior men are virtuous, or is the business person who believes 'good guys finish last' more practical and thus superior?

25. Analects: Book 1, Hsio R

The Master said, 'Is it not pleasant to learn with a constant perseverance and application?

'Is it not delightful to have friends coming from distant quarters?

'Is he not a man of complete virtue, who feels no discomposure though men may take no note of him?'

26. Analects: Book 1, Hsio R

'The superior man bends his attention to what is radical. That being established, all practical courses naturally grow up. Filial piety and fraternal submission, — are they not the root of all benevolent actions?'

27. Analects: Book 4, Le Jin

The Master said, 'The superior man thinks of virtue; the small man thinks of comfort. The superior man thinks of the sanctions of law; the small man thinks of favors which he may receive.'

28. Analects: Book 15, Wei Ling Kung

The Master said, 'What the superior man seeks, is in himself. What the mean man seeks, is in others.'

29. Analects: Book 15, We Ling Kung

The Master said, 'The superior man in everything considers righteousness to be essential. He performs it according to the rules of propriety. He brings it forth in humility. He completes it with sincerity. This is indeed a superior man.'

The Mean Between Two Extremes (the Golden Rule)

Harmony, said Confucius, is essential to a good life. Such harmony is achieved by not doing to others what one does not want done to oneself and by following the other tenets of Confucian ethics. Society supports humans in their quest for harmony and ancestors can help the living; however, people have to do most of the work themselves.

30. Analects: Book 4, Le Jin

The Master said, 'Tsang, my doctrine is that of an all-pervading unity.' The disciple Tsang replied, 'Yes.'

The Master went out, and the other disciples asked, saying, 'What do his words mean?' Tsang said, 'The doctrine of our master is to be true to the principles – of our nature and the benevolent exercise of them to others, – this and nothing more.'

31. Analects: Book 15, Wei Ling Kung

Tsze-kung asked saying, 'Is there one word which may serve as a rule of practice for all one's life?' The Master said, 'Is not RECIPROCITY such a word? What you do not want done to yourself, do not do to others.'

32. The Doctrine of the Mean

While there are no stirrings of pleasure, anger, sorrow, or joy, the mind may be said to be in the state of Equilibrium. When those feelings have been stirred, and they act in their due degree, there ensues what may be called the state of Harmony. This Equilibrium is the great root from which grow all the human actings in the world, and this Harmony is the universal path which they all should pursue.

33. The Virtue of the Mean

The Master said, 'Perfect is the virtue which is according to the Mean! Rare have they long been among the people, who could practice it!

The Master said, 'I know how it is that the path of the Mean is not walked in:– The knowing go beyond it, and the stupid do not come up to it. I know how it is that the path of the Mean is not understood:– The men of talents and virtue go beyond it, and the worthless do not come up to it …

The Master said, 'Alas! How is the path of the Mean untrodden!'

Te: Good Government

Confucius looked to the ancient wise men as his guide to living. He believed superior people should set the example for others by living the good life. All government leaders should follow certain steps:

- Investigate things
- Strive for knowledge
- Be sincere
- Have good hearts
- Live honorable personal lives
- Build close family ties
- Organize the government properly.

Confucius taught when government leaders achieve the above there will be peace in the world.

Reflections

Have you ever known or even heard of a government leader who fits Confucius's description? Should government leaders be virtuous under all circumstances?

Two of the master's fundamental principles concerning government were revolutionary in the Chinese culture of the time: (1) those who govern should be chosen not on the basis of heredity, but on demonstrable characteristics of virtue and ability; (2) the true end of government is the total welfare and happiness of the people.

Rejecting the idea that aristocrats descended from divine ancestors ruled by virtue of heaven's authority, Confucius insisted the right to govern depended on the ruler's moral character and the ability to make his subjects happy. Further, Confucius challenged the very foundations of authoritarian government by insisting on the right of all individuals to make basic decisions for themselves. He did not however indicate that all government is evil. True governing, he said, flows directly from the moral quality of one's character.

The goal of achieving the improvement of government in the interest, and to the advantage of the governed, escaped Confucius during his lifetime. Later, however Confucian kings agreed that they merited the mandate of heaven only by proper conduct; and lesser nobles also expected to thrive or suffer according to whether they followed heaven's will.

34. Analects: Book 12, Yen Yuan

The Duke Ching, of Ch'l, asked Confucius about government. Confucius replied, 'There is government, when the prince is prince, and the minister is minister; when the father is father, and the son is son.'

35. Analects: Book 12, Yen Yuan

Tsze-chang asked about government. The Master said, 'The art of governing is to keep its affairs before the mind without weariness, and to practice them with undeviating consistency.'

36. Analects: Book 12, Yen Yuan

Chi K'ang asked Confucius about government. Confucius replied, 'To govern means to rectify. If you lead the people with correctness, who will dare not be correct?'

37. Analects: Book 12, Yen Yuan

Chi K'ang asked Confucius about government, saying, 'What do you say to killing the unprincipled for the good of the principled?' Confucius replied, 'Sir, in carrying on your government, why should you use killing at all? Let your evinced desires be for what is good, and the people will be good. The relation between superiors and inferiors is like that between the wind and the grass. The grass must bend, when the wind blows across it.'

38. Analects: Book 20, Yao Yueh

Tsze-chang asked Confucius, saying, 'In what way should a person in authority act in order that he may conduct government properly?' The Master replied, 'Let him honor the five excellent, and banish away the four bad, things; — then may he conduct government properly.' Tsze-chang said, 'What are meant by the five excellent things?' The Master said, 'When the person in authority is beneficent without great expenditure; when he lays tasks on the people without their repining; when he pursues what he desires without being covetous; when he maintains a dignified ease without being proud; when he is majestic without being fierce.'

Tsze-chang said, 'What is meant by being beneficent without great expenditure?' The Master replied, 'When the person in authority makes more beneficial to the people the things from which they naturally derive benefit;— is not this being beneficent without great expenditure? When he chooses the labors which are proper, and makes them labor on them, who will repine? When his desires are set on benevolent government, and he secures it, who will accuse him of covetousness? Whether he has to do with many people or few, or with things great or small, he does not dare to indicate any disrespect;— is not this to maintain a dignified ease without any pride? He adjusts his clothes and cap, and throws a dignity into his looks, so that, thus dignified, he is looked at with awe;— is not this to be majestic without being fierce?'

Tsze-chang then asked, 'What are meant by the four bad things?' The Master said, 'To put people to death without having instructed them;— this is called cruelty. To require from them, suddenly, the full tale of work, without having given them warning;— this is called oppression. To issue orders as if without urgency, at first, and, when the time comes, to insist on them with severity; — this is called injury. And, generally, in the giving pay or rewards to men, to do it in a stingy way; — this is called acting the part of a mere official.'

Wen: the Arts

Acknowledging that people vary in their inherent virtues and abilities, Confucius taught that an appropriate education nurtures and cultivates the moral characteristics essential to the superior man. To be fully human, said Confucius, one must love art. Art has the power to transform human nature in the direction of virtue. In education, art includes poetry, music, ritual and dance. Poetry stimulates the emotions, heightens powers of observation, increases sympathy, and moderates resentment of justice. Music expresses the inward, heavenly aspects of the universe. One piece of music cast a spell over Confucius that lasted three months. Rituals are an outward, earthly expression of these worthy concepts. A harmonious relationship among the arts is essential for perfect order.

For Confucius, a nation of excellence has the noblest philosophy, the most lofty poetry and music, and virtuous government leaders. These arts will give a nation such superiority that other leaders will model their country's government and educational systems after it.

39. Music. Li Ki

Music rises from the human heart when the human heart is touched by the external world.

Therefore the ancient kings were ever careful about things that affected the human heart. They tried therefore to guide the people's ideals and aspirations by means of li, establish harmony in sounds by means of music, regulate conduct by means of government, and prevent immorality by means of punishments. Li, music, punishments and government have a common goal, which is to bring about unity in the people's hearts and carry out the principles of political order.

Music expresses the harmony of the universe, while rituals express the order of the universe. Through harmony all things are influenced, and through order all things have a proper place … When rituals and music are well established, we have the Heaven and Earth functioning in perfect order …

Character is the backbone of our human nature, and music is the flowering of character … The poem gives expression to our heart, the song gives expression to our voice, and the dance gives expression to our movements. These three arts take their rise from the human soul, and then are given further expressions by means of the musical instruments.

40. Analects: Book 7, Shu R

When the Master was in Ch'I, he heard the Shao, and for three months did not know the taste of flesh. 'I did not think,' he said, 'that music could have been made so excellent as this.'

41. Analects: Book 16, Xe She

Confucius said, 'There are three things men find enjoyment in which are advantageous, and three things they find enjoyment in which are injurious. To find enjoyment in the discriminating study of ceremonies and music; to find enjoyment in speaking of the goodness of others; to find enjoyment in having many worthy friends;– these are advantageous. To find enjoyment in extravagant pleasures; to find enjoyment in idleness and sauntering; to find enjoyment in the pleasures of feasting;– these are injurious.'

42. Analects 3:3
The Master said, A person who is not Good, what can she or he have to do with ritual? A person who is not Good, what can she or he have to do with music?

The Five Relationships

A consequence of inner harmony is *li*, or proper conduct – an outward manifestation of the moral and social obligations affecting every contact with fellow beings, within the family and within society. These obligations and duties, known as the *Five Relationships*, are fundamental to Confucian teaching:

1. A *husband* is considerate of his wife and a *wife* subservient to her husband.
2. A *father* is kind to his son and a *son* obedient to his father.
3. An *elder brother* is helpful to his younger brother and a *younger brother* respectful of his older brother.
4. A *senior friend* helps a junior friend and a *junior friend* respects his senior.
5. A *ruler* acts beneficently to his subjects and the *subjects* obey their ruler.

43. Right Behavior
Kindness in the father, filial piety in the son
Gentility in the eldest brother, humility and respect in the younger
Righteous behavior in the husband, obedience in the wife
Humane consideration in elders, deference in juniors
Benevolence in rulers, loyalty in ministers and subjects.

44. Family Harmony
When wives and children and their sires are one,
'Tis like the harp and lute in unison.
When brothers live in concord and at peace
The stain of harmony shall never cease.
The lamp of happy union lights the home,
And bright days follow when the children come.

45. Proper Behavior. The Doctrine of the Mean
In the way of the superior man there are four things, to not one of which have I as yet attained. – To serve my father, as I would require my son to serve me: to this I have not attained; to serve my prince as I would require my minister to serve me: to this I have not attained; to serve my elder brother as I would require my younger brother to serve me: to this I have not attained; to set the example in behaving to a friend, as I would require him to behave to me: to this I have not attained …

View of Heaven

In the time of Confucius, the Chinese people considered heaven not a place of salvation but the home of royal ancestor spirits. The ancestor spirits functioned as divine beings, whom the rulers worshipped through complex rituals. Confucius thought it more productive to practice the good life on earth than to spend energy on speculations about life after death. Nevertheless, he recommended the 'way of heaven' as the model by which sages, rulers, and nobles should conduct their lives.

Divination procedures based on the I Ching related directly to the Confucian notion of heaven and the heavenly mandate. Because heaven does not speak directly to humanity, indirect means via the I Ching indicated heaven's approval or disapproval. Confucius himself used the I Ching. Later, Confucian kings who prospered believed they ruled by the mandate of heaven, which they earned by their proper conduct. Lesser nobles also expected to thrive or suffer depending on whether they followed heaven's will.

Confucius did not suggest worship of a personal deity. He taught instead that reverence was best expressed by imitating his example and practicing his teachings in society.

46. The Path. The Doctrine of the Mean
What Heaven has conferred is called The Nature; an accordance with this nature is called The Path of duty; the regulation of this path is called Instruction.

The path may not be left for an instant. If it could be left, it would not be the path …

47. Spiritual Powers. The Doctrine of the Mean
The Master said, 'How abundantly do spiritual beings display the powers that belong to them!

'We look for them, but do not see them; we listen to, but do not hear them; yet they enter into all things, and there is nothing without them.'

48. Sincerity. The Doctrine of the Mean
Sincerity is the way of Heaven. The attainment of sincerity is the way of men. He who possesses sincerity is he who, without an effort, hits what is right, and apprehends, without the exercise of thought;– he is the sage who naturally and easily embodies the right way. He who attains to sincerity is he who chooses what is good, and firmly holds it fast.

49. The Way of Heaven and Earth. The Doctrine of the Mean
The way of Heaven and Earth my be completely declared in one sentence. – They are without any doubleness, and so they produce things in a manner that is unfathomable.

The way of Heaven and Earth is large and substantial, high and brilliant, far-reaching and long-enduring.

50. The Sage. The Doctrine of the Mean
It is only he, possessed of all sagely qualities, that can exist under heaven, who shows himself quick in apprehension, clear in discernment, of far-reaching intelligence, and all-embracing knowledge, fitted to exercise rule; magnanimous, generous, benign, and mild, fitted to exercise forbearance; impulsive, energetic, firm, and enduring, fitted to maintain a firm hold; self-adjusted, grave, never

swerving from the Mean, and correct, fitted to command reverence; accomplished, distinctive, concentrative, and searching, fitted to exercise discrimination.

Call him man in his ideal, how earnest is he! Call him an abyss, how deep is he! Call him Heaven, how vast is he!

Summary

Religion in early China consisted of ancestor worship. Shamans served as medicine men and prophets. Prior to Taoism and Confucianism, three dynasties existed in China: the Hsia Kingdom (2000 BCE), the Shang dynasty (c. 1500–1000 BCE), and the Chou dynasty (c. 1111–700 BCE). The beliefs and customs of these dynasties, especially the Chou dynasty, formed the basis for Chinese philosophy and religion.

An early school of philosophers defined the movements of heaven and earth as *Yang* and *Yin*, the interaction of which produced all phenomena of the universe. The Yang principle, seen in sun and fire, is male. The mysterious, fertile Yin principle is female. Both exist in balance to produce the 'way of nature.'

The Five Classics produced during the Chou period established the foundation of Chinese religion and culture: the *Book of Odes*, the *Book of History*, the *Book of Rites, Spring and Autumn Annals,* and the *I Ching*. The I Ching, the oldest of the Chinese classics, is a manual of divination used throughout the world today.

Taoism

Lao-tzu, born approximately 604 BCE, the founder of Taoism, composed the revered book of the Taoists, the *Tao Te Ching*. Next to the Jewish and Christian Bible, the Tao Te Ching is the most translated book in the English language. The text provides views about the origins of life, the universe, and everything in the universe. Also within the text is a guide to living wisely.

Tao is 'the Way' of nature – the way human beings should follow. All actions should flow in harmony with the laws of nature, respecting the cyclical order of change and reversal, or the complementary energies of Yin-Yang. Through the natural course of things, nature accomplishes its purpose of creating, sustaining, or destroying.

Taking the path of *wu wei* (non-action), the wise person acts without acting, influencing others without aggression. Even the ruler of a state must take the peoples' feelings and opinions as his own so his subjects will feel they have accomplished whatever is done. Competition leads only to strife.

The Tao is Nameable (Being) and Unnameable (Non-being). The two related aspects grow out of one another and are interdependent: The Unnameable produces the Nameable and the Nameable produces nature. In the Tao there are no polar opposites, only standards of value we place on things, because everything is relative. Judgments of right and wrong depend on one's personal stance, situation, and needs. Everything issues out of Tao and everything returns to Tao.

Confucianism

Confucius (551–479 BCE) lived in one of the most intellectually creative periods in the history of China. During this period, Confucius developed and taught the social ethical system for which he has been revered for over two thousand years. Although a great teacher, Confucius was unable to persuade China's leaders to rule according to his philosophy of government. Disciples of Confucius recorded his discourses, conversations, and travels in a collection of twenty books called the *Analects.*

According to the Analects, Confucius considered the world a good place that provides most things people need so long as they work with nature in accordance with the principles of heaven. Rulers, he said, should demonstrate virtue based on proper conduct; then the people would also conduct themselves properly.

Confucius advocated Five Cardinal Virtues: (1) *Jen* – the ideal and unselfish relationship between two people; (2) *Chun tzu* – the 'Superior Person' who treats others with justice and love; (3) *Li* – the mean between two extremes in moral conduct; (4) *Te* – good government leaders; and (5) *Wen* – the art of peace.

Confucius was a strong supporter of 'appropriate' education, which nurtures and cultivates the moral characteristics essential to the superior man. Along with philosophy and ethics, education must include poetry, music, dance, and ritual. A nation of excellence has the noblest philosophy, the most lofty poetry and music, and virtuous government leaders.

Obligations and duties, known as the Five Relationships, are fundamental to Confucius's teachings: (1) a husband is considerate of his wife and a wife subservient to her husband; (2) a father is kind to his son and a son obedient to his father; (3) an elder brother is helpful to his younger brother and a younger brother respectful of his older brother; (4) a senior friend helps a junior friend and a junior friend respects his senior; (5) a ruler acts beneficently to his subjects and the subjects obey their ruler.

Confucius recommended the 'way of heaven,' the home of royal ancestor spirits, as a model by which sages, rulers, and nobles should conduct their lives. Confucius did not suggest worship of a personal deity. Reverence, he said, was best expressed by following his example and his teachings.

Taoism Today

By the mid-twentieth century, Taoism had lost its vital influence among the Chinese people. The dominant religions were those brought in by missionaries from outside China – Buddhism, Christianity, and Islam. The Great Proletarian Cultural Revolution from 1966 to the mid-1970s virtually prohibited all religious practices in China. Religious ideology centered mainly around Marxism in general and Mao Tse-tung in particular. Until his death in 1976, he was revered as 'the red sun in the hearts of people throughout the world.' After the death of Mao Tse-tung, however, a more tolerant religious attitude emerged, and temples, mosques, and churches reopened. In China, Taoism is beginning to flourish again, and around the world intellectuals continue to read the Tao Te Ching.

Confucianism Today

While Confucianism served for many centuries as China's main ethical and religious system, the victory of communism in 1949 and the impact of the Cultural Revolution in 1966 forced Confucius's teachings underground. Communists claimed that Confucianism divided society into two classes: the aristocrats, who possessed wealth, enjoyed leisure, and were the privileged recipients of education – and the masses that lived without education or the benefits enjoyed by the elite.

One must not conclude, however, that Confucianism has no place in Chinese society in the twenty-first century. According to many Chinese scholars, when Mao Tse-tung died, Confucian virtues returned to China. While committed to the modernization and industrialization of China, the current regime has also restored Confucius to a place of honor in schools and in society as a whole. Thus Confucian ideals remain significant to the Chinese people today.

Timeline

Taoism

c. 604 to 500 BCE	Life of Lao-Tzu.
c. 575 BCE	Lao-Tzu composed the Tao Te Ching.
c. 350 BCE	Chuang-Tzu further develops Taoist philosophy.
c. 300 – 213 BCE	Emperor Ch'in Shih burns books including Confucian, Taoist texts and the Five Classics.
400 to 448 CE	Emperor T'ai Wu Ti of Northern Wei dynasty declares Taoism official imperial religion.
618 to 626 CE	Emperor Gaozu builds temple at birthplace of Lao-Tzu.
618 to 907 CE	During T'ang dynasty, Emperor Li Yuan claims descent from Lao-Tzu.
1445 CE	Publication of the Taoist canon.
1912 CE	China becomes a republic.
1949 CE	Establishment of Communist rule in China: repression of religion.

Confucianism

c. 551 to 479 BCE	Life of Confucius.
c. 548 BCE	Death of Confucius's father.
c. 534 BCE	Confucius gains employment as manager of a state granary.
c. 532 BCE	Confucius marries.
c. 534 BCE	Confucius promoted to state husbandry.
c. 528 BCE	Confucius begins teaching.
c. 527 BCE	Death of Confucius's mother.
c. 520 BCE	Confucius meets the Honored Duke, ruler of the neighboring state Qi.

c. 511 BCE	Confucius begins compiling the *Book of History* and the *Book of Songs*.
c. 510 BCE	According to some sources, Confucius divorces his wife.
c. 501 BCE	Confucius becomes chief magistrate of Chung-tu.
c. 499 BCE	Confucius becomes Minister of Justice.
c. 497 BCE	Confucius resigns.
c. 495 to 485 BCE	Confucius travels to several kingdoms in the region, but is unable to find prolonged employment.
c. 484 BCE	Begins editing and adapting Lu's state history, the *Spring and Autumn Annals*.
c. 483 BCE	Death of Confucius's son. Supposed birth date of Confucius's grandson.
c. 479 BCE	Death of Confucius.
c. 300 to 213 BCE	Emperor Ch'in Shih burns Confucian, Taoist texts and the Five Classics.
206 BCE	Han dynasty adopts Confucianism as its state philosophy.
1 CE	Pingdi, Emperor of Peace, confers ducal rank on Confucius in the afterlife.
1645 CE	Shunzhi, Emperor of Unbroken Rule, proclaims Confucius to be 'the Ancient Teacher, Accomplished and Illustrious, the Perfect Sage'.
1949 CE	Establishment of Communist rule in China. Confucian values challenged as patriarchal and oppressive.

Study Questions

1. Which of the three dynasties that existed prior to Taoism and Confucianism did Confucius cite as an example of how society should be governed?
2. Explain the meaning of Yin and Yang.
3. What five classics produced during the Chou period established the foundations of Chinese culture, religion, and philosophy?
4. What is the name of the manual of divination based on sixty-four hexagrams arranged around the symbol of Yin-Yang?
5. What is a book of divination?
6. Who was the founder of Taoism?
7. Next to the Bible, which is the most translated book in the English language?
8. What does the term 'Tao' mean?
9. Why do the Taoists believe that competition corrupts the goodness in people?
10. Do Taoists believe in an absolute morality that everyone must follow, or is morality relative to the situation and individual?
11. What are the Analects of Confucius?
12. What are Confucius's Five Cardinal Virtues?
13. Describe Confucius's view of a good government ruler.

14. What is the 'mandate of heaven'?
15. According to Confucius, what is the major difference between a superior man and an inferior man?
16. What 'Five Relationships' are fundamental to Confucian teaching?
17. What did Confucius consider an appropriate education?

Suggested Reading

Chinese Tradition

1. Chan, Wing-tsit, trans. (1963), *A Source Book in Chinese Philosophy*. New Jersey: Princeton University Press.
2. De Bary, William Theodore, Chan, Wing-tsit, and Watson, Burton, eds. (1960), *Sources of Chinese Tradition*. New York: Columbia University Press.
3. Murphy, Joseph (1976), *Secrets of the I Ching*. Fourth edition, New York: Parker Publishing Company, Inc.
4. Wilhelm, Richard, and Baynes, Cary, trans. (1967), The *I Ching*. Third edition, New Jersey: Princeton University Press.

Taoism

1. Cleary, Thomas (1996), *Practical Taoism*. Boston: Shambala Press.
2. Cleary, Thomas and Po-Tuan, Chang (2001), *The Inner Teachings of Taoism*. Boston: Shambala Press.
3. Kohn, Livia (1993), *The Taoist Experience: An Anthology*. Albany, New York: State University of New York.
4. Schipper, Kristofer M. and Karen Duvball, trans. (1992), *The Taoist Body*. Berkeley: University of California Press.
5. Watts, Alan and Watts, Mark (2001), *Taoism Way Beyond Seeking*. Vermont: Tuttle Publishing.
6. Welch, Holmes (1971), *Taoism: The Parting of the Way*. Boston: Beacon Press.

Confucianism

7. Clements, Jonathan (2004), *Confucius: A Biography*. United Kingdom: Sutton Publishing Limited.
8. Creel, H.G. (1960), *Confucius and the Chinese Way*. New York: Harper & Row.
9. Jaspers, Karl (1957), *Socrates, Buddha, Confucius, Jesus*. New York: Harcourt, Brace & World.
10. Fingarette, Herbert (1990), *Confucius – The Secular as Sacred*. New York: Harper and Row.
11. Taylor, Rodney Leon (1990), *The Religious Dimensions of Confucianism*. New York: State University of New York Press.
12. Tu Wei-mang (1990), *Confucian Thought: Selfhood as Creative Transformation*. Albany: State University of New York Press.
13. Yao, Xinzhong (2000), *An Introduction to Confucianism*. London: Cambridge University Press.

Sources

Taoism

1–4. All selections from the *Tao Te Ching* are from Wing-Tsit Chan, trans. (1970), *A Source Book in Chinese Philosophy*. Princeton, NJ: Princeton University Press.

1. Verses 1, 4, 14, 25, 34, 51.
2. Verses 16, 23, 46, 56, 78.
3. Verses 2, 9, 24, 43, 48, 63.
4. Verses 17, 29, 30, 37, 59.

Confucianism

5. James Legge, trans. (2005), *The Teachings of Confucius*. El Paso, TX: El Paso Norte Press, Analects: Book 2, Wei Chang, p. 9.
6. Legge, *The Teachings of Confucius*. Analects: Book 7, Shu R, p. 34.
7. Arthur Waley, trans. (1938), *The Analects of Confucius*. New York: Random House, p. 26, pp. 7, 16.
8. Legge, *The Teachings of Confucius*. Analects: Book 7, Shu R, p. 36.
9. Legge, *The Teachings of Confucius*. Analects: Book 5, Kung-ye Ch'ang, p. 28.
10. Legge, *The Teachings of Confucius*. Analects: Book 5, Kung-ye Ch'ang, p. 38.
11. James R. Ware, trans. (1955), *The Sayings of Confucius*. New York: The New American Library, Ch. VII. 2, p. 50.
12. Legge, *The Teachings of Confucius*. Analects: Book 7, Shu R, p. 34.
13. Legge, *The Teachings of Confucius*. Analects: Book 7, Shu R, pp. 34–35.
14. Legge, *The Teachings of Confucius*. Analects: Book 7, Shu R, p. 37.
15. W.T. de Bary et al. (1960), *Sources of the Chinese Tradition*. New York: Columbia University Press, p. 90, Book of Rites 2: 11.
16. Legge, *The Teachings of Confucius*. Analects: Book 2, Wei Chang, p. 11.
17. Legge, *The Teachings of Confucius*. Analects: Book 2, Wei Chang, p. 11.
18. Legge, *The Teachings of Confucius*. Analects: Book 15, Wei Ling Kung, p. 90.
19. Legge, *The Teachings of Confucius*. Analects: Book 15, Wei Ling Kung, p. 93.
20. Legge, *The Teachings of Confucius*. Analects: Book 17, Yang Ho, p. 103.
21. Legge, *The Teachings of Confucius*. Analects: Book 4, Le Jin, p. 19.
22. Legge, *The Teachings of Confucius*. Analects: Book 4, Le Jin. P. 19.
23. Legge, *The Teachings of Confucius*. Analects: Book 4, Le Jin, p. 19.
24. Legge, *The Teachings of Confucius*. Analects: Book 1, Hsio R, p. 6.
25. Legge, *The Teachings of Confucius*. Analects: Book 1, Hsio R, p. 5.
26. Legge, *The Teachings of Confucius*. Analects: Book 1, Hsio R, p. 5.
27. Legge, *The Teachings of Confucius*. Analects: Book 4, Le Jin, p. 20.
28. Legge, *The Teachings of Confucius*. Analects: Book15, Wei Ling Kung, p. 91.
29. Legge, *The Teachings of Confucius*. Analects: Book 15, Wei Ling Kung, p. 91
30. Legge, *The Teachings of Confucius*. Analects: Book 4, Le Jin, p. 21.
31. Legge, *The Teachings of Confucius*. Analects: Book 15, Wei Ling Kung, p. 91.
32. Legge, *The Teachings of Confucius*. The Doctrine of the Mean, p. 133.
33. Legge, *The Teachings of Confucius*. The Doctrine of the Mean, p. 134.
34. Legge, *The Teachings of Confucius*. Analects: Book 12, Yen Yuan, p. 68.
35. Legge, *The Teachings of Confucius*. Analects: Book 12, Yen Yuan, p. 68.
36. Legge, *The Teachings of Confucius*. Analects: Book 12, Yen Yuan, p. 69.

37. Legge, *The Teachings of Confucius*. Analects: Book 12, Yen Yuan, p. 69.

38. Legge, *The Teachings of Confucius*. Analects: Book 20, Yao Yueh, pp. 119–120.

39. Lin Yutang. (1943), *The Wisdom of Confucius*. New York: Random House, pp. 229–230, 232, Li Ki, Ch. 19.

40. Legge, *The Teachings of Confucius*. Analects: Book 7, Shu R, p. 35.

41. Legge, *The Teachings of Confucius*. Analects: Book 16, Xe She, p. 97.

42. Lin Yutang, *The Wisdom of Confucius*. Analects3:3.

43. David S. Noss and Noss, John B. (1990), *A History of the World's Religions*. Eighth edition, New York: Macmillan Publishing Co., p. 293.

44. Ku Hung Ming (1906), *The Conduct of Life: A Translation of the Doctrine of the Mean*. In *Wisdom of the East Series*. London: John Murray, p. 28 (SV).

45. Legge, *The Teachings of Confucius*. The Doctrine of the Mean, p. 137.

46. Legge, *The Teachings of Confucius*. The Doctrine of the Mean, p. 133.

47. Legge, *The Teachings of Confucius*. The Doctrine of the Mean, p. 139.

48. Legge, *The Teachings of Confucius*. The Doctrine of the Mean, p. 146.

49. Legge, *The Teachings of Confucius*. The Doctrine of the Mean, p. 149.

50. Legge, *The Teachings of Confucius*. The Doctrine of the Mean, pp. 153, 154

Jewish Wisdom 6

The Star of David
*The primary emblem of the Jewish religion.
Legend has it that the symbol was first
used by the biblical King David.*

The Hebrew Bible

The wisdom of Judaism lies in the Hebrew Bible or *Tanakh*, which is made up of thirty-nine sacred books in three sections: (1) the Torah; (2) the Prophets; and (3) the Writings. The Bible evolved out of a rich oral tradition. Its vast library of materials was compiled over the centuries by unknown authors, and authenticated by Jewish scholars. It contains Jewish history, poetry, songs, stories, prayers, philosophy, and spiritual, moral, and civil law.

The Torah

According to the Jewish tradition, the Torah is a letter written by God to human beings. The word Torah means Law or Teachings, and is the foundation of the Jewish religion. It is also called the *Pentateuch*, because it consists of the first five books of the Bible: Genesis, Exodus, Leviticus, Numbers, and Deuteronomy. Some scholars believe the Torah took between six hundred and seven hundred years to complete. However, according to Jewish tradition, God revealed the Torah to Moses during Moses's lifetime. In any case, this remarkable work tells of the history, culture, religion, and nation of the Hebrew people. The Torah also includes God's directions for the conduct of humankind.

Genesis relates the creation of the world and of man and woman. It also describes paradise, the origin and diversity of language, and the origin of sin. Genesis recounts time from the creation to the death of Joseph and the fall of Judah in 586 BCE.

Exodus tells the colorful story of the liberation of the Hebrews (Israelites) from Egyptian bondage, the revelation to Moses of the Ten Commandments, and the covenant between Yahweh and His Chosen People.

Leviticus contains the laws given by Moses in the desert to his followers.

Numbers concerns genealogies, the wandering of the Jews in the wilderness, and the waging of wars.

Deuteronomy repeats much of Leviticus written in the first person in the form of addresses by Moses before he died.

Every week portions of the Torah are read aloud in the synagogue or Temple. The Torah scrolls are kept in a curtained ark on the wall facing Jerusalem. They are hand-lettered in Hebrew and treated with reverence. The scrolls are brought ceremoniously to the center of the congregation for the reading, symbolizing the need to keep the Torah and its teachings in the heart of the community. It is a great honor to be called upon to read from the sacred scripture.

The Creation

1. In the Beginning: The First Day of Creation. Genesis 1: 1–5

In the beginning God created the heavens and the earth. The earth was without form and void, and darkness was upon the face of the deep; and the Spirit of God was moving over the face of the waters.

And God said, 'Let there be light'; and there was light. And God saw that the light was good; and God separated the light from the darkness. God called the light Day, and the darkness he called Night. And there was evening and there was morning, one day.

2. The Sixth Day: God Created Humankind. Genesis 1: 26–31

Then God said, 'Let us make man in our image, after our likeness; and let them have dominion over the fish of the sea, and over the birds of the air, and over the cattle, and over all the earth, and over every creeping thing that creeps upon the earth.' So God created man in his own image, in the image of God he created him; male and female he created them. And God blessed them, and God said to them, 'Be fruitful and multiply, and fill the earth and subdue it; and have dominion over the fish of the sea and over the birds of the air and over every living thing that moves upon the earth.' And God said, 'Behold, I have given you every plant yielding seed which is upon the face of all the earth, and every tree with seed in its fruit; you shall have them for food. And to every beast of the earth, and to every bird of the air, and to everything that creeps on the earth, everything that has the breath of life, I have given every green plant for food.' And it was so. And God saw everything that he had made, and behold, it was very good. And there was evening and there was morning, a sixth day.

3. The Seventh Day: God Rested. Genesis 2: 1–3

Thus the heavens and the earth were finished, and all the host of them. And on the seventh day God finished his work which he had done, and he rested on the seventh day from all his work which he had done. So God blessed the seventh day and hallowed it, because on it God rested from all his work which he had done in creation.

The Garden of Eden

4. The Garden and the Tree of Knowledge. Genesis 2: 8–9, 15–17, 18, 21–22, 25
And the Lord God planted a garden in Eden, in the east; and there he put the man whom he had formed. And out of the ground the Lord God made to grow every tree that is pleasant to the sight and good for food, the tree of life also in the midst of the garden, and the tree of knowledge of good and evil.

… The Lord God took the man and put him in the garden of Eden to till it and keep it. And the Lord God commanded the man, saying, 'You may freely eat of every tree of the garden; but of the tree of the knowledge of good and evil you shall not eat, for in the day that you eat of it you shall die.'

Then the Lord God said, 'It is not good that the man should be alone' … So the Lord God caused a deep sleep to fall upon the man, and while he slept took one of his ribs and closed up its place with flesh; and the rib which the Lord God had taken from the man he made into a woman and brought her to the man … And the man and his wife were both naked, and were not ashamed.

Disobedience

5. Adam and Eve Expelled from the Garden. Genesis 3: 1–7, 8–11, 16, 19, 22–23
Now the serpent was more subtle than any other wild creature that the Lord God had made. He said to the woman, 'Did God say, "You shall not eat of any tree of the garden"'? And the woman said to the serpent, 'We may eat of the fruit of the trees of the garden; but God said, "You shall not eat of the fruit of the tree which is in the midst of the garden, neither shall you touch it, lest you die."' But the serpent said to the woman, 'You will not die. For God knows that when you eat of it your eyes will be opened, and you will be like God, knowing good and evil.' So when the woman saw that the tree was good for food, and that it was a delight to the eyes, and that the tree was to be desired to make one wise, she took of its fruit and ate; and she also gave some to her husband, and he ate. Then the eyes of both were opened, and they knew that they were naked.

And they heard the sound of the Lord God walking in the garden … and the man and his wife hid themselves from the presence of the Lord God among the trees of the garden. But the Lord God called to the man, and said to him, 'Where are you?' And he said, 'I heard the sound of thee in the garden, and I was afraid, because I was naked; and I hid myself.' He said, 'Who told you that you were naked? Have you eaten of the tree of which I commanded you not to eat?'

To the woman he said,
'I will greatly multiply your pain in childbearing;
… in pain you shall bring forth children …
And to Adam he said,
'In the sweat of your face
You shall eat bread
till you return to the ground,
for out of it you were taken;
you are dust,

and to dust you shall return.'

Then the LORD GOD said, 'Behold, the man has become like one of us, knowing good and evil; and now, lest he put forth his hand and take also of the tree of life, and eat, and live forever' – therefore the LORD GOD sent him forth from the garden of Eden to till the ground from which he was taken.

The Story of the Great Flood

The story of the Great Flood is similar to a Mesopotamian myth, the *Epic of Gilgamesh*. According to the Hebrew Bible, to show his distaste for the immorality of the human race, God sends a flood to wash away all of humanity with the exception of the righteous Noah and his family. God has Noah build an ark and fill it with animals, because only those in the boat will survive the coming deluge. With Noah, God makes the first of three covenants (the second covenant was with Abraham and the third with Moses). God makes a promise to Noah never again to destroy the earth by water. As a sign of this promise, God places his 'bow' into the sky. The 'rainbow' is a reminder of God's solemn oath.

6. Noah Found Favor With God. Genesis 6: 5, 8 9: 8–13

The LORD saw that the wickedness of man was great in the earth … But Noah found favor in the eyes of the LORD.

7. God's Covenant with Noah. Genesis 9: 8–13

Then God said to Noah and to his sons with him, 'Behold, I establish my covenant with you and your descendants after you, and with every living creature that is with you, the birds, the cattle, and every beast of the earth with you, as many as came out of the ark. I establish my covenant with you, that never again shall all flesh be cut off by the waters of a flood, and never again shall there be a flood to destroy the earth.' And God said, 'This is the sign of the covenant which I make between me and you and every living creature that is with you, for all future generations: I set my bow in the cloud, and it shall be a sign of the covenant between me and the earth.'

The Story of Abraham

The Hebrew Bible records that the roots of Judaism go back to a nomadic people sometimes called Hebrews and more commonly called Israelites, who traced themselves to an ancestor named Abraham (or Abram). About 1800 BCE, God directed Abraham to emigrate from the Sumerian city of Ur to an area near the Sea of Galilee and the Dead Sea. There, he was to establish a nation that would live by the will of God. God's covenant, or promise, to Abraham was that if Abraham proved faithful to God, his descendants would inherit this land.

Recognizing that the One God rejected the idolatry, which had been practiced by his tribal father and country, Abraham followed God's instructions. The covenant between God and Abraham was sealed with the blood of sacrificial animals. Thus,

Abraham, with his wife Sarah and his brother's son, Lot, began his journey to the Land of Promise.

After many years of marriage, Abraham still had no son to carry on the tribal name, so his wife Sarah, believing she was too old to have children, directed Abraham to take their servant Hagar as his wife and have a son by her. However, shortly after Hagar gave birth to Abraham's son Ishmael, Sarah became pregnant with Isaac and insisted that Abraham banish Hagar and Ishmael from the tribe.[*]

Later, God tested Abraham by commanding him to take his son Isaac to a mountain and kill him. But before the faithful act took place, God replaced Isaac with a ram.

Abraham's son Isaac grew up to father a son Jacob (who was given the name Israel by God). Jacob had twelve sons whose families upheld the covenant with God and became the twelve tribes of Israel – thus called Israelites. From one of the sons, Judah, comes the word Jew.

Another son, Joseph, became viceroy of Egypt, where his father, brothers, and their families eventually joined him. But many centuries later, Egypt's new Pharaoh enslaved the Israelites, who remained in bondage there for five hundred years, until God chose Moses to deliver them.

8. God Said To Abraham, 'I Will Make of You a Great Nation.'
Genesis 12: 1–2, 6–7

Now the LORD said to Abram, 'Go from your country and your kindred and your father's house to the land that I will show you. And I will make of you a great nation, and I will bless you, and make your name great, so that you will be a blessing.

Abram passed through the land to the place at Shechem … At that time the Canaanites were in the land. Then the LORD appeared to Abram, and said, 'To your descendants I will give this land.' So he built there an altar to the LORD, who had appeared to him.

9. God's Covenant with Abraham. Genesis 17: 1–3, 5, 7–8, 10–12

When Abram was ninety-nine years old the LORD appeared to Abram, and said to him, 'I am God Almighty; walk before me, and be blameless. And I will make my covenant between me and you, and will multiply you exceedingly.' Abram fell on his face, and God said to him … 'I have made you the father of a multitude of nations … And I will establish my covenant between me and you and your descendants after you throughout their generations for an everlasting covenant, to be God to you and to your descendants after you. And I will give to you, and to your descendants after you, the land of your sojournings, all the land of Canaan, for an everlasting possession; and I will be their God.'

'… This is my covenant, which you shall keep, between me and you and your descendants after you: Every male among you shall be circumcised. You shall be

---

[*] According to Islamic tradition, Abraham accompanied Hagar and Ishmael to Arabia, where Ishmael became a leader of the Arabs. According to the Jews, however, Abraham stayed with Sarah and their son Isaac in Sumer.

circumcised in the flesh of your foreskins, and it shall be a sign of the covenant between me and you. He that is eight days old among you shall be circumcised ...'

10. The Lord Tests Abraham. Genesis 22: 1–2, 9–13

... God tested Abraham, and said to him, 'Abraham!' And he [Abraham] said, 'Here am I.' He said, 'Take your son, your only son Isaac, whom you love, and go to the land of Mori'ah, and offer him there as a burnt offering upon one of the mountains of which I shall tell you.' ...

When they came to the place of which God had told him, Abraham built an altar there ... and bound Isaac his son, and laid him on the altar ... Then Abraham put forth his hand, and took the knife to slay his son. But the angel of the LORD called to him from heaven, and said, 'Abraham, Abraham!' ... 'Do not lay your hand on the lad or do anything to him; for now I know that you fear God, seeing you have not withheld your son, your only son, from me.' And Abraham lifted up his eyes and looked, and behold, behind him was a ram, caught in a thicket by his horns; and Abraham went and took the ram, and offered it up as a burnt offering instead of his son.

Reflections

If God is omniscient, what importance could Abraham's willingness to take his son Issac's life have to Him? Could this event be understood in more than one way?

The Story of Moses

Fearing that the rapidly multiplying Israelites would conspire with Egypt's enemies against him, Pharaoh ordered that all newborn Israelite males must be killed. To protect her infant, Moses's mother placed him in a cradle in the reeds at the edge of the river. While bathing in the river Pharaoh's daughter found the Hebrew baby, named him Moses, and raised him as her son.

Thus Moses spent his childhood in the Egyptian court and received his education from Egyptian teachers and priests. While still a young man, however, he was sentenced to death for killing an Egyptian overseer who was beating a Hebrew slave. Escaping to Midian, Moses became a shepherd, married and raised a family.

One day while Moses was herding his flock, God appeared to him through a burning bush that miraculously remained unconsumed by the flames. From out of the bush, God sent Moses to the Egyptian Pharaoh to demand the release of the Hebrew people.

Following God's directions, Moses pleaded with Pharaoh for release of the Israelites, but Pharaoh refused to let them go. Then God sent a series of ten plagues on Egypt, the last of which killed all of Egypt's first-born sons. Following God's instructions, the Israelites smeared the blood of a sacrificial lamb on the doors as a sign for the angel of death to spare them, and their infant sons remained unharmed. Each spring since the year 1300 BCE, the Jews have celebrated Passover to honor God for having the angel of death 'pass over' their infant sons and for the Israelites' exodus from slavery.

Obeying God's orders, Moses led the Israelites to the Red Sea. There, God parted the waters of the Red Sea allowing Moses to lead them safely through. The waters closed over Pharaoh's pursuing armies, drowning them. God guided the Israelites with a pillar of cloud by day and a pillar of fire by night as they journeyed through the Sinai wilderness back toward the Promised Land.

When they reached Mt. Sinai, God told them that He was the Lord their God who brought them out of the land of Egypt, and out of the house of bondage. Then He gave to Moses the Ten Commandments. On the mountain, God also renewed the covenant with His people: If they obeyed Him, God would make them a great nation and lead them to the Promised Land. Before reaching the Promised Land called Canaan, an area roughly corresponding to modern Palestine, Moses appointed Joshua his successor, according to the Lord's instructions. Then he went up to Mount Nebo, looked out over the Promised Land, and was never seen again.

11. The Burning Bush. Exodus 3: 4–8, 10, 13–14

God called to him out of the bush, 'Moses, Moses!' And he said, 'Here am I.' Then he said, 'Do not come near; put off your shoes from your feet, for the place on which you are standing is holy ground... And Moses hid his face, for he was afraid to look at God...

The LORD said, 'I have seen the affliction of my people who are in Egypt, and have heard their cry ... I know their sufferings, and I have come down to deliver them out of that land to a ... land flowing with milk and honey ... Come, I will send you to Pharaoh that you may bring forth my people, the sons of Israel out of Egypt.' ... But Moses said to God, 'If I come to the people of Israel and say to them, 'The god of your fathers has sent me to you,' and they ask me, 'What is his name?' what shall I say to them?' God said to Moses, 'I AM WHO I AM.' And he said, 'Say this to the people of Israel, "I AM has sent me to you".'

12. God's Passover Instructions. Exodus 12: 1–2, 6–8, 11–14, 37, 40–42

The LORD said to Moses and Aaron in the land of Egypt, 'This month shall be for you the beginning of months; it shall be the first month of the year for you. Tell all the congregation of Israel that on the tenth day of this month they shall take every man a lamb according to their fathers' houses, a lamb for a household ... and you shall keep it until the fourteenth day of this month, when the whole assembly of the congregation of Israel shall kill their lambs in the evening. Then they shall take some of the blood, and put it on the two doorposts and the lintel of the houses in which they eat them.

'In this manner you shall eat it: your loins girded, your sandals on your feet, and your staff in your hand; and you shall eat it in haste. It is the LORD's Passover. For I will pass through the land of Egypt that night and I will smite all the first-born in the land of Egypt, both men and beast; and on all the gods of Egypt I will execute judgments: I am the LORD. The blood shall be a sign for you, upon the houses where you are; and when I see the blood, I will pass over you, and no plague shall fall upon you to destroy you, when I smite the land of Egypt.

'This day shall be for you a memorial day, and you shall keep it as a feast to the LORD; throughout your generations you shall observe it as an ordinance for ever ...'

And the people of Israel journeyed from Ram'eses to Succoth, about six hundred thousand men on foot, besides women and children … The [length of] time that the people of Israel dwelt in Egypt was four hundred and thirty years. And at the end of four hundred and thirty years, on that very day, all the hosts of the LORD went out from the land of Egypt. It was a night of watching kept to the LORD by all the people of Israel throughout their generations.

> **Reflections**
>
> Jews often consider the exodus 'out of Egypt' an inner journey as well as an external journey. What do Jews mean by an 'inner journey'?

13. Parting of the Red Sea. Exodus 14: 8–9, 21–23, 26–28, 30

And the LORD hardened the heart of Pharaoh king of Egypt and he pursued the people of Israel as they went forth defiantly. The Egyptians pursued them, all Pharaoh's horses and chariots and his horsemen and his army, and overtook them encamped at the sea …

Then Moses stretched out his hand over the sea; and the LORD drove the sea back by a strong east wind all night, and made the sea dry land, and the waters were divided. And the people of Israel went into the midst of the sea on dry ground, the waters being a wall to them on their right hand and on their left. The Egyptians pursued, and went in after them into the midst of the sea, all Pharaoh's horses, his chariots, and his horsemen.

Then the LORD said to Moses, 'Stretch out your hand over the sea, that the water may come back upon the Egyptians, upon their chariots, and upon their horsemen.' So Moses stretched forth his hand over the sea, and the sea returned to its wonted flow when the morning appeared; and the Egyptians fled into it, and the LORD routed the Egyptians in the midst of the sea. The waters returned and covered the chariots and the horsemen and all the hosts of Pharaoh that had followed them into the sea; not so much as one of them remained. But the people of Israel walked on dry ground through the sea, the waters being a wall to them on their right hand and on their left.

Thus the LORD saved Israel that day from the hand of the Egyptians; and Israel saw the Egyptians dead upon the seashore.

14. The Pillar of Cloud and the Pillar of Fire. Exodus 13: 21–22

And the LORD went before them [the Israelites] by day in a pillar of cloud to lead them along the way, and by night in a pillar of fire to give them light, that they might travel by day and by night; the pillar of cloud by day and the pillar of fire by night did not depart from before the people.

When they reached Mt. Sinai, God proposed through Moses, a final covenant to the Israelites – I will be your God if you will be a moral people.

15. 'Keep My Covenant.' Exodus 19: 3–6

And Moses went up to God, and the LORD called to him out of the mountain, saying, 'Thus you shall … tell the people of Israel: You have seen what I did to the

Egyptians, and how I bore you on eagles' wings and brought you to myself. Now therefore, if you will obey my voice and keep my covenant, you shall be my own possession among all peoples; for all the earth is mine, and you shall be to me a kingdom of priests and a holy nation. These are the words which you shall speak to the children of Israel.'

Reflections

Imagine that the exodus is an inner journey. What, then, did God mean when he said, 'You have seen what I did to the Egyptians, and how I bore you on eagles' wings and brought you to myself'?

---

16. The Ten Commandments. Exodus 20: 1–14

And God spoke all these words, saying,

I am the LORD your God, who brought you out of the land of Egypt, out of the house f bondage.

'You shall have no other gods before me.

'You shall not make for yourself a graven image, or any likeness of anything that is in heaven above, or that is in the earth beneath, or that is in the water under the earth; you shall not bow down to them or serve them; for I the LORD your God am a jealous God, visiting the iniquity of the fathers upon the children to the third and the fourth generation of those who hate me, but slowing steadfast love to thousands of those who love me and keep my commandments.

'You shall not take the name of the LORD your God in vain; for the LORD will not hold him guiltless who takes his name in vain.

'Remember the Sabbath day, to keep it holy. Six days you shall labor, and do all your work; but the seventh day is a Sabbath to the LORD your God; in it you shall not do any work, you, or your son, or your daughter, your manservant, or your maidservant, or your cattle, or the sojourner who is within your gates; for in six days the LORD made heaven and earth, the sea, and all that is in them, and rested the seventh day; therefore the LORD blessed the Sabbath day and hallowed it.

'Honor your father and your mother, that your days may be long in the land which the LORD your God gives you.

'You shall not kill.

'You shall not commit adultery.

'You shall not steal.

'You shall not bear false witness against your neighbor.

'You shall not covet your neighbor's house; you shall not covet your neighbor's wife, or his manservant, or his maidservant, or his ox, or his ass, or anything that is your neighbor's.'

17. The Blood of the Covenant. Exodus 24: 7–8

… {Moses} took the book of the covenant, and read it in the hearing of the people; and they said, 'All that the LORD has spoken we will do, and we will be obedient.' And Moses took the blood [of sacrificial oxen] and threw it upon the people, and said, 'Behold the blood of the covenant which the LORD has made with you in accordance with all these words.'

18. The Death of Moses. Deuteronomy 34: 1–2, 4–6, 10–12

And Moses went up from the plains of Moab to Mount Nebo, to the top of Pisgah, which is opposite Jericho. And the LORD showed him all the land … of Judah as far as the Western Sea … And the LORD said to him, 'This is the land of which I swore to Abraham, to Isaac, and to Jacob, "I will give it to your descendants." I have let you see it with your eyes, but you shall not go over there.' So Moses the servant of the LORD died there in the land of Moab, according to the word of the LORD, and he buried him in the valley in the land of Moab opposite Beth-pe'or; but no man knows the place of his burial to this day.

… And there has not arisen a prophet since in Israel like Moses, whom the LORD knew face to face, none like him for all the signs and the wonders which the LORD sent him to do in the land of Egypt, to Pharaoh and to all his servants and to all his land, and for all the mighty power and all the great and terrible deeds which Moses wrought in the sight of all Israel.

The Prophets

The second section of the Hebrew Bible is called the Prophets. Hebrew prophets believed they had been especially appointed by God to bring His message to the people. Some prophets experienced mystical visions; others had a more intellectual or ethical approach, but all prescribed the religious, moral, and righteous life, predicting personal and national calamity for those who defied God's will. Especially the prophets told the rulers to change their selfish ways, devote themselves to the God of Abraham, Isaac, Jacob, and Moses, and follow the teachings of the Torah.

In the Hebrew Bible, the Prophet books are subdivided into the books of the Former Prophets – Joshua, Judges, First and Second Samuel, and First and Second Kings; the Latter Prophets – Isaiah, Jeremiah, Ezekiel; and twelve 'minor' prophets – Hosea, Joel, Amos, Obadiah, Jonah, Micah, Nahum, Habakkuk, Zephaniah, Haggai, Zachariah, and Malachi.

Settlement in Canaan

The Lord aided the Israelites to conquer the Canaanites, who were polytheists and worshipped human/animal statues symbolic of their many deities. Chapter 6 of the Book of Joshua vividly describes the Israelites' victory over Jericho.

19. The City Wall Fell Down. Joshua 6: 12–16, 20

Then Joshua rose early in the morning, and the priests took up the ark of the LORD. And the seven priests bearing the seven trumpets of rams' horns before the ark of the LORD passed on, blowing the trumpets continually; and the armed men went before them, and the rear guard came after the ark of the LORD, while the trumpets blew continually. And the second day they marched around the city once, and returned into the camp. So they did for six days.

On the seventh day they rose early at the dawn of day, and marched around the city in the same manner seven times; it was only on that day that they marched around the city seven times. And at the seventh time, when the priests had blown the trumpets, Joshua said to the people, 'Shout; for the LORD has given you the city … As soon as the people heard the sound of the trumpet, the people raised a great shout, and the wall fell down flat, so that the people went up into the city, every man straight before him, and they took the city.

The Next Generation

The Book of Judges, which may contain the oldest biblical material on Hebrew history, describes the development of the Hebrew nation.

20. The Lord Raised up Judges. Judges 2: 16–17

And the people of Israel did what was evil in the sight of the LORD and served the Ba'als; and they forsook the LORD, the God of their fathers …

Then the LORD raised up judges, who saved them out of the power of those who plundered them. And yet they did not listen to their judges, for they played the harlot after other gods and bowed down to them …

21. The Lord's Anger. Judges 3: 7–8

And the people of Israel did what was evil in the sight of the LORD, forgetting the LORD their God, and serving the Ba'als and the Ashe'roth. Therefore the anger of the LORD was kindled against Israel, and he sold them into the hand of Cau'shan-risha-tha'im king of Mesopota'mia; and the people of Israel served Cau'shan-risha-tha'im eight years.

> **Reflections**
> If God's presence is everywhere, how does one account for evil in the world?

The Prophets

When the Hebrews decided they would prefer kings to rule their nation, God reluctantly consented to anoint Saul; but Saul proved inept and was replaced by David (c. 1013–973 BCE). In the Book of Kings, we read that David's son Solomon succeeded him. Under Solomon, the Hebrews reached their height of political and economic power. Northern tribes revolted, however, against the high taxes required by Solomon's lavish spending on palaces, state and military structures, and his elaborate temple – the first temple of worship at Jerusalem. The revolt led to a split between the north, thereafter called Israel, and the south or Judah.

An explanation for the destruction came from prophets of the time, who spoke in God's name. These prophets usually experienced a life-changing revelation from God and a call to communicate God's message to the people. The prophets took Israel to task for its failures to measure their immorality against the ideals of the covenant between God and His people. They advised the people, including their kings, to live morally, uphold social justice, and to follow God's commandments.

22. Isaiah's Vision and Call to be a Prophet. Isaiah 6: 1–3, 5–8

In the year that King Uzzi'ah died I saw the LORD sitting upon a throne, high and lifted up; and his train filled the temple. Above him stood the seraphim; each had six wings; with two he covered his face, and with two he covered his feet, and with two he flew. And one called to another and said:
'Holy, holy, holy is the LORD of hosts;
The whole earth is full of his glory.'
  ... And I said: 'Woe is me! For I am lost; for I am a man of unclean lips, and I dwell in the midst of a people of unclean lips; for my eyes have seen the King, the LORD of hosts!'
  Then flew one of the seraphim to me, having in his hand a burning coal which he had taken with tongs from the altar. And he touched my mouth, and said: 'Behold, this has touched your lips; your guilt is taken away, and your sin forgiven.' And I heard the voice of the LORD saying, 'Whom shall I send, and who will go for us?' Then I said, 'Here am I! Send me.'

23. Jeremiah's Call to be a Prophet. Jeremiah 1: 4–8

Now the word of the LORD came to me saying,
'Before I formed you in the womb I knew you,
And before you were born I consecrated you;
I appointed you a prophet to the nations.'
  Then I said, 'Ah, LORD GOD Behold, I do not know how to speak,
For I am only a youth.' But the LORD said to me,
'Do not say, 'I am only a youth';
For to all to whom I send you, you shall go,

And whatever I command you, you shall speak.
Be not afraid of them, for I am with you to deliver you,
   Says the LORD.'

24. Isaiah Chastises Israel for Rebelling Against God. Isaiah 1: 2–4, 7

Hear, O heavens, and give ear, O earth,
For the LORD has spoken:
'Sons have I reared and brought up,
But they have rebelled against me.
The ox knows its owner, and the ass its master's crib;
But Israel does not know, my people do not understand.'

Ah, sinful nation, a people laden with iniquity,
Offspring of evildoers, sons who deal corruptly!
They have forsaken the LORD, they have despised the
Holy One of Israel, they are utterly estranged.

Your country lies desolate, your clothes are burned with fire;
Your very presence aliens [strangers] devour your land;
It is desolate, as overthrown by aliens.

25. Ezekiel's Vision and Call to be a Prophet. Ezekiel 1: 1–14, 28; 2: 1–7

In the thirtieth year in the fourth month, on the fifth day of the month, as I was among the exiles by the river Cahebar, the heavens were opened, and I saw visions of God.

As I looked, behold, a stormy wind came out of the north, and a great cloud, with brightness round about it, and fire flashing forth continually, and in the midst of the fire, as it were gleaming bronze. And from the midst of it came the likeness of four living creatures. And this was their appearance; they had the form of men, but each had four faces, and each of them had four wings. Their legs were straight, and the soles of their feet were like the sole of a calf's foot; and they sparkled like burnished bronze. Under their wings on their four sides they had human hands. And the four had their faces and their wings thus; their wings touched one another; they went every one straight forward, without turning as they went.

As for the likeness of their faces, each had the face of a man in front; the four had the face of a lion on the right side, the four had the face of an ox on the left side, and the four had the face of an eagle at the back. Such were their faces. And their wings were spread out above; each creature had two wings, each of which touched the wing of another, while two covered their bodies. And each went straight forward; wherever the spirit would go, they went, without turning as they went. In the midst of the living creatures there was something that looked like burning coals of fire, like torches moving to and fro among the living creatures; and the fire was bright, and out of the fire went forth lightning. And the living creatures darted to and fro, like a flash of lighting.

Like the appearance of the bow that is in the cloud on the day of rain, so was the appearance of the brightness round about.

Such was the appearance of the likeness of the glory of the LORD. And when I saw it, I fell upon my face, and I heard the voice of one speaking.

And he said to me, 'Son of man, stand upon your feet, and I will speak with you.' And when he spoke to me, the Spirit entered into me and set me upon my feet; and I heard him speaking to me. And he said to me, 'Son of man, I send you to the people of Israel, to a nation of rebels, who have rebelled against me; they and their fathers have transgressed against me to this very day. The people also are impudent and stubborn: I send you to them; and you shall say to them, 'thus says the LORD GOD.' And whether they hear or refuse to hear (for they are a rebellious house) they will know that there has been a prophet among them. And you, son of man, be not afraid of them, nor be afraid of their words, though briers and thorns are with you and you sit upon scorpions; be not afraid of their words, nor be dismayed at their looks, for they are a rebellious house.'

26. The Prophet Nathan Rebukes King David. Samuel 12: 1–9

And the LORD sent Nathan to David. He came to him, and said to him, 'There were two men in a certain city, the one rich and the other poor. The rich man had very many flocks and herds; but the poor man had nothing but one little ewe lamb, which he had bought. And he brought it up, and it grew up with him and with his children; it used to eat of his morsel and drink from his cup, and lie in his bosom, and it was like a daughter to him. Now there came a traveler to the rich man, and he was unwilling to take one of his own flock or herd to prepare for the wayfarer who had come to him, but he took the poor man's lamb, and prepared it for the man who had come to him: Then David's anger was greatly kindled against the man; and he said to Nathan, 'As the LORD lives, the man who has done this deserves to die; and he shall restore the lamb fourfold, because he did this thing, and because he had no pity.'

Nathan said to David, 'You are the man. Thus says the LORD, the God of Israel, 'I anointed you king over Israel … I gave you your master's house, and your master's wives into your bosom, and gave you the house of Israel and of Judah … Why have you despised the word of the LORD, to do what is evil in his sight? …'

27. Hosea Chastises the People of Israel. Hosea 4: 1–3, 12–13

Hear the word of the LORD, O people of Israel;
for the LORD has a controversy with the inhabitants
    of the land.
There is no faithfulness or kindness, and no
    knowledge of God in the land;
there is swearing, lying, killing, stealing,
    and committing adultery;
they break all bounds and murder
    follows murder.
Therefore the land mourns,
    and all who dwell in it languish,
and also the beasts in the field,
    and the birds of the air;
    and even the fish of the sea are taken away …

My people inquire of a thing of wood;
    and their staff gives them oracles.
For a spirit of harlotry has led them astray,
    and they have left their God to play the harlot.
They sacrifice on the tops of the mountains,
    and make offerings upon the hills, under oak,
        poplar, and terebinth, because their shade is good.

28. Israel Has Spurned the Good. Hosea 8: 4, 7–8

They made kings, but not through me.
They set up princes, but without my knowledge.
With their silver and gold they made idols
    for their own destruction …

For they sow the wind,
    and they shall reap the whirlwind.
The standing grain has no heads,
    it shall yield no meal; if it were to yield,
    aliens would devour it.
Israel is swallowed up; already they are
    among the nations as a useless vessel.

Reflections

Do you agree that our immoral actions can bring on calamities?

---

29. Isaiah: God Abhors Blood Sacrifices. Isaiah 1: 11–17

What to me is the multitude of your sacrifices?
Says the LORD;
I have had enough of burnt offerings of rams
    and the fat of fed beasts;
I do not delight in the blood of bulls,
    or of lambs, or he-goats.

When you come to appear before me,
who requires of you this trampling of my courts?
Bring no more vain offerings;
Incense is an abomination to me.
New moon and Sabbath and the calling of assemblies –
I cannot endure iniquity and solemn assembly.
Your new moons and your appointed feasts my soul hates;
They have become a burden to me,
I am weary of bearing them.
When you spread forth your hands,
I will hide my eyes from you;
Even though you make many prayers,

I will not listen;
Your hands are full of blood.
Wash yourselves clean;
Remove the evil of your doings
From before my eyes;
Cease to do evil, learn to do good;
Seek justice, correct oppression;
Defend the fatherless, plead for the widow.

30. Isaiah: Against the Elders and Princes. Isaiah 3: 14–15

The LORD enters into judgment
With the elders and princes of his people:
It is you who have devoured the vineyard,
The spoil of the poor is in your houses.
What do you mean by crushing my people,
By grinding the face of the poor?'
Says the LORD GOD of hosts.

31. The LORD Has Shown You What is Good. Micah 6: 6–8

'With what shall I come before the LORD,
And bow myself before God on high?
Shall I come before him with burnt offerings,
With calves a year old?
Will the LORD be pleased with thousands of rams,
with ten thousands of rivers of oil?
Shall I give my first-born for my transgressions,
the fruit of my body for the sin of my soul?'
He has showed you, O man, what is good;
and what does the LORD require of you
but to do justice, and to live kindness,
and to walk humbly with your god?'

32. Prophecy: The Messiah Will Bring Forth Light, Joy, Peace, and Justice. Isaiah 11: 1–9

There shall come forth a shoot from the stump of Jesse,
and a branch shall grow out of his roots.
And the Spirit of the LORD shall rest upon him,
the spirit of wisdom and understanding,
the spirit of counsel and might,
the spirit of knowledge and the fear of the LORD.

He shall not judge by what his eyes see,
or decide by what his ears hear;
but with righteousness he shall judge the poor,
and decide with equity for the meek of the earth;
and he shall smite the earth with the rod of his mouth,
and with the breath of his lips he shall slay the wicked.

Righteousness shall be the girdle of his waist,
and faithfulness the girdle of his loins.

The wolf shall dwell with the lamb,
and the leopard shall lie down with the kid,
and the calf and the lion and the fatling together,
and a little child shall lead them.
The cow and the bear shall feed;
their young shall lie down together;
and the lion shall eat straw like the ox.
The sucking child shall play over the hole of the asp,
and the weaned child shall put his hand on the adder's den.
They shall not hurt or destroy in all my holy mountain.
For the earth shall be full of the knowledge of the LORD
as the waters cover the sea.

Reflections
Could our world ever be a place where the last verse (above) will bear fruit?

Wisdom Literature (The Writings)

The official canon called the Writings, was prepared by Hebrew spiritual leaders or rabbis in approximately 90 CE. This portion of the Bible includes the Psalms, Proverbs, Book of Job, Song of Solomon, Ruth, Lamentations, Ecclesiastes, Esther, Daniel, Ezra, Nehemiah, and the Chronicles.

Psalms

Some of the most beautiful biblical verses are found in Psalms. Many of these verses are sung at religious services or in private devotions and cover such subjects as mourning, praise, hope, and thanksgiving. All of them express a deep awareness of the individual's relationship to God.

33. The Lord is My Shepherd. Psalms 23: 1–6
The LORD is my shepherd, I shall not want;
He makes me lie down in green pastures.
He leads me beside still waters;
    he restores my soul.
He leads me in paths of
    righteousness for his name's sake.

Even though I walk through the
    valley of the shadow of death,
    I fear no evil;
        for thou art with me;

thy rod and thy staff,
they comfort me.

Thou preparest a table before me
in the presence of my enemies;
thou anointest my head with oil,
my cup overflows.
Surely goodness and mercy shall
follow me
all the days of my life;
And I shall dwell in the house of the LORD
forever.

34. The Heavens Tell the Glory of God. Psalms 19: 1–4

The heavens are telling the glory of God;
and the firmament proclaims his handiwork.
Day to day pours forth speech,
and night to night declares knowledge.
There is no speech, nor are there words;
their voice is not heard;
yet their voice goes out through all the earth,
and their words to the end of the world.

35. Rejoice the Day. Psalms 118: 24

This is the day which the LORD has made;
let us rejoice and be glad in it.

36. A Prayer of Moses. Psalms 90: 1–6

Lord, thou hast been our dwelling place
in all generations.
Before the mountains were brought forth,
or ever thou hadst formed the earth and the world,
from everlasting to everlasting thou art God.

Thou turnest man back to the dust, and sayest,
'Turn back, O children of men!'
For a thousand years in thy sight are
but as yesterday when it is past,
or as a watch in the night.

Thou dost sweep men away; they are like a dream,
like grass which is renewed in the morning;
in the morning it flourishes and is renewed;
in the evening it fades and withers.

> **Reflections**
> What does the above Psalm mean that men are like a dream? Do you agree?

Proverbs

Proverbs emphasizes the importance of living a happy life. A father explains to his sons that happiness and harmony do not come easily. They require self-discipline and reverence for God. A special combination of humility and insight help the wise to understand the world and their place in it.

37. A Father's Instruction. Proverbs 4: 1–9

Hear, O sons, a father's instruction, and be attentive that you may gain insight;
for I give you good precepts; do not forsake my teaching.
When I was a son with my father, tender, the only one in the sight of my mother,
he taught me, and said to me,
    'Let your heart hold fast my words; keep my commandments, and live;
do not forget, and do not turn away from the words of my mouth.
Get wisdom; get insight.
Do not forsake her, and she will keep you;
love her, and she will guard you.
The beginning of wisdom is this:
    Get wisdom,
and whatever you get, get insight
Prize her highly, and she will exalt you;
she will honor you if you embrace her.
She will place on your head a fair garland;
she will bestow on you a beautiful crown.'

> **Reflections**
> Why do you think the Jewish scriptures refer to 'wisdom' as 'she'?

38. A Gentle Tongue. Proverbs 15: 1–5

A soft answer turns away wrath, but a harsh word stirs up anger.
The tongue of the wise dispenses knowledge,
but the mouths of fools pour out folly.
The eyes of the LORD are in every place,
keeping watch on the evil and the good.
A gentle tongue is a tree of life,
but perverseness in it breaks the spirit.
A fool despises his father's instruction,
but he who heeds admonition is prudent.

Book of Job

One of the most frequently discussed stories in the Bible is the Book of Job. The story begins with a discussion between God and Satan. God praises the good and faithful Job, but Satan claims that if evil were to befall Job, he as so many others, would soon curse God. God agrees to test Job, first by allowing his cattle and his servants to die. Finally Job's sons are killed. Job is very sad, but his faith does not waver.

Refusing defeat, Satan argues that if God brought physical harm to Job, the man would curse Him. So God tests Job again by covering his entire body with painful boils.

Job's friends suggest that he must have brought his troubles on himself, that God must be punishing him for something. Even Job's wife advises him to curse God. Although Job questions his fate, he remains strong in faith. In the end, God rewards him.

Reflections

If God is omniscient, why would He wager with the devil about Job's faith? Eastern religions might say everything that happened to Job was his karma. What do you think?

---

39. Job's Faith. Book of Job 1:21

And he [Job] said, 'Naked I came from my mother's womb, and naked shall I return; the LORD gave, and the LORD has taken away, blessed be the name of the LORD.

40. The Disease of His Body Tests Job's Patience. Book of Job 21: 4–17

Why should I not be impatient?
Look at me and be appalled, and lay your hand upon your mouth.
When I think of it I am dismayed, and shuddering seizes my flesh.

Why do the wicked live, reach old age, and grow mighty in power?
Their children are established in their presence, and their offspring
before their eyes.
Their houses are safe from fear, and no rod of God is upon them.
Their bull breeds without fail; their cow calves, and does not cast her calf.
They send forth their little ones like a flock, and their children dance.
They sing to the tambourine and the lyre, and rejoice to the sound of the lyre.
They spend their days in prosperity, and in peace they go down to Sheol.
They say to God, 'Depart from us! We do not desire the knowledge of thy ways.
What is the Almighty that we should serve him?
And what profit do we get if we pray to him?'
Behold, is not their prosperity in their hand?
The counsel of the wicked is far from me.

'How often is it that the lamp of the wicked is put out?
That their calamity comes upon them?
That God distributes pains in his anger? ...'

41. God Answers Job Out of the Whirlwind. Book of Job 38: 1–7, 12–13, 16–17, 25–28, 34–37; 39: 1–2, 26–28

Then the LORD answered Job out of the whirlwind:
'Who is this that darkens counsel by words without knowledge?
Gird up your loins like a man,
I will question you, and you shall declare to me.

'Where were you when I laid the foundation of the earth?
Tell me, if you have understanding.
Who determined its measurements – surely you know!
Or who stretched the line upon it?
On what were its bases sunk, or who laid its cornerstone,
   when the morning stars sang together,
   and all the sons of God shouted for joy? ...

'Have you commanded the morning since your days began,
   and caused the dawn to know it place,
that it might take hold of the skirts of the earth,
   and the wicked be shaken out of it? ...

'Have you entered into the springs of the sea,
   or walked in the recesses of the deep?
Have the gates of death been revealed to you,
   or have you seen the gates of deep darkness?

'Who has cleft a channel for the torrents of rain,
   and a way for the thunderbolt
   to bring rain on a land where no man is,
   on the desert in which there is no man:
to satisfy the waste and desolate land, and to make
   the ground put forth grass?

'Has the rain a father, or who has begotten the drops of dew? ...

'Can you lift up your voice to the clouds,
   that a flood or waters may cover you?
Can you send forth lightnings, that they may go
   and say to you, "Here we are?"
Who has put wisdom in the clouds,
   or given understanding to the mists?
Who can number the clouds by wisdom?

'Who provides for the raven its prey,
  when its young ones cry to God,
  and wander about for lack of food?

'Do you know when the mountain goats bring forth?
Do you observe the calving of the hinds?
Can you number the months that they fulfil,
  and do you know the time when they bring forth? ...

'Is it by your wisdom that the hawk soars,
  and spreads its wings toward the south?
Is it at your command that the eagle mounts up
  and makes his nest on high?
On the rock he dwells and makes his home
  In the fastness of the rocky crag ...'

42. Job's Answer to God. Book of Job 42: 1–6

Then Job answered the LORD:
'I know that thou canst do all things,
and that no purpose of thine can be thwarted.
'Who is this that hides counsel without knowledge?'
Therefore I have uttered what I did not understand,
things too wonderful for me, which I did not know.
'Hear, and I will speak;
I will question you, and you declare to me.'
I had heard of thee by the hearing of the ear,
but now my eye sees thee;
therefore I despise myself, and repent in dust and ashes.'

Ecclesiastes

Ecclesiastes, which in Greek means 'the preacher' suggests that life is fleeting and people should live fully aware.

43. For Everything, There is a Season. Ecclesiastes 3: 1–8

For everything there is a season, and a time for every matter under heaven;
a time to be born and a time to die;
a time to plant, and a time to pluck up what is planted;
a time to kill, and a time to heal;
a time to weep, and a time to laugh;
a time to cast away stones, and a time to gather stones together;
a time to embrace, and a time to refrain from embracing;
a time to seek, and a time to lose;
a time to keep, and a time to cast away;
a time to rend, and a time to sew;
a time to keep silence, and a time to speak;
a time to love, and a time to hate;
a time for war, and a time for peace;

The Talmud

Although Judaism became a religion exiled from its homeland, Jewish rabbi scholars working in Babylon and Palestine prepared two versions of the compilation of Torah commentaries called the *Talmud*, in effect accomplishing the change from the ancient Hebrew previously described to Judaism as it is today. For modern Orthodox Jews, the Babylonian Talmud is recognized as the authoritative commentary.

The oldest portion of the Talmud is the *Mishnah*, which summarized Jewish laws, customs, and creeds. Later, as the need for interpretation of the Mishnah grew, scholars wrote commentaries known as the *Gemara*. Although these books are not part of the Bible, they are examples of the Jews' unquenchable thirst for knowledge and wisdom.

The sixty-three chapters of the Mishnah were written by the Pharisees (Rabbis), a group particularly devoted to the study and practice of the Torah. The Sadducees, a rival group, accepted only the written law of the Torah, while the Pharisees believed that the oral law as expressed in the Talmud should also influence Judaism.

44. Mark Well Three Things. Mishnah, Abot 2.1

Mark well three things and you will not fall into the clutches of sin: Know what is above you – an eye that sees, an ear that hears, and all your actions recorded in the book.

45. Judge Not in Haste. Mishnah, Abot 2.5

Do not judge thy comrade until thou hast stood in his place.

46. Good Deeds. Mishnah, Abot 4.13

He who carries out one good deed acquires one advocate in his own behalf, and he who commits one transgression acquires one accuser against himself. Repentance and good works are like a shield against calamity.

Summary

Jewish wisdom lies in the Hebrew Bible or *Tanakh*, which is made up of thirty-nine sacred books in three sections: (1) the Torah; (2) the Prophets; and (3) the Writings. The Torah is the foundation of the Jewish religion and consists of the first five books of the Bible: Genesis, Exodus, Leviticus, Numbers, and Deuteronomy.

Genesis relates the creation of the world and of man and woman. It also describes paradise, the origin and diversity of language, the origin of sin, the Great Flood, and the story of Abraham. Genesis recounts time from the creation to the death of Joseph and the fall of Judah in 586 BCE.

Exodus tells the story of the liberation of the Hebrews (Israelites) from Egyptian bondage, the revelation to Moses of the Ten Commandments, and the covenant between Yahweh and the Chosen People.

Leviticus contains the laws given by Moses in the desert to his followers.

Numbers concerns genealogy, the wandering of the Jews in the wilderness, and the waging of wars.

Deuteronomy repeats much of Leviticus written in the first person in the form of addresses by Moses before he died.

The second section of the Hebrew Bible is called the Prophets, who were appointed by God to bring His message to the people. The Prophet books are subdivided into the books of the Former Prophets – Joshua, Judges, First and Second Samuel, and First and Second Kings; the Latter Prophets – Isaiah, Jeremiah, and Ezekiel; and the 'Minor' Prophets – Hosea, Joel, Amos, Obadiah, Jonah, Micah, Habakkuk, Zephaniah, Haggai, Zachariah, and Malachi.

The official canon called the Writings or Wisdom Literature was prepared by Hebrew spiritual leaders or rabbis in approximately 90 CE. This portion of the Bible includes the Psalms, Proverbs, Book of Job, Song of Solomon, Ruth, Lamentations, Ecclesiastes, Ester, Daniel, Ezra, Nehemiah, and the Chronicles.

Jewish rabbi scholars prepared two versions of Torah commentaries called the *Talmud*. The oldest portion of the Talmud is the *Mishnah*, which summarized Jewish laws, customs, and creeds. Later, scholars wrote commentaries on the Mishnah known as the *Gemara*.

Judaism Today

Judaism is in a state of transition today, as Jews choose between Reconstruction, Reform, Conservative, or Orthodox observance and between life in Israel, the spiritual center of Judaism, or as part of another culture. While early Judaism was patriarchal and the woman's place was in the home, in the twentieth century Jewish women were active in political life. Golda Meir, for example, was a strong and widely admired Prime Minister of Israel from 1969–1974.

In the twentieth century, there were few fields where Jews were not deeply involved. The famous psychiatrist Sigmund Freud was a Jew and that century's pre-eminent scientist was Einstein, again Jewish. Also in that century no other ethnic or national group approached the proportionate number of Jewish Nobel

Laureates. In the twenty-first century Jews continue to excel in fields of science, literature, business, and the arts.

Timeline

c. 1800 BCE	Abraham, Sarah, Isaac, Hagar, Ishmael.
c. 1250 BCE	Exodus of Hebrews from Egypt led by Moses through Sinai to Promised Land.
c. 1200 to 1000 BCE	Oral Torah.
c. 1050 to 450 BCE	Hebrew Prophets (Samuel-Malachi).
c. 1030 to 1010 BCE	King Saul.
c. 1010 to 970 BCE	David makes Jerusalem his Capital.
c. 950 BCE	*Song of Songs.*
c. 970 to 931 BCE	Solomon and the building of the Temple.
c. 750 to 250 BCE	Age of classical prophets: Isaiah, Jeremiah, Ezekiel and twelve Minor Prophets.
c. 586 to 539 BCE	Destruction of First Temple. Exile of Jews to Babylonia.
c. 520 to 515 BCE	Second Temple rebuilt in Jerusalem.
c. 450 to 430 BCE	First public reading of Torah.
c. 90 CE	Canon of Tanakh agreed by consensus.
c. 200 CE	Compilation of Mishnah.
c. 500 CE	Jerusalem Talmud.
c. 600 CE	Babylonian Talmud.
c. 1200 to 1300 CE	Zohar written. Contributes to Jewish Kabalah.
c. 1492 CE	Expulsion of Jews and Muslims from Spain.
c. 1700 to 1760 CE	Life of Baal Shem Tov. Founder of Jewish Hasidism.
1939 to 1945 CE	Nazi German Holocaust against Jews.
1948 CE	Beginning of Israel as an independent Jewish state.
1972 CE	Ordination of first (Reform) Jewish woman Rabbi.
1984/1985 CE	Ordination of first Conservative Jewish Woman Rabbi.

Study Questions

1. Describe the three major divisions of the *Tanakh*.
2. What is the *Pentateuch*?
3. According to Genesis, on which day did God create humankind?
4. The story of Noah and the Great Flood is similar to which Mesopotamian myth?
5. What is a Jewish Covenant? Describe the three major Covenants.
6. How did the Lord test Abraham?
7. To whom did God give the name Israel?

8. What were God's 'Passover' instructions to Moses?
9. What happened at Mt. Sinai in the Book of Exodus? Why is this important?
10. Which city's wall fell down? Why?
11. Discuss the Jewish scriptures as a drama of the relation of God and humanity.
12. Discuss the importance of the Prophets.
13. What was the essence of God's answer to Job when he was suffering?
14. What is the *Talmud*? Why do the Jews consider it important?
15. Why is the Holocaust such a memorable occasion?

Suggested Reading

1. Becher, Mordechai (2005), *Gateway to Judaism: The What, How, and Why of Jewish Life.* New York: Mesorah Publications.
2. De Lange, Nicholas (2000), *An Introduction to Judaism.* London: Cambridge University Press.
3. Flanders, Henry Jackson, Robert Wilson Crapps, and David Anthony Smith (1996), *People of the Covenant.* Fourth edition, New York: Oxford University Press.
4. Frank, Anne (1993), *The Diary of a Young Girl.* New York: Bantam.
5. Frankl, Viktor (1988), *Man's Search for Meaning.* New York: Pocketbooks.
6. Heschel, Abraham J. (1959), *Between God and Man: An Interpretation of Judaism.* Fritz A. Rothschild, New York: The Free Press.
7. Scholem, Gershom (1995), *Major Trends in Jewish Mysticism.* New York: Schocken Books.
8. Seltzer, Robert M. (1980), *Jewish People, Jewish Thought.* New York: Macmillan.
9. Solomon, Norman (2000), *Judaism: A Very Short Introduction.* New York: Oxford University Press.
10. Wiesel, Elie (1960), *Night.* New York: Bantam Books.
11. Wosick, Wayne D. (1998), *Living Judaism: The Complete Guide to Jewish Belief. Tradition, and Practice.* San Francisco: HarperOne.

Sources

All biblical quotations are from: Herbert G. May and Bruce M. Metzer, eds. (1977), *The New Oxford Annotated Bible with the Apocrypha* (Revised Standard Version). New York: Oxford University Press.

1. Genesis 1: 1–5.
2. Genesis 1: 26–31.
3. Genesis 2: 1–3.
4. Genesis 2: 8–9, 15–17, 18, 21–22, 25.
5. Genesis 3: 1–7, 8–11, 16, 19, 22–23.
6. Genesis 6: 5, 8; 9: 8–13.
7. Genesis 9: 8–15.
8. Genesis 12: 1–2, 6–7.
9. Genesis 17: 1–3, 5, 7–8, 10–12.
10. Genesis 22: 1–3, 9–13.
11. Exodus 3: 4–8, 10, 13–14.

12. Exodus 12: 1–2, 6–8, 11–14, 37, 40–42.
13. Exodus 14: 8–9, 21–23, 26–28, 30.
14. Exodus 13: 21–22.
15. Exodus 19: 3–6.
16. Exodus 20: 1–14.
17. Exodus 24: 7–8.
18. Deuteronomy 34: 1–2, 4–6, 10–12.
19. Joshua 6: 12–16, 20.
20. Judges 2: 16–17.
21. Judges 3: 7–8.
22. Isaiah 6: 1–3, 5–8.
23. Jeremiah 1: 4–8.
24. Isaiah 1: 2–4, 7.
25. Ezekiel 1: 1–14, 28; 2: 1–7.
26. Samuel 2, 12: 1–9.
27. Hosea 4: 1–3, 12–13.
28. Hosea 8: 4, 7–8.
29. Isaiah 1: 11–17.
30. Isaiah 3: 14–15.
31. Micah 6: 6–8.
32. Isaiah 11: 1–9.
33. Psalms 23: 1–6.
34. Psalms 19: 1–4.
35. Psalms 118: 24.
36. Psalms 90: 1–6.
37. Proverbs 4: 1–9.
38. Proverbs 15: 1–5.
39. Book of Job 1: 21.
40. Book of Job 21: 4–17.
41. Book of Job 38: 1–7, 12–13, 16–17, 25–28, 34–37; 39: 1–2, 26–28.
42. Book of Job 42: 1–6.
43. Ecclesiastes 3: 1–8.
44. Judah Goldin, trans. (1957), *The Living Talmud: The Wisdom of the Fathers*. New York: New American Library, Mishnah, Abot 2.1.
45. Judah Goldin, trans., *The Living Talmud*. Mishnah, Abot 2.5.
46. Judah Goldin, trans., *The Living Talmud*. Mishnah, Abot 4.13.

7 Christian Wisdom

The Cross
The Christian cross represents the cross
of Christ's crucifixion. When shown with the
image of Christ, it is called a crucifix.

Early Christianity

Christians and historians of Christianity recognize Jesus as the founder of the Christian religion. Like the Buddha, Moses, and Muhammad, however, Jesus never referred to himself as the founder of a religion. Most scholars believe that Jesus understood his mission to be the fulfillment of Judaism.

Christians agree that the historical figure of Jesus (c. 4 BCE–30 CE[*]), was the Christ, the Son of God, who died on the cross to atone for the sins of humanity. According to the New Testament, his body was sealed in a tomb that was miraculously empty three days later. The resurrection of Jesus was the final sign to his followers that he was the chosen one of God, the Messiah. The early preaching about Jesus was simple: Jesus, who was crucified, has been raised from the dead; therefore repent and believe that he is Lord and Messiah.

> **Reflections**
> Why do you think the resurrection of Jesus was the final sign to his followers that he was the Messiah?

---

[*] In the sixth century, a Christian monk related the birth of Jesus to the ancient Roman calendar by dividing history into events occurring Before Christ [BC] and after the year of his birth [Anno Domini, year of our Lord or AD]. Because non-Christians as well as Christians use this calendar, modern historians have changed BC to BCE. [Before the Common Era] and AD to CE [Common Era].

Christian Scripture

Christians followed the Jewish precedent in creating a scripture, which they called the New Testament. While Jews consider the Hebrew Bible the *only* testament of the covenant between God and humankind, Christians believe that God made a new covenant with humanity through Jesus the Christ.**

1. The New Covenant. John 3: 16
For God so loved the world that he gave his one and only Son,
that whoever believes in him should not perish but have eternal life.

Epistles

The oldest literature in the New Testament may be the Epistles (Letters) of Paul to Christians scattered in cities throughout the Roman Empire. Prior to 65 CE, Paul's letters were in circulation to the Thessalonians, Corinthians, Galatians, Romans, Philippians, and to Philemon. Later, other letters in a style similar to Paul's were written to the Colossians, the Ephesians, Timothy, and Titus. The Epistles reflect the life, questions and conflicts of the early Christian community, and show a developing theology about Jesus and his mission.

The Gospels

The first four books of the New Testament, called the Gospels ('good news'), reflect on the life, death, and resurrection of Jesus the Christ. Each is written from a different perspective and emphasizes particular things about him. The first three gospels, Matthew, Mark, and Luke, are similar in content and therefore called the Synoptic Gospels – Greek for 'seeing together'. The fourth, John, is quite different in style and content from the others.

The Gospel of Mark is the shortest and was probably the first written, about 60–70 CE. This gospel presents Jesus as the tragic and misunderstood Son of God: a Messiah who must suffer. However, his resurrection is a sign of the power he has over his own death. Mark wrote as if he expected the end of the age to come soon.

Matthew and Luke used much of Mark in their gospels, though in some passages Matthew and Luke agree word for word on information not found in Mark. Scholars think it possible that Matthew and Luke copied from a common source called Q, which stands for the German word for source, *Quelle*. Matthew emphasized that Jesus fulfilled prophecies of the Jewish scriptures, concerning where the Messiah would be born, how he would enter Jerusalem, and the delivery of the new Law in the Sermon on the Mount (as Moses delivered the old Law on Mt. Sinai). Matthew saw Jesus as the new Moses, that is, the giver of the new Law. The Gospel of Luke added accounts showing Jesus among the common people. (Many scholars believe the Gospel of Luke and the Book of Acts were written by the same author and should be read together as the first conscious history of the Christian movement). Luke traces the genealogy of Jesus back to Adam, the father of all humans, rather than Abraham, father of the Jews, as Matthew does. Luke

** Although Christians continued to read and receive guidance from the Hebrew Bible, or Old Testament, for them the New Testament became the word of God.

emphasizes the universality of Jesus's message, tells stories about the poor and downcast, and gives women a place of importance in his account.

John's gospel, probably written about 90 CE, focuses on the mystery, eternal origin and divine nature of the Christ. For John, Jesus is more powerful than death even before his resurrection: Jesus is God become Man.

Reflections
If you are familiar with the New Testament, which gospel is the most meaningful for you?

Book of Revelation

The last book of the New Testament is the Book of Revelation, written between 95 and 150 CE. Revelation is an example of *Apocalyptic* literature describing in highly symbolic language the end of the world as revealed to John. Some contemporary Christians use this book to predict the end of the world, while others speculate that the purpose of the book may be to discover what these symbols mean in the lives of human beings.

The Jewish Legacy

The Christians retained the Hebrew Bible, viewing the New Testament as the fulfillment and continuation of the prophetic hopes of Judaism itself. The theology of the New Testament can only be understood with reference to the Hebrew Scriptures (called the Old Testament by Christians), especially the Psalms, the Wisdom literature, the Prophets and the moral codes.

Reflections
Why do you think the Jews refuse to call the Hebrew Bible the Old Testament?

The Story of Jesus

The date and place of Jesus's birth are uncertain: the gospels of Matthew, Mark, Luke, and John do not concur with each other on the subject, and Jesus was not referred to in non-Christian literature until the end of the first century CE, when the dates could no longer be certain. However, the gospels of Matthew and Luke present Jesus as a miraculous conception by the Spirit of God in the Virgin Mary.

According to Luke, Jesus's parents Mary and Joseph lived in Nazareth, about eighty miles north of Bethlehem, and were in Bethlehem at the time of Jesus's birth to register for tax purposes. Matthew also says Jesus was born in Bethlehem but later moved to Nazareth because his parents feared Herod, who had been told of the birth of a new 'king of the Jews'.

Mark and John make no mention of Jesus's virgin birth. Matthew and Luke agree that Jesus was conceived by the Holy Spirit and born of the Virgin Mary, and that supernatural events occurred at the time of his birth. Matthew tells of the coming of Wise Men from the East, the murder of the male children of Bethlehem (ordered by Herod), the flight of the holy family to Egypt, and their return to Nazareth. Luke describes Jesus's circumcision rite when he was eight days old.

Little is known of the childhood and youth of Jesus. Luke tells of the boy's learned conversation with the Jewish rabbis in the Temple at Jerusalem when he was twelve years old. Mark and Matthew imply that Jesus's trade, like that of his father Joseph, was carpentry and that he had brothers and sisters.

Matthew, Mark, and Luke agree that John the Baptist, a stern Jewish ascetic (and a cousin of Jesus), baptized Jesus. John appeared in Galilee, announcing the coming judgment of God in the person of a Messiah who would deliver the Jews from Roman rule. Standing by the River Jordan, John proclaimed, 'Repent, for the kingdom of heaven is at hand.'

Reflections

Because he was God's son, Jesus was pure and in no need of baptism. Why do you think he had John baptize him?

After his baptism, Jesus withdrew to the wilderness beyond the Jordan. What actually happened during his forty days in the wilderness is a mystery. Mark states that Jesus lived there with the wild beasts, and angels ministered to him. Matthew and Luke write that Satan appeared and challenged Jesus with three temptations. These temptations represent the moral struggle of the spiritual life. Hebrew writers dealt with this struggle through the temptation of Adam and Eve, to whom evil appeared in the form of a serpent in the Garden of Eden. In another section of the Bible, the Book of Job, Satan appears as one of the sons of God, able to do only what God permits him to do. But in the New Testament, Satan talks to Jesus face to face as the enemy of both God and humankind.

After his baptism, Jesus gathered disciples and started a ministry of his own, choosing twelve who followed him to be his apostles, or messengers. His fame and healing powers attracted men and women from many places who witnessed his healing of fever, leprosy, paralysis, a shriveled hand, demon possession, blindness and epilepsy. He stilled a storm, multiplied loaves and fishes, walked on water, and withered a fig tree.

The disciples of Jesus came from various social groups, but most were poor and uneducated. Among his followers were two women, Mary Magdalene and Mary of Bethany, the sister of Jesus's friend Lazarus. Having women followers marked a departure from the Jewish tradition, which excluded women from most religious rituals.

Reflections

Is there a reason Jesus chose poor and uneducated people as his disciples rather than rich and educated people?

Gospel accounts focus on the weeks before Jesus's death. The celebration of Palm Sunday recalls Jesus's entry into Jerusalem for the feast of the Passover. People waved branches and spread their garments on the road before him as he rode into the city on a donkey colt. The next morning, Jesus went into the Temple and drove out the moneychangers and the buyers and sellers. This act greatly antagonized the Jewish religious leaders.

The last supper Jesus shared with his disciples has special meaning for Christians. During the meal, Jesus took a piece of bread and blessed and broke it, saying, 'Take, eat: this is my body.' Then he took a cup of wine and blessed it saying, 'Drink of it, all of you, for this is my blood of the covenant, which is poured out for many for the forgiveness of sins.' Christians recall these acts during the celebration of the Eucharist or Holy Communion also called the Lord's Supper.

Reflections

When Jesus blessed the bread and wine saying the bread was his body and the wine his blood, did he mean bread was literally his body and wine was literally his blood? Or was he using such language symbolically?

At the close of this meal, Judas, the disciple who was to betray Jesus, left to meet with the priests, while Jesus and the remaining disciples went to the Garden of Gethsemane. Jesus asked his disciples to watch for him while he prayed, but then Judas arrived with the soldiers of the high priest and arrested Jesus.

The next day, the high priest tried Jesus and found him guilty of blasphemy. Only Romans could pronounce the death sentence; thus Pontius Pilate ordered Jesus's execution to take place on the hill of Golgotha outside Jerusalem. There, Jesus and two criminals were crucified.

The arrest and trial of Jesus frightened his followers: Peter denied even knowing him, and only a few women disciples and the apostle John are reported to have stood at the foot of his cross. Jesus was crucified on a Friday and placed in his tomb that evening, but on Sunday morning, women visiting the tomb to mourn his death found it empty. Death could not hold him. Jesus had been resurrected.

Over the next forty days, Jesus appeared to several disciples in Jerusalem and Galilee. Then, he brought his friends together at the Mount of Olives outside Jerusalem and he ascended into heaven. Fifty days after the ascension (celebrated now as Pentecost), the Holy Spirit descended on the disciples while they were visiting together, and they went into the streets of Jerusalem to proclaim that Jesus was the Christ.

The Life of Jesus (from Scripture)

2. Announcement of the Birth of Jesus. Luke 1: 26–28, 30–33, 46–47

In the sixth month, the angel Gabriel was sent from God to a city of Galilee named Nazareth, to a virgin betrothed to a man whose name was Joseph, of the house of David; and the virgin's name was Mary. And he came to her and said,: 'Hail, O favored one, the Lord is with you!' ... And the angel said to her, 'Do not be afraid, Mary, for you have found favor with God. And behold, you will conceive in your womb and bear a son, and you shall call his name Jesus.

He will be great, and will be called the Son of the Most High; and the Lord God will give to him the throne of his father David, and he will reign ... for ever.

And Mary said, 'My soul magnifies the Lord, and my spirit rejoices in God my Savior ...

3. The Birth of Jesus. Matthew 1: 18–23

Now the birth of Jesus Christ took place in this way. When his mother Mary had been betrothed to Joseph, before they came together, she was found to be with child of the Holy Spirit; and her husband Joseph, being a just man and unwilling to put her to shame, resolved to divorce her quietly. But as he considered this, behold, an angel of the Lord appeared to him in a dream, saying, 'Joseph, son of David, do not fear to take Mary your wife, for that which is conceived in her is of the Holy Spirit; she will bear a son, and you shall call his name Jesus, for he will save his people from their sins.' All this took place to fulfil what the Lord had spoken by the prophet:

'Behold, a virgin shall conceive and bear a son,
And his name shall be called Emmanuel' (which means God with us).

Reflections

What is the significance of Jesus being born of a virgin? Would it have made any difference to Christians if Joseph had been his father?

---

4. The Birth of Jesus. Luke 2: 7–11

And she gave birth to her first-born son and wrapped him in swaddling clothes, and laid him in a manger, because there was no room for them in the inn.

And in that region there were shepherds out in the field, keeping watch over their flock by night. And an angel of the Lord appeared to them, and the Lord shone around them, and they were filled with fear. And the angel said to them, 'Be not afraid; for behold, I bring you good news of a great joy which will come to all the people; for to you is born this day in the city of David a Savior, who is Christ the Lord ...'

5. Finding Jesus in the Temple. Luke 2: 41–50

Now his parents went to Jerusalem every year at the feast of the Passover. And when he was twelve years old, they went up according to custom; and when the feast was ended, as they were returning, the boy Jesus stayed behind in Jerusalem. His parents did not know it, but supposing him to be in the company they went a day's journey, and they sought him among their kinsfolk and acquaintances; and when they did not find him, they returned to Jerusalem, seeking him. After three days they found him in the temple, sitting among the teachers, listening to them and asking them questions; and all who heard him were amazed at his understanding and his answers. And when they saw him they were astonished;

and his mother said to him, 'Son, why have you treated us so? Behold, your father and I have been looking for you anxiously.' And he said to them, 'How is it that you sought me? Did you not know that I must be in my father's house?' And they did not understand the saying which he spoke to them.

5. The Baptism of Jesus. Matthew 3: 13, 16–17

Then Jesus came from Galilee to the Jordan to John, to be baptized by him ... And when Jesus was baptized, he went up immediately from the water, and behold, the heavens were opened and he saw the Spirit of God descending like a dove, and alighting on him; and lo, a voice from heaven, saying, 'This is my beloved Son, with whom I am well pleased.'

6. The Temptations of Jesus. Matthew 4: 1–11

Then Jesus was led up by the Spirit into the wilderness to be tempted by the devil. And he fasted forty days and forty nights, and afterward he was hungry. And the tempter came and said to him, 'If you are the Son of God, command these stones to become loaves of bread.'

But he answered, 'It is written, "Man shall not live by bread alone, but by every word that proceeds from the mouth of God".'

Then the devil took him to the holy city, and set him on the pinnacle of the temple, and said to him, 'If you are the Son of God, throw yourself down; for it is written, "He will give his angels charge of you," and "On their hands they will bear you up, lest you strike your foot against a stone".'

Jesus said to him, 'Again it is written, "You shall not tempt the Lord your God".' Again, the devil took him to a very high mountain, and showed him all the kingdoms of the world and the glory of them; and he said to him, 'All these I will give you, if you will fall down and worship me.' Then Jesus said to him. 'Begone, Satan! For it is written, "You shall worship the Lord your God and him only shall you serve".'

Then the devil left him, and behold, angels came and ministered to him.

7. Jesus's First Disciples. Matthew 4: 18–19

As he walked by the Sea of Galilee, he saw two brothers, Simon who is called Peter and Andrew his brother, casting a net into the sea; for they were fishermen. And he said to them, 'Follow me, and I will make you fishers of men.'

8. Jesus Casts Out Unclean Spirits. Luke 4: 31, 33–37

And he went down to Capernaum, a city of Galilee. And he was teaching them on the Sabbath; and they were astonished at his teaching, for his word was with authority.

And in the synagogue there was a man who had the spirit of an unclean demon; and he cried out with a loud voice, 'Ah! What have you to do with us, Jesus of Nazareth? Have you come to destroy us? I know who you are, the Holy One of God.' But Jesus rebuked him, saying, 'Be silent, and come out of him!'

And when the demon had thrown him down in the midst, he came out of him, having done him no harm. And they were all amazed and said to one another, 'What is this word? For with authority and power he commands the unclean spirits, and they come out.' And reports of him went out into every place in the surrounding region.

9. Your Sins Are Forgiven. Luke 5: 17–25

On one of those days, as he was teaching, there were Pharisees and teachers of the law sitting by, who had come from every village of Galilee and Judea and from Jerusalem; and the power of the Lord was with him to heal. And behold, men were bringing on a bed a man who was paralyzed, and they sought to bring him in and lay him before Jesus; but finding no way to bring him in, because of the crowd, they went up on the roof and let him down with his bed through the tiles into the midst before Jesus. And when he saw their faith he said, 'Man, your sins are forgiven you.' And the scribes and the Pharisees began to question, saying, 'Who is this that speaks blasphemies? Who can forgive sins but God only?'

When Jesus perceived their questionings, he answered them, 'Why do you question in your hearts? Which is easier, to say, 'Your sins are forgiven you,' or to say, 'Rise and walk'? But that you may know that the Son of man has authority on earth to forgive sins – he said to the man who was paralyzed – 'I say to you, rise, take up your bed and go home.' And immediately he rose before them, and took up that on which he lay, and went home, glorifying God.

10. 'Your Faith Has Made You Well.' Matthew 9: 20–22

And behold, a woman who had suffered from a hemorrhage for twelve years came up behind him and touched the fringe of his garment; for she said to herself, 'If I only touch his garment, I shall be made well.' Jesus turned, and seeing her he said, 'Take heart, daughter; your faith has made you well.' And instantly the woman was made well.

11. Jesus Gives Sight to a Blind Man. Luke 18: 35–43

As he drew near to Jericho, a blind man was sitting by the roadside begging; and hearing a multitude going by, he inquired what this meant. They told him, 'Jesus of Nazareth is passing by.' And he cried, 'Jesus, Son of David, have mercy on me!'

And those who were in front rebuked him, telling him to be silent; but he cried out all the more, 'Son of David, have mercy on me!' And Jesus stopped, and commanded him to be brought to him; and when he came near, he asked him, 'What do you want me to do for you?' He said, 'Lord, let me receive my sight.' And Jesus said to him, 'Receive your sight; your faith has made you well.' And immediately he received his sight and followed him, glorifying God; and all the people, when they saw it, gave praise to God.

Reflections
Is the above a literal story of physical sight, or could Jesus have restored the man's spiritual sight? What do you think?

11. His Fame Spread. Matthew 4: 23–25

And he went about all Galilee, teaching in their synagogues and preaching the gospel of the kingdom and healing every disease and every infirmity among the people. So his fame spread throughout all Syria, and they brought him all the sick, those afflicted with various diseases and pains, demoniacs, epileptics, and paralytics, and he healed them. And great crowds followed him from Galilee and the Decapolis and Jerusalem and Judea and from beyond the Jordan.

12. Rejected in Nazareth. Matthew 13: 54–58

… and coming to his own country he taught them in their synagogue, so that they were astonished, and said, 'Where did this man get this wisdom and these mighty works? Is not this the carpenter's son? Is not his mother called Mary? And are not his brothers James and Joseph and Simon and Judas? And are not all his sisters with us? Where then did this man get all this?' And they took offense at him. But Jesus said to them, 'A prophet is not without honor except in his own country and in his own house.' And he did not do many mighty works there, because of their unbelief.

> **Reflections**
> Why do you think Jesus refused to heal anyone in Nazareth? By performing miracles, wouldn't he have made believers out of them?

13. Jesus's Entry into Jerusalem. Luke 19: 35–38

And they brought it [the donkey colt] to Jesus, and throwing their garments on the colt they set Jesus upon it. And as he rode along, they spread their garments on the road. As he was now drawing near, at the descent of the Mount of Olives, the whole multitude of the disciples began to rejoice and praise God with a loud voice for all the mighty works that they had seen, saying, 'Blessed is the King who comes in the name of the Lord! Peace in heaven and glory in the highest!'

14. Cleansing the Temple. Luke 19: 45–46

And he entered the temple and began to drive out those who sold, saying to them, 'It is written, 'My house shall be a house of prayer'; but you have made it a den of robbers.'

15. The Last Supper. Jesus Washes the Feet of His Disciples. John 13: 1, 3–5, 12–15

Now before the feast of the Passover, when Jesus knew that his hour had come to depart out of this world to the Father, having loved his own who were in the world, he loved them to the end.

Jesus, knowing that the Father had given all things into his hands, and that he had come from God and was going to God, rose from supper, laid aside his garments, and girded himself with a towel. Then he poured water into a basin, and began to wash the disciples' feet, and to wipe them with the towel with which he was girded.

When he had washed their feet, and taken his garments, and resumed his place, he said to them, 'Do you know what I have done to you? You call me

Teacher and Lord; and you are right, for so I am. If I then, your Lord and Teacher, have washed your feet, you also ought to wash one another's feet. For I have given you an example, that you also should do as I have done to you ...'

16. The Last Supper. This is My Body. This is My Blood. Luke 22: 19–20
And he took bread, and when he had given thanks he broke it and gave it to them, saying, 'This is my body which is given for you. Do this in remembrance of me.' And likewise the cup after supper, saying, 'This cup which is poured out for you is the new covenant in my blood.'

17. Jesus Prays in the Garden of Gethsemane. Luke 22: 41–42
And he withdrew from them about a stone's throw, and knelt down and prayed, 'Father, if thou art willing, remove this cup from me; nevertheless not my will, but thine, be done.'

Reflections
According to scripture, Jesus knew of his coming betrayal and crucifixion. Why then would he ask God to 'remove this cup' from him?

---

18. The Kiss of Betrayal. Luke 22: 47–48
… there came a crowd, and the man called Judas, one of the twelve, was leading them. He drew near to Jesus to kill him; but Jesus said to him, 'Judas, would you betray the Son of man with a kiss?'

19. Jesus's Trial. Matthew 27: 11–15, 20–23
Now Jesus stood before the governor, and the governor asked him, 'Are you the King of the Jews?' Jesus said, 'You have said so.' But when he was accused by the chief priests and elders, he made no answer. Then Pilate said to him, 'Do you not hear how many things they testify against you?' But he gave him no answer, and even to a single charge, so that the governor wondered greatly.

Now at the feast the governor was accustomed to release for the crowd any one prisoner whom they wanted … Now the chief priest and the elders persuaded the people to ask for Barabbas and destroy Jesus.

The governor again said to them, 'Which of the two do you want me to release for you?' And they said, 'Barabbas.' Pilate said to them, 'Then what shall I do with Jesus who is called Christ?' They all said, 'Let him be crucified.' And he said, 'Why, what evil has he done?' But they shouted all the more, 'Let him be crucified.'

20. The Soldiers Mocked Him. Matthew 27: 27–31
Then the soldiers of the governor took Jesus into the praetorium, and they gathered the whole battalion before him. And they stripped him and put a scarlet robe upon him, and plaiting a crown of thorns they put it on his head, and put a reed in his right hand. And kneeling before him they mocked him, saying, 'Hail King of the Jews!' And they spat upon him, and took the reed and struck him on the head. And when they had mocked him, they stripped him of the robe, and put his own clothes on him, and led him away to crucify him.

21. The Crucifixion. John 19: 17–19

So they took Jesus, and he went out, bearing his own cross, to the place called the place of a skull, which is called in Hebrew Golgotha. There they crucified him, and with him two others, one on either side, and Jesus between them. Pilate also wrote a title and put it on the cross; it read, 'Jesus of Nazareth, the King of the Jews.'

Reflections
Why do you think Pilate wrote, 'Jesus of Nazareth, the King of the Jews' rather than 'Jesus of Nazareth, the Messiah, Savior, or Prophet of the Jews'?

22. 'Forgive Them.' Luke 23: 34

And Jesus said, 'Father, forgive them; for they know not what they do.'

23. 'You Will Be With Me in Paradise.' Luke 23: 39–43

One of the criminals who were hanged railed at him, saying, 'Are you not the Christ? Save yourself and us!' But the other rebuked him, saying, 'Do you not fear God, since you are under the same sentence of condemnation? And we indeed justly; for we are receiving the due reward of our deeds; but this man has done nothing wrong.' And he said, 'Jesus, remember me when you come into your kingdom.' And he said to him, 'Truly, I say to you, today you will be with me in Paradise.'

24. 'Behold Your Son. Behold Your Mother.' John 19: 25–27

So the soldiers did this. But standing by the cross of Jesus were his mother, and his mother's sister, Mary the wife of Clopas, and Mary Magdalene. When Jesus saw his mother, and the disciple whom he loved standing near, he said to his mother, 'Woman, behold, your son!' Then he said to the disciple, 'Behold, your mother!' And from that hour the disciple took her to his own home.

Reflections
To which disciple do you think Jesus said, 'Behold your mother!'?

25. Jesus's Last Words. Matthew 27: 45–46, 50

Now from the sixth hour there was darkness over all the land until the ninth hour. And about the ninth hour Jesus cried with a loud voice, 'Eli, Eli, lama sabachthani?' that is, 'My God, my God, why hast thou forsaken me?' And Jesus cried again with a loud voice and yielded up his spirit.

Reflections
What do you think happened to make Jesus cry out, 'My God, my God, why hast thou forsaken me'?

26. The Resurrection. John 20: 11–18

... Mary stood weeping outside the tomb, and as she wept she stooped to look into the tomb; and she saw two angels in white, sitting where the body of Jesus had lain, one at the head and one at the feet. They said to her, 'Woman, why are you weeping?' She said to them, 'Because they have taken away my Lord, and I do not know where they have laid him.' Saying this, she turned round and saw Jesus standing, but she did not know that it was Jesus. Jesus said to her, 'Woman, why are you weeping? Whom do you seek?' Supposing him to be the Gardner, she said to him, 'Sir, if you have carried him away, tell me where you have laid him, and I will take him away.' Jesus said to her, 'Mary.' She turned and said to him in Hebrew, 'Rabboni!' (which means Teacher). Jesus said to her, 'Do not hold me, for I have not yet ascended to the Father, but go to my brethren and say to them, I am ascending to my Father and your Father, to my God and your God.' Mary Magdalene went and said to the disciples, 'I have seen the Lord,' and she told them that he had said these things to her.

27. Jesus Appears to His Disciples. Luke 24: 13–16, 30–31, 33–43

That very day two of them were going to a village named Emmaus, about seven miles from Jerusalem, and talking with each other about all these things that had happened. While they were talking and discussing together, Jesus himself drew near and went with them. But their eyes were kept from recognizing him ... When he was at table with them, he took the bread and blessed, and broke it, and gave it to them. And their eyes were opened and they recognized him; and he vanished out of their sight ...

And they rose that same hour and returned to Jerusalem; and they found the eleven gathered together and those who were with them, who said, 'The Lord has risen indeed, and has appeared to Simon!' Then they told what had happened on the road, and how he was known to them in the breaking of the bread. As they were saying this, Jesus himself stood among them. But they were startled and frightened and supposed that they saw a spirit. And he said to them, 'Why are you troubled, and why do questionings rise in your hearts? See my hands and my feet, that it is I myself; handle me, and see; for a spirit has not flesh and bones as you see that I have.' And while they still disbelieved for joy, and wondered, he said to them, 'Have you anything here to eat?' They gave him a piece of broiled fish, and he took it and ate before them.

28. Doubting Thomas. John 20: 26–29

Eight days later, his disciples were again in the house, and Thomas was with them. The doors were shut, but Jesus came and stood among them, and said, 'Peace be with you.' Then he said to Thomas, 'Put your finger here, and see my hands; and put out your hand, and place it in my side; do not be faithless, but believing.' Thomas answered him, 'My Lord and my God!' Jesus said to him, 'Have you believed because you have seen me? Blessed are those who have not seen and yet believe.'

The Holy Spirit

The Christian doctrine of the Trinity says that God has three natures: Father, Son, and Holy Spirit (or Holy Ghost). Christians believe that each of the three 'beings' in the Trinity has unique characteristics and has revealed something distinct to humanity about the nature of God.

In the Bible, the Holy Spirit is described variously as fire, as water, and as the breath of life, but the most striking images are violent wind and the peaceful dove. Like the wind, the Holy Spirit cannot be seen, but it can be felt. The New Testament describes the Holy Spirit descending at Jesus's baptism in the form of a dove – the symbol of peace.

Many Christians claim to have been healed by the Holy Spirit, and others believe the Holy Spirit helps them to know the presence of God in their daily lives.

Reflections

Have you experienced the presence of the Holy Spirit? If so, how would you describe it?

In the Acts of the Apostles, Paul describes how Jesus promised his disciples that he would leave them a helper – the Holy Spirit.

29. The Ascension of Jesus. Acts 1: 8–11

[Jesus said to them] '... You shall receive power when the Holy Spirit has come upon you; and you shall be my witnesses in Jerusalem and in all Judea and Samaria and to the end of the earth.' And when he had said this, as they were looking on, he was lifted up, and a cloud took him out of their sight. And while they were gazing into heaven as he went, behold, two men stood by them in white robes, and said, 'Men of Galilee, why do you stand looking into heaven? This Jesus, who was taken up from you into heaven, will come in the same way as you saw him go into heaven.'

30. Descent of the Holy Spirit. Acts 2: 1–4

When the Day of Pentecost had come, they were all together in one place. And suddenly a sound came from heaven like the rush of a mighty wind, and it filled all the house where they were sitting. And there appeared to them tongues as of fire, distributed and resting on each one of them. And they were all filled with the Holy Spirit and began to speak in other tongues, as the Spirit gave them utterance.

Jesus Appoints Peter the Founder of the Church and Sends the Disciples on a Mission

Jesus renamed Simon as Peter, the rock on which the church is founded. Jesus gave Peter the 'the keys of the kingdom of heaven.' After Jesus's death, he directed his disciples to Galilee where he gave them instructions.

31. The Keys of the Kingdom. Matthew 16: 18–19

'And I tell you, you are Peter, and on this rock I will build my church, and the powers of death shall not prevail against it. I will give you the keys of the kingdom of heaven, and whatever you bind on earth shall be bound in heaven, and whatever you loose on earth shall be loosed in heaven.'

32. The Mission. Matthew 28: 16–20

Now the eleven disciples went to Galilee, to the mountain to which Jesus had directed them. And when they saw him they worshiped him; but some doubted. And Jesus came and said to them, 'All authority in heaven and on earth has been given to me. Go therefore and make disciples of all nations, baptizing them in the name of the Father and of the Son and of the Holy Spirit, teaching them to observe all that I have commanded you; and lo, I am with you always, to the close of the age.'

Jesus's Teachings

Jesus despised the petty regulations easily obeyed by the rich but difficult for the ordinary working person: 'To eat with unwashed hands does not defile a man,' he said. What you do matters less than the thoughts that come from your heart.

33. What Matters is in the Heart. Mark 7: 5, 9, 18, 20–23

And the Pharisees and the scribes asked him, 'Why do your disciples not live according to the tradition of the elders, but eat with hands defiled?'

And he said to them, 'You have a fine way of rejecting the commandment of God, in order to keep your tradition! … Do you not see that whatever goes into a man from outside cannot defile him, since it enters, not his heart but his stomach, and so passes on?' And he said, 'What comes out of a man is what defiles a man. For from within, out of the heart of man, come evil thoughts, fornication, theft, murder, adultery, coveting, wickedness, deceit, licentiousness, envy, slander, pride, foolishness. All these evil things come from within, and they defile a man.

> **Reflections**
> Do you agree that nothing that comes into us from outside can pollute us unless we allow it?

Beatitudes

According to Matthew, Jesus defined the kingdom of heaven in the famous passages from the Sermon on the Mount known as the Beatitudes (Blesseds).

34. The Kingdom of God. Matthew 5: 1–10

Seeing the crowds, he went up on the mountain, and when he sat down his disciples came to him. And he opened his mouth and taught them, saying:

'Blessed are the poor in spirit, for theirs is the kingdom of heaven.

'Blessed are those who mourn, for they shall be comforted.

'Blessed are the meek, for they shall inherit the earth.

'Blessed are those who hunger and thirst for righteousness, for they shall be satisfied.

'Blessed are the merciful, for they shall obtain mercy.

'Blessed are the pure in heart, for they shall see God.

'Blessed are the peacemakers, for they shall be called sons of God.

'Blessed are those who are persecuted for righteousness' sake, for theirs is the kingdom of heaven.'

God's Love and the Importance of Serving God

For Jesus, the essential element of God's kingdom is love. We must love God, our neighbors, and even our enemies. The principle of human love for God is based on God's prior love for humanity – God took the initiative in forming a covenant with humankind. Jesus emphasized the universality of God's kingdom, which could begin whenever two or more were gathered in his name. God's love and perfection is the kingdom Jesus asked us to seek. And he taught us how to express our love through serving God.

35. Love One Another. John 13: 34–35

A new commandment I give to you, that you love one another; even as I have loved you, that you also love one another. By this all men will know that you are my disciples, if you have love for one another.

36. Turn the Other Cheek. Matthew 5: 38–41

'You have heard that it was said, "An eye for an eye and a tooth for a tooth." But I say to you, Do not resist one who is evil. But if any one strikes you on the right cheek, turn to him the other also; and if any one would sue you and take your coat, let him have your cloak as well; and if any one forces you to go one mile, go with him two miles ...'

37. Love Your Enemies. Matthew 5: 43–45

'You have heard that it was said, "You shall love your neighbor and hate your enemy." But I say to you, Love your enemies and pray for those who persecute you, so that you may be sons of your Father who is in heaven; for he makes his sun rise on the evil and on the good, and sends rain on the just and on the unjust.'

> **Reflections**
>
> According to Matthew, Jesus said, 'Turn the other cheek.' He also said, 'Love your enemy.' Is the question, 'Could a soldier be a Christian without resigning from the army?' valid in today's world?

38. The Golden Rule. Matthew 7: 12

So whatever you wish that men would do to you, do so to them; for this is the law and the prophets.

39. I Was Hungry and You Gave Me Food. Matthew 25: 34–36, 40

The King will say to those at his right hand, 'Come, O blessed of my Father, inherit the kingdom prepared for you from the foundation of the world; for I was hungry and you gave me food, I was thirsty and you gave me drink, I was a stranger and you welcomed me, I was naked and you clothed me, I was sick and you visited me, I was in prison and you came to me.

And the King will answer them, 'Truly, I say to you, as you did it to one of the least of these my brethren, you did it to me.'

40. Before Offering Your Gift. Matthew 5: 23–25

So if you are offering your gift at the altar, and there remember that your brother has something against you, leave your gift there before the altar and go; first be reconciled to your brother, and then come and offer your gift.

41. Forgive Seventy Times Seven. Matthew 18: 21–22

Then Peter came up and said to him, 'Lord, how often shall my brother sin against me, and I forgive him? As many as seven times?' Jesus said to him, 'I do not say to you seven times, but seventy times seven.'

42. He Who is Without Sin Throw the First Stone. John 8: 4–11

… they said to him, 'Teacher, this woman has been caught in the act of adultery. Now in the law Moses commanded us to stone such. What do you say about her?' This they said to test him, that they might have some charge to bring against him. Jesus bent down and wrote with his finger on the ground.

And as they continued to ask him, he stood up and said to them, 'Let him who is without sin among you be the first to throw a stone at her.' And once more he bent down and wrote with his finger on the ground. But when they heard it, they went away, one by one, beginning with the eldest, and Jesus was left alone with the woman standing before him. Jesus looked up and said to her, 'Woman, where are they? Has no one condemned you?' She said, 'No one, Lord.' And Jesus said, 'Neither do I condemn you; go, and do not sin again.'

43. Do Not Store Up Treasures on Earth. Matthew 6: 19–21

'Do not lay up for yourselves treasures on earth, where moth and rust consume and where thieves break in and steal, but lay up for yourselves treasures in heaven, where neither moth nor rust consumes and where thieves do not break in and steal. For where your treasure is, there will your heart be also.'

Reflections
The world assumes it is the rich, the powerful, and the famous that are happy. Would Jesus agree?

44. No One Serve Two Masters. Matthew 6: 24

'No one can serve two masters; for either he will hate the one and love the other, or he will be devoted to the one and despise the other. You cannot serve God and mammon.

45. Consider the Lilies of the Field. Matthew 6: 25–30

'Therefore I tell you, do not be anxious about your life, what you shall eat or what you shall drink, nor about your body, what you shall put on. Is not life more than food, and the body more than clothing? Look at the birds of the air; they neither sow nor reap nor gather into barns, and yet your heavenly Father feeds them. Are you not of more value than they? And which of you by being anxious can add one cubit to his span of life? And why are you anxious about clothing? Consider the lilies of the field, how they grow; they neither toil nor spin; yet I tell you, even Solomon in all his glory was not arrayed like one of these. But if God so clothes the grass of the field, which today is alive and tomorrow is thrown into the oven, will he not much more clothe you, O men of little faith? ...'

46. Take Up Your Cross. Matthew 16: 24–25

Then Jesus told his disciples, 'If any man would come after me, let him deny himself and take up his cross and follow me. For whoever would save his life will lose it, and whoever loses his life for my sake will find it.'

Reflections

What do you think Jesus meant when he said, 'For whoever would save his life will lose it, and whoever loses his life for my sake will find it'?

---

47. You Are the Light of the World. Matthew 5: 14–16

'You are the light of the world. A city set on a hill cannot be hid. Nor do men light a lamp and put it under a bushel, but on a stand, and it gives light to all in the house. Let your light so shine before men, that they may see your good works and give glory to your Father who is in heaven.'

48. Ask and You Will Receive. Matthew 7: 7

'Ask, and it will be given you; seek, and you will find; knock, and it will be opened to you ...'

49. Pray Like This. Matthew 6: 9–13

Pray then like this:
Our Father who art in heaven,
Hallowed be thy name.
Thy kingdom come.
Thy will be done, on earth as it is in heaven.
Give us this day our daily bread;
And forgive us our debts,
As we also have forgiven our debtors;
And lead us not into temptation,
But deliver us from evil.

God's Law

Though God loves all unconditionally, until we cease to rebel and defy Him, we cannot fully love God. We are responsible for allowing God's love into, or keeping it out of, our lives. God's law is the law of justice: 'Judge not that you be not judged,' 'Whatsoever you sow, you also reap.'

Early in the Gospels, John the Baptist introduces us to the idea of justice. In prophetic language, he calls the multitude flocking to him a brood of vipers, warning them of a wrath to come. In the Gospel of Mark, Jesus uses fire as a symbol of justice when he speaks of those who are thrown into hell where the fire is not quenched. The Greek word for hell in this passage is *Ghenna*, derived from *Hinnom* and referring to the valley of Hinnom, south of Jerusalem, where people of the city dumped their garbage and trash. Flies bred there, and the smoking flames never died out.

50. The Log in Your Own Eye. Matthew 7: 1–3

'Judge not, that you be not judged. For with the judgment you pronounce you will be judged, and the measure you give will be the measure you get. Why do you see the speck that is in your brother's eye, but do not notice the log that is in your own eye?'

51. Do Unto Others. Matthew 7: 12

So whatever you wish that men would do to you, do so to them; for this is the law and the prophets.

52. Where the Fire is Not Quenched. Mark 9: 43–50

'... And if your hand causes you to sin, cut it off; it is better for you to enter life maimed than with two hands to go to hell, to the unquenchable fire. And if your foot causes you to sin, cut it off; it is better for you to enter life lame than with two feet to be thrown into hell. And if your eye causes you to sin, pluck it out; it is better for you to enter the kingdom of God with one eye than with two eyes to be thrown into hell, where their worm does not die, and the fire is not quenched. For every one will be salted with fire. Salt is good; but if the salt has lost its saltness, how will you season it? Have salt in yourselves, and be at peace with one another.'

Parables

Jesus often conveyed his teachings through parables – stories that made a point and helped people understand profound religious concepts by comparison with familiar situations. His stories acknowledged human nature and left some puzzles unresolved. For example, in the parable of the Prodigal Son, a wayward son rebels against his father and leaves home to seek a more exciting, worldly life. Later, penniless and friendless, he returns to seek his father's forgiveness. Seeing him approach, the happy father runs to meet his son, embraces him, and prepares a great feast to celebrate his return. The good son, who has not rebelled or got into trouble, is disturbed when his wayward brother receives more praise and attention than he does.

53. The Parable of the Prodigal Son. Luke 15: 11–32

'There was a man who had two sons; and the younger of them said to his father, "Father, give me the share of property that falls to me." And he divided his living between them. Not many days later the younger son gathered all he had and took his journey into a far country, and there he squandered his property in loose living. And when he had spent everything, a great famine arose in that country, and he began to be in want. So he went and joined himself to one of the citizens of that country, who sent him into his fields to feed swine. And he would gladly have fed on the pods that the swine ate; when he came to himself he said, "How many of my father's hired servants have bread enough and to spare, but I perish here with hunger! I will arise and go to my father, and I will say to him, 'Father, I have sinned against heaven and before you; I am no longer worthy to be called your son; treat me as one of your hired servants.'" And he arose and came to his father. But while he was yet at a distance, his father saw him and had compassion, and ran and embraced him and kissed him. And the son said to him, "Father, I have sinned against heaven and before you; I am no longer worthy to be called your son." But the father said to his servants, "Bring quickly the best robe and put it on him; and put a ring on his hand, and shoes on his feet; and bring the fatted calf and kill it, and let us eat and make merry; for this my son was dead, and is alive again; he was lost, and is found." And they began to make merry.

'Now his elder son was in the field; and as he came and drew near to the house, he heard music and dancing. And he called one of the servants and asked what this meant. And he said to him, "Your brother has come, and your father has killed the fatted calf, because he has received him safe and sound." But he was angry and refused to go in. His father came out and entreated him, but he answered his father, "Lo, these many years I have served you, and I never disobeyed your command; yet you never gave me a kid that I might make merry with my friends. But when this son of yours came, who has devoured your living with harlots, you killed for him the fatted calf!" And he said to him, "'Son, you are always with me, and all that is mine is yours. It was fitting to make merry and be glad, for this your brother was dead, and is alive; he was lost, and is found."'

Reflections
Why do Christians consider the parable of the Prodigal Son so significant?

54. The Parable of the Mustard Seed. Matthew 13: 31–32
'The kingdom of heaven is like a grain of mustard seed which a man took and sowed in his field; it is the smallest of all seeds, but when it has grown it is the greatest of shrubs and becomes a tree, so that the birds of the air come and make nests in its branches.'

55. The Parable of Sowing Good Seed. Matthew 13: 24–30
'The kingdom of heaven may be compared to a man who sowed good seed in his field; but while men were sleeping, his enemy came and sowed weeds among the wheat, and went away. So when the plants came up and bore grain, then the weeds appeared also. And the servants of the householder came and said to him, "Sir, did you not sow good seed in your field? How then has it weeds?" He said to them, "An enemy has done this." The servants said to him, "Then do you want us

to go and gather them?" But he said, "No; lest in gathering the weeds you root up the wheat along with them. Let both grow together until the harvest; and at harvest time I will tell the reapers, Gather the weeds first and bind them in bundles to be burned, but gather the wheat into my barn." '

56. The Parable of the Pearl. Matthew 13: 45
'The kingdom of heaven is like a merchant in search of fine pearls, who, on finding one pearl of great value, went and sold all that he had and bought it.'

57. The Parable of the Vineyard Laborers. Matthew 20: 1–15
'For the kingdom of heaven is like a householder who went out early in the morning to hire laborers for his vineyard. After agreeing with the laborers for a denarius a day, he sent them into his vineyard. And going out about the third hour he saw others standing idle in the market place; and to them he said, "You go into the vineyard too, and whatever is right I will give you." So they went. Going out again about the sixth hour and the ninth hour, he did the same. And about the eleventh hour he went out and found others standing, and he said to them, "Why do you stand here idle all day?" They said to him, "Because no one has hired us." He said to them, "You go into the vineyard too."

And when evening came, the owner of the vineyard said to his steward, "Call the laborers and pay them their wages, beginning with the last, up to the first." And when those hired about the eleventh hour came, each of them received a denarius. Now when the first came, they thought they would receive more; but each of them also received a denarius. And on receiving it they grumbled at the householder, saying, "These last worked only one hour, and you have made them equal to us who have borne the burden of the day and the scorching heat." But he replied to one of them, "Friend, I am doing you no wrong; did you not agree with me for a denarius? Take what belongs to you, and go; I choose to give to this last as I give to you. Am I not allowed to do what I choose with what belongs to me? Or do you begrudge my generosity?" So the last will be first, and the first last.'

58. The Parable of the Wedding Feast. Matthew 22: 1–14
'The kingdom of heaven may be compared to a king who gave a marriage feast for his son, and sent his servants to call those who were invited to the marriage feast; but they would not come. Again he sent other servants, saying, "Tell those who are invited, Behold I have made ready my dinner, my oxen and my fat calves are killed, and everything is ready; come to the marriage feast." But they made light of it and went off, one to his farm, another to his business, while the rest seized his servants, treated them shamefully, and killed them. The king was angry, and he sent his troops and destroyed those murderers and burned their city. Then he said to his servants, "The wedding is ready, but those invited were not worthy. Go therefore to the thoroughfares, and invite to the marriage feast as many as you find." And those servants went out into the streets and gathered all whom they found, both bad and good; so the wedding hall was filled with guests.

'But when the king came in to look at the guests, he saw there a man who had no wedding garment; and he said to him, "Friend, how did you get in here without a wedding garment?" And he was speechless. Then the king said to the attendants, "Bind him hand and foot, and cast him into the outer darkness; there men will weep and gnash their teeth." For many are called, but few are chosen.'

> **Reflections**
> If we are to love our enemy, turn the other cheek, and practice forgiveness, what meaning could the above parable have?

59. The Parable of the Good Samaritan. Luke 10: 25–37

And behold, a lawyer stood up to put him to the test, saying, 'Teacher what shall I do to inherit eternal life?' He said to him, 'What is written in the law? How so you read?' And he answered, 'You shall love the Lord your God will all your heart, and with all your soul, and with all your strength, and with all your mind; and your neighbor as yourself.' And he said to him, 'You have answered right; do this, and you will live.'

But he, desiring to justify himself, said to Jesus, 'And who is my neighbor?' Jesus replied, 'A man was going down from Jerusalem to Jericho, and he fell among robbers, who stripped him and beat him, and departed, leaving him half dead. Now by chance a priest was going down that road; and when he saw him he passed by on the other side. So likewise a Levite, when he came to the place and saw him, passed by on the other side. But a Samaritan, as he journeyed, came to where he was; and when he saw him, he had compassion, and went to him and bound up his wounds, pouring on oil and wine; then he set him on his own beast and brought him to an inn, and took care of him. And the next day he took out two denarii and gave them to the innkeeper, saying, "Take care of him; and whatever more you spend, I will repay you when I come back." Which of these three, do you think, proved neighbor to the man who fell among the robbers?' He said, 'The one who showed mercy on him.' And Jesus said to him, 'Go and do likewise.'

Selected New Testament Passages

60. The Light of the World. John 1: 1–5, 12–14

In the beginning was the WORD, and the Word was with God, and the Word was God. He was in the beginning with God; all things were made through him, and without him was not anything made that was made. In him was life, and the life was the light of men. The light shines in the darkness, and the darkness has not overcome it.

... to all who received him, who believed in his name, he gave power to become children of God; who were born not of blood nor of the will of the flesh nor of the will of man, but of God.

And the Word became flesh and dwelt among us, full of grace and truth; we have beheld his glory, glory as of the only Son from the Father.

61. Christ in the World. John 3: 16–17

For God so loved the world that he gave his only Son, that whoever believes in him should not perish but have eternal life. For God sent the Son into the world, not to condemn the world, but that the world might be saved through him.

62. Atonement. I Corinthians 15: 21–22

For as by a man came death, by a man has come also the resurrection of the dead. For as in Adam all die, so also in Christ shall all be made alive.

63. Between God and Men. Timothy 2: 5–6

For there is one God and there is one mediator between God and men, the man Christ Jesus, who gave himself as a ransom for all, the testimony to which was borne at the proper time.

64. Atonement. Romans 6: 8–11

But if we have died with Christ, we believe that we shall also live with him. For we know that Christ being raised from the dead will never die again; death no longer has dominion over him. The death he died he died to sin, once for all, but the life he lives he lives to God. So you also must consider your selves dead to sin and alive to God in Christ Jesus.

65. Death, Where Is Thy Sting? I Corinthians 15: 51–56

Lo! I tell you a mystery. We shall not all sleep, but we shall all be changed, in a moment, in the twinkling of an eye, at the last trumpet. For the trumpet will sound, and the dead will be raised imperishable, and we shall be changed. For this perishable nature must put on the imperishable, and the mortal nature must put on immortality. When the perishable puts on the imperishable, and the mortal puts on immortality, then shall come to pass the saying that is written:
'Death is swallowed up in victory.'
'O death, where is they victory?
O death, where is thy sting?'
The sting of death is sin, and the power of sin is the law. But thanks be to God, who gives us the victory through our Lord Jesus Christ.

66. Love Is Patient. Love Is Kind. I Corinthians 13: 1–7, 11–13

If I speak in the tongues of men and of angels, but have not love, I am a noisy gong or a changing cymbal. And if I have prophetic powers, and understand all mysteries and all knowledge, and if I have all faith, so as to remove mountains, but have not love, I am nothing. If I give away all I have, and if I deliver my body to be burned, but have not love, I gain nothing.

When I was a child, I spoke like a child, I thought like a child, I reasoned like a child; when I became a man, I gave up childish ways. For now we see in a mirror dimly, but then face to face. Now I know in part; then I shall understand fully, even as I have been fully understood. So faith, hope, love abide, these three; but the greatest of these is love.

67. Have Your Mind in Christ Jesus. Philippians 2: 4–11

Let each of you look not only to his own interests, but also to the interests of others. Have this mind among yourselves, which is yours in Christ Jesus, who though he was in the form of God, did not count equality with God a thing to be grasped, but emptied himself, taking the form of a servant, being born in the likeness of men. And being found in human form he humbled himself and became obedient unto death, even death on a cross. Therefore God has highly exalted him and bestowed on him the name which is above every name, that at the name of Jesus every knee should bow, in heaven and on earth and under the earth, and every tongue confess that Jesus Christ is Lord, to the glory of God the Father.

Summary

Christians and historians of Christianity recognize Jesus as the founder of the Christian religion. Christians agree that the historical figure of Jesus was the Christ, the Son of God, who died on the cross to atone for the sins of humanity. According to the New Testament, his body was sealed in a tomb that was miraculously empty three days later. The resurrection of Jesus was the final sign to his followers that he was the chosen one of God, the Messiah.

Christians followed the Jewish precedent in creating a scripture, which they called the New Testament. While Jews consider the Hebrew Bible the only testament of the covenant between God and humankind, Christians believe that God made a new covenant with humanity through Jesus the Christ. The Christians retained the Hebrew Bible, viewing the New Testament as the fulfillment and continuation of the prophetic hopes of Judaism itself. The theology of the New Testament can only be understood with reference to the Hebrew Scriptures.

The oldest literature in the New Testament may be the Epistles (Letters) of Paul to Christians scattered throughout the Roman Empire. The Epistles showed a developing theology about Jesus and his mission.

The first four books of the New Testament, called the gospels ('good news'), reflect on the life, death, and resurrection of Jesus the Christ. The first three gospels, Matthew, Mark, and Luke, are similar in content and therefore called the Synoptic gospels – from the Greek for 'seeing together.' The fourth, John, is quite different in style and content from the others.

The last book of the New Testament is the Book of Revelation, written between 95 and 150 CE. Revelation is an example of *apocalyptic* literature and describing in highly symbolic language the end of the world as revealed to John.

The Christian doctrine of the Trinity says that God has three natures: Father, Son, and Holy Spirit (or Holy Ghost). Christians believe that each of the three 'beings' in the Trinity has unique characteristics and has revealed something distinct to humanity about God.

For Jesus, the essential element of God's kingdom was love. People must love God, their neighbors, and even their enemies. God's love and perfection is the kingdom Jesus asked people to seek. And he taught them how to express their love through serving God.

Christianity Today

During the twentieth century, mainstream Christianity worked together to find a common ground in a movement called ecumenism, which in Greek means 'household.' The ecumenical movement views all mainstream Christian churches as part of a 'household' of Christianity with the objective of encouraging dialogue between them. Today, groups involved in ecumenism continue to discuss with all Christians the best way of restoring the lost unity of Christendom, as well as problems of common Christian action in the twenty-first century. Frequently denominations participate together in community welfare projects. It is no longer unusual for individuals of different Christian denominations to marry, and sometimes ministers from both churches witness the marriage.

After the Second Vatican Council, which first met in 1960, major changes took place in the Roman Catholic Church. First, the churches used living languages of the people instead of Latin in church services. Second, the Catholic Church agreed to endorse the value of other major religions and dialogue with Christian groups. Third, the lay people were given more authority, and fourth, the church buildings have been stripped of inessentials and their decoration simplified. Changes made by the Second Vatican Council spurred debate about other church traditions such as celibacy of priests, the ordination of women, and positions on divorce, sex, and birth control. These topics continue to be debated in the twenty-first century.

Also in the twentieth century evangelical denominations emerged. Evangelicals stressed biblical authority and human sinfulness, and insisted that Christians must be 'born again,' live a life of purity, and bear personal witness to their religious belief. During services, evangelicals express their emotions and place a strong emphasis on healing. Within the evangelical movement there has been a worldwide growth in the number of Pentecostals and Charismatics. The word 'charismatic' comes from the Greek 'charisma,' meaning 'gifts.' There has always been charismatic worship, but in the past few decades, particularly in North America, charismatic worship has been on the increase. Charismatic worship places great emphasis on practicing the gifts of the Holy Spirit, such as healing and speaking in tongues. Charismatics formed new churches and appear in traditional churches throughout the world.

Women of various religious persuasion have observed that the teaching and institutional power of the major Christian religions, from their founding to the present, have been almost exclusively male. God is traditionally portrayed in Western cultures as male, and the language of the Bible is masculine. Some men and women question whether that means that God is indeed masculine or whether women should be excluded from religious rites and power.

Women are questioning their exclusion from ordination on the basis of sex and the use of sexist language in scripture and worship. In America, Roman Catholics are divided on issues involving the role of women in the church, married priests, and family matters; but within religious institutions change is occurring. The language of worship and new translations of scripture often avoid sexist vocabulary. Because women are eligible for ordination in many Protestant denominations, the number of women ministers is rapidly growing.

Timeline

c. 4 BCE to 30 CE	Life of Jesus.
c. 4 BCE	Birth of Jesus, visit by the Magi, escape to Egypt, return to Nazareth.
c. 8 CE	Jesus and family journey to Jerusalem temple.
c. 26 CE	Jesus baptized by John the Baptist. Jesus tempted by Satan.
c. 27 CE	Jesus begins ministry.
c. 27 CE	Jesus rejected by his own people in Nazareth.
c. 27 to 29 CE	Ministry in Galilee. Four fishermen become Jesus's followers. Teaches parables.
c. 28 CE	Jesus chooses twelve disciples. Preaches Sermon on the Mount.
c. 28 CE	Jesus sends his twelve followers out to preach and heal. John the Baptist killed by Herod.
c. 29 CE	Jesus is transfigured.
c. 29 CE	Ministry in Judea/Jerusalem
c. 29 CE	Ministry in Perea.
c. 29 CE	Raises Lazarus from the dead.
c. 30 CE	Jesus enters Jerusalem on small donkey.
c. 30 CE	Final week in Jerusalem: Last Supper, arrest, trial, crucifixion and death.
c. 30 CE	Resurrection from the dead and final appearances.
c. 30 CE	Ascends to his Father in heaven.
c. 35 CE	Conversion of Paul.
c. 48 to 55 CE	Paul writes Galatians
c. 50 to 52 CE	Paul writes letter to the Thessalonians.
c. 53 to 55 CE	Paul writes letter to the Philippians.
c. 57 CE	Paul writes Letter to the Romans.
c. 57 to 58 CE	Paul? writes Acts of the Apostles.
c. 59 to 63 CE	Paul writes letters to Philemon and first and second letters to the Corinthians. Paul? writes letters to Ephesians and Colossians.
c. 66 to 67 CE	First and Second letters to Timothy, and letter to Titus (author or authors unknown).
c. 65 to 70 CE	Gospel of Mark.
c. 68 CE	Martyrdom of Paul.
c. 65 to 70 CE	Letter to the Hebrews.
c. 64 to 95 CE	Letters of Peter written. c. 95 CE The Letter of James.
c. 90 CE	Gospel of John.
c. 95 to 150 CE	Book of Revelations.
380 CE	Christianity made official religion of Roman Empire.
c. 400 CE	Jerome's *Vulgate* (translation of Greek Bible into Latin).

1054 CE	Schism between East and West.
1517 CE	Luther posts 95 theses. Founder of Lutheran religion.
1536 CE	Calvin's Institutes of the Christian Religion.
1609 CE	Baptist church founded by John Smyth.
1611 CE	King James version of the Bible.
1729 CE	Methodist church founded by John Wesley.
1830 CE	Joseph Smith produces Book of Mormon.
1869 CE	First Vatican Council.
1875 CE	Mary Baker Eddy writes *Science and Health*.
1914 CE	Assemblies of God founded.
1945 CE	Nag Hammadi Library discovered in Egypt.
1948 CE	World Council of Churches founded.
1962 to 1965 CE	Second Vatican Council.
1988 CE	First woman ordained in an apostolic-succession church (Episcopal church).

Study Questions

1. According to tradition, what did Jesus consider as his mission?
2. What beliefs do Christians and Jews continue to share?
3. Explain the importance of the Hebrew Bible or Old Testament to Christianity.
4. How does the Christian view of God differ from Judaism's view of God?
5. Compare and contrast the Christian concept of God with those of Hinduism, Buddhism, and Taoism.
6. What do Christians understand by the term 'original sin'? Explain the relation of this concept to the biblical story of Adam and Eve.
7. In what ways do the Jews and Christians differ in their view of Jesus?
8. According to Christianity what was the 'new covenant' that God made with humanity through Jesus the Christ?
9. Which two gospels make no mention of Jesus's virgin birth?
10. What convinced Jesus's disciples that he was the Messiah?
11. What is the oldest literature in the New Testament?
12. Why are the gospels of Matthew, Mark, and Luke called the Synoptic gospels?
13. Which gospel is the shortest and when was it written?
14. Why is the Book of Revelation an example of apocalyptic literature?
15. Which gospel traces the genealogy of Jesus back to Adam?
16. Following Jesus's baptism by John the Baptist, what were his three temptations?
17. Explain the importance of Jesus's resurrection to Christianity.
18. Discuss the significance of 'signs' and 'parables' in Jesus's ministry.
19. Explain the importance of the Last Supper to Christianity.
20. Explain the meaning of Pentecost.
21. Discuss the significance of the Holy Spirit.
22. What effects have scientific developments of the past two centuries had on Christianity in Western culture?

Suggested Reading

1. Abbott, Walter M., ed. (1966), *The Documents of Vatican II*. New York: The American Press.
2. Donovan, Vincent J. (2003), *Christianity Rediscovered*. New York: Orbis Books.
3. Henry, Francoise, ed. (1977), *The Book of Kells*. New York: Knopf.
4. Lewis, C.S. (2001), *Mere Christianity*. Third edition, New York: HarperCollins Publisher.
5. Nystrom, Bradley P. and Nystrom, David P. (2003), *The History of Christianity: An Introduction*. New York: McGraw-Hill.
6. Pelikan, Jaroslav (1985), *Jesus Through the Centuries*. New Haven: Yale University Press.
7. Price, James L. (1971), *Interpreting the New Testament*. Second edition, New York: Holt, Rinehart and Winston.
8. Progoff, Ira, ed. and trans. (1976), *The Cloud of Unknowing*. New York: Image/Doubleday.
9. Ware, Timothy (1984), *The Orthodox Church*. Middlesex, England and Baltimore, Maryland: Penguin Books.
10. Woodhead, Linda (2005), *Christianity: A Very Short Introduction,* New York: Oxford University Press.

Sources

All biblical quotations are from Herbert G. May and Bruce M. Metzger, editors. (1977), *The New Oxford Annotated Bible With the Apocrypha,* (Revised Standard Version). New York: Oxford University Press.
1. John 3: 16.
2. Luke 1: 26–28, 30–33, 46–47.
3. Matthew 1: 18–22.
4. Luke 2: 7–11.
5. Mathew 3: 13, 16–17.
6. Matthew 4: 1–11.
7. Matthew 4: 18–19.
8. Luke 4: 31, 33–37.
9. Luke 5: 17–25.
10. Matthew 9: 20–22.
11. Matthew 4: 23–25.
12. Matthew 13: 54–58.
13. Luke 19: 35–38.
14. Luke 19: 45–46.
15. John 13: 1, 4–5, 12–15.
16. Luke 22: 19–20.
17. Luke 22: 41–42.
18. Luke 22: 47–48.
19. Matthew 27: 11–15, 20–23.
20. Matthew 27: 27–31.
21. John 19: 17–19.
22. Luke 23: 34.
23. Luke 23: 39–43.
24. John 19: 25–27.

25. Matthew 27: 45–46, 50.
26. John 20: 11–18.
27. Luke 24: 13–16, 30–31, 33–43.
28. John 20: 26–29.
29. Acts I: 8–11.
30. Acts 2: 1–4.
31. Matthew 16: 18–19.
32. Matthew 28: 16–20.
33. Mark 7: 5, 9, 18, 20–23.
34. Matthew 5: 1–10.
35. John 13: 34–35.
36. Matthew 5: 38–41.
37. Matthew 5: 43–45.
38. Matthew 7: 12.
39. Matthew 25: 34–36, 40.
40. Matthew 5: 23–25.
41. Matthew 18: 21–22.
42. John 8: 4–11.
43. Matthew 6: 19–21.
44. Matthew 6: 24.
45. Matthew 6: 25–30.
46. Matthew 16: 24–25.
47. Matthew 5: 14–16.
48. Matthew 7: 7.
49. Matthew 6: 9–13.
50. Matthew 7: 1–3.
51. Matthew 7: 12.
52. Mark 9: 43–50.
53. Luke 15: 11–32.
54. Matthew 13: 31–32.
55. Matthew 13: 24–30.
56. Matthew 13: 45.
57. Matthew 20: 1–15.
58. Matthew 22: 1–14.
59. Luke 10: 25–37.
60. John 1: 1–5, 12–14.
61. John 3: 16.
62. I Corinthians 15: 21–22.
63. Timothy 2: 5–6.
64. Romans 6: 8–11.
65. I Corinthians 15: 51–56.
66. I Corinthians 13: 1–7, 11–13.
67. Philippians 2: 4–11.

8 Islamic Wisdom

Star and Crescent of Islam
Widely accepted symbol of the Islamic faith.
It is, however, not accepted by all Muslims,
because there is no mention of this symbol
in the Holy Koran.

The Final Revelation

Islam, which means 'surrendering oneself to God' (*Allah* in Arabic), is the youngest and fastest-growing organized religion in the world today. Followers of Islam are found in all parts of the world, and number about one-fifth of the world's present population.

Muslims, as believers in Islam are called, acknowledge the other great monotheistic religions Judaism and Christianity. Muslims believe that Islam was the religion revealed to all the prophets including Moses and Jesus, however the revelation given to the prophet Muhammad was the final and complete revelation from God.

1. Islam: The Chosen Religion. Sura 3: 85
In the Name of God, the Compassionate, the Merciful
He that chooses a religion other than Islam, it will not be accepted
from him and in the world to come he will surely be among the losers.

As a way of life, nothing in Islam is considered secular. Islamic moral principles guide social, political and economic decision, which are all equal before God.

Reflections
Do you agree with the Muslims that religious moral principles should guide social, political and economic decisions?

Origins of Islam

Unlike the Jews who believe that Abraham stayed with Sarah and their son Isaac, Muslims believe that God called Abraham to leave Palestine with his wife Hagar and son Ishmael travel to the Arabian valley. According to Muslim tradition, while journeying across the desert, Hagar and Ishmael got lost. Hagar, frantic for water to give her child, searched in every direction until Ishmael struck the sand with his heel and a well sprang up miraculously.

On arriving in the valley where the city of Mecca is located today, Abraham was instructed by God to build a cubical shrine called the Ka'bah or Kaaba. According to Islam, the angel Gabriel brought a black stone from heaven and placed it in the corner of the shrine.

Next, God issued a devastating commandment: Abraham must kill his beloved son Ishmael as a sacrifice to God. As Abraham obediently led his son to the place of sacrifice, Satan tempted Ishmael to reject his awful fate, but the boy stoutly refused. At the last moment, God ordered a ram to be sacrificed instead.

2. A Bitter Test. Sura 37: 99–110

In the Name of God, the Compassionate, the Merciful

He [Abraham] said: I will take refuge with my Lord; He will give me guidance. Lord, grant me a righteous son.'

We gave him news of a gentle son. And when he reached the age when he could work with him, his father said to him: 'My son, I dreamt that I was sacrificing you. Tell me what your think.'

He replied: 'Father, do as you are bidden. God willing, you shall find me steadfast.'

And when they had both submitted to God's will, and Abraham had laid down his son prostrate upon his face, We* called out to him, saying: 'Abraham, you have fulfilled your vision.' Thus do We reward the righteous. That was indeed a bitter test. We ransomed his son with a noble sacrifice and bestowed on him the praise of later generations. 'Peace be on Abraham!'

Thus do We reward the righteous. He was one of Our believing servants.

Reflections

What would you do if you heard a voice that you thought was God ask you to take the life of a loved one?

Mecca

Mecca soon became a sanctuary for members of the many combative Arabian tribes and a center for worship: the Kaaba held 360 images of pagan gods worshiped by Arabs of various tribes and cultures. The city was also an important trading center where Meccan merchants organized large caravans for trade with Syria, south Arabia and Ethiopia. Here, members of various Arab tribes and religious beliefs could combine business and religious pilgrimage, worshiping their particular gods in peace.

---

* In the Koran, God refers to himself interchangeably as 'We,' 'He,' 'Our,' and 'I.'

The Life of Muhammad

Muhammad (c. 570–632 CE) was born into a poor but influential Arabian clan. His father having died before Muhammad was born and his mother soon after, the boy was adopted and raised by relatives. When old enough, he became a camel driver, leading caravans in and out of Mecca. He soon built a reputation as a quiet, serious, thoughtful man and an honest and trustworthy merchant. Kadijah, a wealthy widow hired him to conduct a caravan to Syria. As the caravan was returning from Syria, she saw two angels over Muhammad protecting him from the sun. Impressed by the way he handled the caravan, and by his kindness, Kadijah offered him her hand in marriage. The marriage with Kadijah, fifteen years his senior, was a happy one. They had six children, and though it was the custom of an Arab man to have more than one wife, Muhammad took no other woman as long as Kadijah lived. After her death, Muhammad had many wives, but no male heirs. (According to the Koran as God's will.)

At age forty, having withdrawn from the business life to spend more time meditating in secluded mountain places, Muhammad began to have visions of the archangel Gabriel bringing him revelations from God. 'There is one God,' said Gabriel, 'and that God is God (Allah).' Told by Gabriel to read God's message, Muhammad apologized that he was unable to read, but at the angel's command, Muhammad discovered to his own amazement that he could miraculously read the word of God.

As Gabriel instructed, Muhammad carried to the people the message that God was the one and only God, but for three years they responded with scorn and ridicule. Finally a few people of wealth and influence were converted and began to organize the new religion. This roused the ire of jealous enemies, who would have killed Muhammad had he not fled to the city of Yathrib (now Medina). The night of the flight, Muhammad and his disciple Abu Bakr hid in a cave while the enemy searched for them. One legend tells how God watched over His prophet by having a pair of doves build their nest in the entrance of the cave. Another legend relates that God had a spider weave her web across the entrance of the cave. When the enemy saw the undisturbed bird nest (or spider web), they assumed the cave was empty. Muhammad's flight, called the Hegira, marks the beginning of the Muslim calendar: the date was 622 CE.

As the Islam community spread and grew strong in Yathrib, Muhammad, at Gabriel's command, tried to force all Arabia into Islam. He led military raids on traders and their tribal allies and freed the conquered if they promised to join Islam. In 628, a truce was negotiated with Mecca allowing Muslims to make a yearly pilgrimage to the Kaaba. Then, eight years later, offered the choice of war or converting to Islam, the Meccans prudently chose to convert.

Immediately Muhammad smashed the idols of the Kaaba, for Islam now embraced nearly all Arabs, who worshipped the one God. Ever since, Muslims have revered Mecca as the navel of the world, the place where creation began.

> **Reflections**
> How difficult do you think it would be to switch from worshiping an idol that you could see with your physical eye to worshiping an invisible God?

The Koran (Qur'an)

Muslims consider the Old and New Testaments sacred scripture, rejecting, however, the Christian Trinity, which, like the Jews, they consider polytheistic.

Muslims believe in the virgin birth of Jesus but consider him a prophet only: even Muhammad, the true prophet of Islam, was only a messenger from God and not a god himself. There are 114 suras or chapters in the Koran and all the verses are understood by Muslims as the direct speech of God, not of Muhammad. (For this reason, Muslims request that their religion not be called Muhammadanism.)

For Muslims, the Koran (*Qur'an* in Arabic) is the purest, most complete, and most authentic scripture in the world. It is the final and complete message of the infinite divine mind to all humanity. With one exception, each sura begins with: *In the Name of God, the Compassionate, the Merciful.* In the Koran, God refers to himself interchangeably as 'We,' 'He,' 'Our,' and 'I.'

(For descriptive purposes, most of the headings given below are mine.)

3. The Book. Sura 2: 1–2
In the Name of God, the Compassionate, the Merciful
    This Book [the Koran] is not to be doubted. It is a guide for the righteous, who believe in the unseen and are steadfast in prayer …

4. People of the Book. Sura 5: 15
In the Name of God, the Compassionate, the Merciful
    People of the Book! Our apostle has come to reveal to you much of what you have hidden of the Scriptures, and to forgive you much. A light has come to you from God and a glorious Book, with which God will guide to the paths of peace those that seek to please Him; He will lead them to His will from darkness to the light; He will guide them to a straight path.

Twenty-three Year Revelation

Over a period of twenty-three years, the angel Gabriel revealed the Koran to Muhammad, who called it 'the standing miracle' because it came from God to an illiterate man. Muslims consider the Koran ('Reading') untranslatable from its original Arabic, in which it has been carefully preserved. Muslims believe that all 114 of its chapters, called *suras*, came to Muhammad as revelations from God. As Muhammad received each portion of the Koran, he learned it by heart, and never forgot it.

5. You Shall Not Forget. Sura 87: 6

In the Name of God, the Compassionate, the Merciful
We shall make you recite Our revelations, so that you
shall not forget any of them except what God pleases.

Reflections

Why do you think that in the Koran, God refers to 'Himself' in the plural as well as
the singular?

God's Revealed Words

God's revealed words are held to be holy by Muslims. Muhammad's other remarks
are preserved in the Hadith ('Tradition'), which is considered important, but not
Holy Scripture.

The Koran proclaims the oneness and sovereignty of God and humanity's need
to submit to him alone: thus *Islam* is Arabic for 'surrendering oneself to God,' and
a *Muslim* is 'one who submits.'

For Muslims, the Koran is God's eternal attribute of speech given in words
and verbal images that can be understood by all people. It includes Muhammad's
beautifully poetic speeches recorded by the faithful, apparently in random
order and further revelations collected after his death. The Koran describes the
wonders of creation, such as the making of humans out of clots of blood. It also
discusses human fate in the hereafter, with its last judgment and its rewards
and punishments: the beautiful garden of Paradise, the terrors of hell. But more
importantly, the Koran gives clear directions for human behavior in this world.
True believers must honor their parents, help the poor, protect orphans, be honest
and just in all dealings, avoid strong drink, pork, and gambling, and be humble
before God. The structure of Muslim society and its laws covering marriage,
almsgiving, relations with non-Muslims, punishment for criminals, and moral
codes, are also proclaimed in this scripture.

Because Muhammad could neither read nor write, his followers took down what
he recited, using pieces of parchment and leather, tablets of stone, ribs of palm
branches, and deceased camels' shoulder blades. Soon after Muhammad's death,
these fragments were collected and made into the Koran.

According to scholars, no translation of the Koran has ever fully conveyed the
eloquence of the original Arabic. The first sura has been called 'essence of the
Koran.' It is an essential part of all Muslim worship and no contract or transaction
is complete unless it is recited.

6. The Exordium. Sura 1: 1–7

IN THE NAME OF GOD THE COMPASSIONATE THE MERCIFUL
Praise be to God, Lord of the Universe,
  The Compassionate, the Merciful,
    Sovereign of the Day of Judgement!
You alone we worship, and to You alone
        We turn for help.

Guide us to the straight path
The path of those whom You have favoured,
Not of those who have incurred Your wrath,
    Nor of those who have gone astray.

Muhammad's Call and Mission (from the Koran)

7. The First revelation. Sura 96: 1–5; 19
In the Name of God, the Compassionate, the Merciful
    Recite in the name of your Lord who created – created man from clots of blood!
    Recite! Your Lord is the Most Bountiful One, who by the pen taught man what he did not know.
    … Prostrate yourself and come nearer.

8. The Night of Glory. Koran 97: 1–5
In the Name of God, the Compassionate, the Merciful
    We revealed this [the Koran] on the Night of Qadr [Glory]. Would that you knew what the Night of Qadr is like!
    Better is the Night of Qadr than a thousand months. On that night the angels and the Spirit by their Lord's leave come down with each decree.
    That night is peace, till break of dawn.

9. Muhammad Speaks the Truth. Sura 53: 1–15
In the Name of God, the Compassionate, the Merciful
    By the declining star your compatriot [Muhammad] is not in error, nor is he deceived! He does not speak out of his own fancy. This is an inspired revelation. He is taught by one who is powerful and mighty [Gabriel] …
    His own heart did not deny his vision. How can you [unbelievers], then, question what he sees? He beheld him once again at the sidra-tree, beyond which no one may pass. (Near it is the Garden of Repose.) When that tree was covered with what covered it, his eyes did not wander, nor did they turn aside: for he saw some of his Lord's greatest signs.

10. Muhammad's Mission. Sura 11: 2, 10–12
In the Name of God, the Compassionate, the Merciful
    Serve none but God. I am [Gabriel] sent to you by Him to warn you and to give good tidings …
    But you are only to give warning. God is the guardian of all things. If they say: 'He has invented it [the Koran] himself,' say to them: 'Produce ten invented chapters like it. Call on whom you will among your idols, if what you say be true. But if they fail you, know that it is revealed with God's knowledge, and that there is no god but Him. Will you then accept Islam?'

11. God's Instructions. Sura 93: 1–11

In the Name of God, the Compassionate, the Merciful

By the light of day, and by the dark of night, your Lord has not forsaken you [Muhammad], nor does He abhor you.

The life to come holds a richer prize for you than this present life. You shall be gratified with what your Lord will give you.

Did He not find you an orphan and give you shelter?

Did He not find you in error and guide you?

Did He not find you poor and enrich you?

Therefore do not wrong the orphan, nor chide away the beggar. But proclaim the goodness of your Lord.

12. Opposition to Muhammad. Sura 52: 30–49

In the Name of God, the Compassionate, the Merciful

Therefore give warning. By the grace of God, you are neither soothsayer nor madman.

Do they [those who oppose Muhammad] say: 'He is a poet: we are waiting for some misfortune to befall him'? Say: 'Wait if you will; I too am waiting.'

Does their reason prompt them to say this? Or is it merely that they are wicked men?

Do they say: 'He has invented it [the Koran] himself'? Indeed, they have no faith. Let them produce a scripture like it, if what they say be true!

Were they created out of the void? Or were they their own creators?

Did *they* create the heavens and the earth? Surely they have no faith!

Do they hold the treasures of your Lord or have control over them?

Have they a ladder by means of which they overhear Him? Let their eavesdropper bring a positive proof!

… Are you [Muhammad] demanding payment of them, that they should fear to be weighed down with debts?

Have they knowledge of what is hidden? Can they write it down?

Are they seeking to ruin you? It is the unbelievers who shall be ruined.

… Let them be, until they face the day when they shall stand dumbfounded; the day when their designs will avail them nothing and none will help them.

And besides this a scourge awaits the wrongdoers, though most of them do not know it.

Therefore wait the judgement of your Lord: We are watching over you. Give glory to your Lord when you awaken; in the night-time praise Him, and at the setting of the stars.

13. The Flight to Yathrib (Medina). Sura 9: 40

In the Name of God, the Compassionate, the Merciful

If you [citizens of Yathrib] do not help him [Muhammad], God will help him as He helped him when he was driven out by the unbelievers with one other [Abu Bakr]. In the cave he said to his companion: 'Do not despair, God is with us.' God caused His tranquility to descend upon him and sent to his aid invisible warriors, so that he routed the unbelievers and exalted the Word of God. God is mighty and wise.

Muhammad's Wives

The Koran speaks of Muhammad's wives after the death of Kadijah. While married to Kadijah, the prophet took no other wives. In Yathrib, Muhammad had many wives and it is to these women the Koran refers.

14. The Wives of Muhammad. Sura 33: 28–36, 39

In the Name of God, the Compassionate, the Merciful

Prophet, say to your wives; 'If you seek this nether life and all its finery, come, I will make provision for you and release you honourably. But if you seek God and His apostle and the abode of the hereafter, know that God has prepared a recompense for those of you who do good works.'

Wives of the Prophet! Those of you who clearly commit a lewd act shall be doubly punished. That is easy enough for God. But those of you who obey God and His apostle and do good works shall be doubly recompensed; for them We have made a rich provision.

Wives of the Prophet, you are not like other women. If you fear God, do not be too complaisant in your speech, least the lecherous-hearted should lust after you. Show discretion in what you say. Stay in your homes and do not display your finery as women used to do in the days of ignorance [pre-Islamic days]. Attend to your prayers, give alms and obey God and His apostle.

Women of the Household, God seeks only to remove uncleanness from you and to purify you. Commit to memory the revelations of God and the wise sayings that are recited in your dwellings. Gracious is God and all-knowing.

Those who submit to God and accept the true Faith; who are devout, sincere, patient, humble, charitable, and chaste; who fast and are ever mindful of God – on these, both men and women, God will bestow forgiveness and a rich recompense.

It is not for true believers – men or women – to order their own affairs if God and His apostle decree otherwise. He that disobeys God and His apostle strays far indeed.

Muhammad is the father of no man among you [Muhammad left no male heirs]. He is the Apostle of God and the Seal of the Prophets. Surely God has knowledge of all things.

15. The Idolaters. Sura 9: 2–5

[This is the only chapter in the Koran that does not begin with the invocation: *In the Name of God*, etc.]

God and His apostle are under no obligation to the idolaters. If you repent, it shall be well with you; but if you pay no heed, know that you shall not be immune from God's judgement.

Proclaim a woeful punishment to the unbelievers, except those idolaters who have honoured their treaties with you in every detail and aided none against you. With these keep faith, until their treaties have run their term. God loves the righteous.

When the sacred months are over slay the idolaters wherever you find them. Arrest them, besiege them, and lie in ambush everywhere for them. If they repent and take to prayer and render the alms levy, let them go their way. God is forgiving and merciful.

16. The Death of Muhammad. Sura 21: 34–37

In the Name of God, the Compassionate, the Merciful

No man before you [Muhammad] have We made immortal. If you yourself are doomed to die, will they live on forever?

Every soul shall taste death. We will prove [provide] you all with evil and good. To Us you shall return.

When the unbelievers see you, they only mock you, saying: 'Is this the man who fulminates against your gods?' And they deny all mention of the Merciful.

Impatience is the very stuff man is made of. I shall show you My signs: do not ask Me to hurry them on.

The Teachings

God

For Muslims, God is the one and supreme Reality and the experience of God's presence is the most important experience we can have. God is just, but He is merciful to repentant sinners, and we should reflect God's justice and mercy in our lives. God, says the Koran, is closer to man than his jugular vein.

Reflections

What is meant by the statement: God is closer to man than his jugular vein?

---

17. Praise Be to God. Sura 34: 1

In the Name of God, the Compassionate, the Merciful

PRAISE BE to God, to whom belongs all that the heavens and the earth contain! Praise be to Him in the world to come. He is the Wise One, the All-knowing.

He has knowledge of all that goes into the earth and all that springs up from it; all that comes down from heaven and all that ascends to it. He is the Forgiving One, the Merciful.

18. God, the Creator. Sura 6: 96–99, 102–103

In the Name of God, the Compassionate, the Merciful

He kindles the light of dawn. He has ordained the night for rest and the sun and the moon for reckoning. Such is the ordinance of God, the Mighty One, the All-knowing.

It is He that has created for you the stars, so that they may guide you in the darkness of land and sea …

It was He that created you from a single being and furnished you with a dwelling and a resting-place …

It is He who sends down water from the sky with which We bring forth the buds of every plant. From these We bring forth green foliage and close-growing grain, palm-trees laden with clusters of dates, vineyards and olive groves and all manner of pomegranates …

Such is God, your Lord. There is no god but Him, the Creator of all things. He is the Guardian.

19. The Creation, Angels and Satan. Sura 15: 16–48

In the Name of God, the Compassionate, the Merciful

We have decked the heavens with constellations and made them lovely to behold. We have guarded them from every cursed devil. Eavesdroppers are pursued by fiery comets.

We have spread out the earth and set upon it immovable mountains. We have planted it with every seasonable fruit, providing sustenance for yourselves and for those whom you do not provide for. We hold the store of every blessing and send it down in appropriate measure. We let loose the fertilizing winds and bring down water from the sky for you to drink; its stores are beyond your reach.

It is surely We who ordain life and death. We are the Heir of all things. We know those who have gone before you, and know those who will come hereafter. It is your Lord who will gather them all before Him. He is wise and all-knowing.

We created man from dry clay, from black moulded loam, and before him Satan from smokeless fire. Your Lord said to the angels: 'I am creating man from dry clay, from black moulded loam. When I have fashioned him and breathed of My spirit into him, kneel down and prostrate yourselves before him.'

The angels, one and all, prostrated themselves, except Satan. He refused to prostrate himself as the others did.

'Satan.' Said God, 'why do you not prostrate yourself?'

He replied: 'I will not bow to a mortal whom You created of dry clay, of black moulded loam.'

'Get you hence,' said God, 'you are accursed. The curse shall be on you till Judgement-day.'

'Lord,' said Satan, 'reprieve me till the Day of Resurrection.'

He answered: 'You are reprieved till the Appointed Day.'

'Lord,' said Satan, 'since You have thus seduced me, I will tempt mankind on earth: I will seduce them all, except those of them who are your faithful servants.'

He replied: 'This is My straight path. You shall have no power over My servants, only the sinners who follow you. They are all destined for Hell. It has seven gates, and through these they shall come in separate bands. But the righteous shall dwell amongst gardens and fountains; in peace and safety they shall enter them. We shall remove all hatred from their hearts, and they shall take their ease on couches face to face, a band of brothers. Toil shall not weary them, nor shall they ever be driven out.'

20. One God. Sura 112: 1–4

In the Name of God, the Compassionate, the Merciful

SAY: 'GOD is One, the Eternal God. He begot none, nor was He begotten. None is equal to Him.'

21. God Has No Son. Sura 17: 111

In the Name of God, the Compassionate, the Merciful
Say: 'Praise be to God who has never begotten a son;
who has no partner in His Kingdom; who needs none to defend Him from humiliation.' Proclaim His greatness.

God's Names

According to Islamic tradition, God has ninety-nine most gracious names listed in the Koran. With the exception of Chapter 9: Repentance, each chapter of the Koran begins with two of these names, *'compassionate'* and *'merciful.'* Fifteen of the glorious ninety-nine names are listed below.

22. A Few of God's Ninety-Nine Names. Sura 59: 22–24

In the Name of God, the Compassionate, the Merciful
He is God, besides whom there is no other deity. He knows the unknown and the manifest. He is the Compassionate, the Merciful.

He is God, besides whom there is no other deity. He is the Sovereign Lord, the Holy One, the Giver of Peace, the Keeper of Faith; the Guardian, the Mighty One, the All-powerful, the Most High! Exalted be God above their idols!

He is God, the Creator, the Originator, the Modeller. His are the most gracious names. All that is in the heavens and the earth gives glory to Him. He is the Mighty, the Wise One.

God's Angels and Prophets

Angels, according to Islam, are God's messengers. As 'creatures of light,' they praise and obey God always. Some of the angels have special duties. Gabriel, the highest angel, brought God's message to the prophet Muhammad and to all other prophets. Angels pray for human beings, support the faithful, and accompany every individual and record their deeds for Judgment Day.

Muslims believe that God sent angels as messengers to prophets who would relay these messages to help guide human beings through life. The first messenger was the first man, Adam, and the last messenger was Muhammad. According to Islam there have been 124,000 messengers in all. Twenty-eight of them are mentioned by name in the Koran, which also states there were several others not mentioned in the Koran, but mentioned in the other revealed books such as the Torah, Psalms, and the Four Gospels.

Muslims also believe that, while the previous prophets were sent to their respective peoples and times, Muhammad was sent to all humanity. Because his message will last until the end of time, no prophet would follow after him. Through Muhammad the Koran was revealed for the benefit of all humankind.

> **Reflections**
>
> Why would God send angels and prophets as messengers rather than deliver the message first-hand?

23. God's Will Revealed. Sura 4: 163–165

In the Name of God, the Compassionate, the Merciful

We have revealed Our will to you [Muhammad] as We revealed it to Noah and to the prophets who came after him; as We revealed it to Abraham, Ishmael, Isaac, Jacob, and the tribes; to Jesus, Job, Jonah, Aaron, Solomon and David, to whom We gave the Psalms. Of some apostles We have already told you, but there are others of whom We have not yet spoken (God spoke directly to Moses): apostles who brought good news to mankind and admonished them, so that they might have no plea against God after their coming. God is mighty and wise.

Satan (Iblis)

According to the Koran, Iblis, the devil or Satan and enemy of humankind, was not really an angel, but a different creature called a *jinn*.

> **Reflections**
>
> According to the Koran, God is wise and all-knowing. Did God then purposefully create Iblis (the devil)?

24. Satan. Sura 18: 50

In the Name of God, the Compassionate, the Merciful

When We said to the angels: 'Prostrate yourselves before Adam,' all prostrated themselves except Satan, who was a jinnee disobedient to his Lord.

The Five Doctrines of Faith

First Doctrine of Faith

The first Muslim doctrine of faith is, 'There is no god but God.' God sits in the seventh heaven on a high throne surrounded by angels who serve him as ministers and attendants serve their kings. The devil (*Iblis*), who fell from grace through pride, is now an accursed tempter who with his helpers tries to block God's plans and lead people astray.

25. No Other god but God. Sura 72: 19–20

In the Name of God, the Compassionate, the Merciful

Temples are built for God's worship; invoke in them no other god besides Him … Say: 'I will pray to my Lord and worship none besides Him.'

26. Faith in God. Sura 4: 136

In the Name of God, the Compassionate, the Merciful

Believers, have faith in God and His apostle, in the Book He has revealed to His apostle, and in the Scriptures He formerly revealed. He that denies God, His angels, His Scriptures, His apostles, and the Last Day, has strayed far.

Second Doctrine of Faith

Second, 'Muhammad is the messenger (or prophet) of God.' Muslims accept twenty-eight prophets from the Bible, principally Abraham, Moses, and Jesus, but the last and greatest of the prophets is Muhammad.

27. God's Prophets. Sura 5: 44, 46–48

In the Name of God, the Compassionate, the Merciful

We have revealed the Torah, in which there is guidance and light. By it the prophets who submitted to God judged the Jews, and so did the rabbis and the divines, according to God's Book which had been committed to their keeping and to which they themselves were witnesses.

After them We sent forth Jesus son of Mary, confirming the Torah already revealed, and gave him the Gospel, in which there is guidance and light, corroborating that which was revealed before it in the Torah, a guide and an admonition to the righteous. Therefore let those who follow the Gospel judge according to what God has revealed therein.

And to you We have revealed the Book with the truth. It confirms the Scriptures which came before it and stands as a guardian over them.

Third Doctrine of Faith

Third, God reveals his will through Muhammad, the Koran, and the angels, especially the chief angel Gabriel, the agent of revelation.

28. God's Angels. Sura 2: 98, 285

In the Name of God, the Compassionate, the Merciful

... 'Whoever is an enemy of God, His angels, or His apostles, or of Gabriel or Michael, will surely find that God is the enemy of the unbelievers.'

The Apostle believes in what has been revealed to him by his Lord, and so do the faithful. They all believe in God and His angels....

Fourth Doctrine of Faith

Fourth, there will be a Last Day and final judgment. 'Every soul shall taste death, and in the end you shall return to us.' The faithful shall enter the gardens of Paradise. Angels will greet them, saying: 'Peace be to you for all that you have steadfastly endured. Blessed is the reward of Paradise.' The unfaithful will enter the gates of Hell where they shall remain forever. 'Scalding water shall be poured upon their heads, melting their skins and that which is in their bellies.' Evil is the home of the arrogant – those who delighted in falsehoods and lived selfish lives.

> **Reflections**
> How do you view heaven and hell?

29. Judgment. Sura 3: 30

In the Name of God, the Compassionate, the Merciful

The day will surely come when each soul will be confronted with whatever good it did. As for its evil deeds, it will wish they were a long way off.

30. Day of Resurrection. Sura 39: 67–70

In the Name of God, the Compassionate, the Merciful

They underrate the might of God, but on the Day of Resurrection He will hold the entire earth in His grasp and fold up the heavens in His right hand. Glory be to Him! Exalted be He above their idols!

The Trumpet shall be blown, and all who are in the heavens and on earth shall fall down fainting, except those that shall be spared by God. Then the Trumpet will be blown again and they shall rise and gaze around them. The earth will shine with the light of her Lord, and the Book will be laid open. The prophets and the witnesses shall be brought in, and all shall be judged with fairness: none shall be wronged. Every soul shall be recompensed according to its deeds, for He best knows all that they did.

31. The Last Judgment. Sura 82: 1–5

In the Name of God, the Compassionate, the Merciful

WHEN THE SKY is rent asunder; when the stars scatter and the oceans merge together; when the graves are hurled about: each soul shall know what it has done and what it has failed to do.

O man! What evil has enticed you from your gracious Lord who created you, and gave you due proportions and an upright form? In whatever shape He willed He could have moulded you.

Yet you deny the Last Judgement. Surely there are guardians watching over you, noble recorders who know of all your actions.

The righteous will surely dwell in bliss. But the wicked shall burn in Hell upon the Judgement-day: nor shall they ever escape from it.

Would that you knew what the Day of Judgement is! Oh, would that you knew what the Day of Judgement is! It is the day when every soul will stand alone and God will reign supreme.

Fifth Doctrine of Faith

The fifth doctrine is one's faith in the Divine Will and Providence. God, as the creator of the heavens and the earth, has all knowledge. He bestows grace on those whom He chooses. God's grace is infinite. God alone is wise and forgiving.

32. Divine Will and Providence. Sura 2: 117
In the Name of God, the Compassionate, the Merciful
Creator of the heavens and the earth! When He decrees a thing, He need only say 'Be,' and it is.

33. God's Grace. Sura 3: 73–74
In the Name of God, the Compassionate, the Merciful
Say, 'Grace is in the hands of God: He bestows it on whom He will. God is munificent and all-knowing. He is merciful to whom He will. God's grace is infinite.'

34. God is Bountiful. Sura 10: 107
In the Name of God, the Compassionate, the Merciful
If God afflicts you with a misfortune, none can remove it but He; and if he bestows on you a favour, none can withhold His bounty. He is bountiful to whom He will. He is the Forgiving One, the Merciful.

35. God's Will. Sura 23: 62
In the Name of God, the Compassionate, the Merciful
We charge no soul with more than it can bear. Our Book records the truth: none shall be wronged.

The Five Pillars of Faith
The Five Pillars of Faith are exercises used by faithful Muslims to help them put the doctrines of faith into practice. These are: (1) *Shahadah* (the declaration of faith); (2) *Salat* (ritual prayers performed five times daily); (3) *Zakah* (the payment of alms); (4) *Sawm* (fasting in the month of Ramadan); and (5) *Hajj* (pilgrimage to Mecca at least once in a lifetime).

The Declaration of Faith
Muslims recite the *Shahadah* many times a day. It is the first statement spoken into the ears of a newborn Muslim baby and the last words a Muslim should utter before death.

36. Recitation of *Shahadah* (Traditional)
'I bear witness that there is not god but God, and that Muhammad is the messenger of God.'

Ritual Prayer
Five times a day – at daybreak, noon, mid-afternoon, before sunset, and after dark – the faithful say prayers. Each of these times a crier (*muezzin*) climbs to the platform of the mosque tower (*minaret*) and chants the call to prayer. The following is the traditional call to prayer, but there are variations

> God is great! God is great!
> There is no god but God,
> And Muhammad is his prophet!
> Come to prayer! Come to salvation!

At daybreak, the muezzin adds:

> Prayer is better than sleep!
> Prayer is better than sleep!
> God is great! God is great!
> There is no god but God!

Before entering the mosque for prayer, the faithful must wash their hands and feet in water fountains on the mosque grounds. This cleansing of the body symbolizes the cleansing of the soul from sin. If the faithful are unable to go to a mosque, they may pray anywhere by facing Mecca. Women and girls may go to a mosque that has a room or balcony set aside for them. But most of the time they pray at home. All, however, must face Mecca while they pray.

Salat is always conducted in Arabic, the language of the Koran. Thus Muslims from different countries can worship together. Prayer follows a series of formal actions, which include bowing and prostrating (a sign of submission to God).

Saying prayers frequently during the day reminds the faithful of God and is a direct communication with Him.

37. *Salat* or Daily Prayer. Sura 1: 1–7
IN THE NAME OF GOD
THE COMPASSIONATE
THE MERCIFUL
Praise be to God, Lord of the Universe,
The Compassionate, the Merciful,
Sovereign of the Day of Judgement,
we turn for help.
Guide us to the straight path,
The path of those whom You have favoured.
Not of those who have incurred Your wrath,
Nor of those who have gone astray.

38. Recommendations for Prayer. Sura 20: 14
In the Name of God, the Compassionate, the Merciful
'I am God. There is no god but Me. Serve Me, and recite your prayers in My remembrance.'

39. Remember God. Sura 7: 205
In the Name of God, the Compassionate, the Merciful
Remember your Lord deep in your soul with humility and reverence, and without ostentation: in the morning and in the evening; and do not be negligent.

40. Praise God Day and Night. Sura 20: 130

In the Name of God, the Compassionate, the Merciful

Give glory to your Lord before sunrise and before sunset. Praise Him night and day, so that you may find comfort.

41. Face Holy Mecca. Sura 2: 144

In the Name of God, the Compassionate, the Merciful

Turn your face towards the Holy Mosque [Mecca]; wherever you be, turn your faces towards it.

Reflections

Would the world be a different place, and would people have different attitudes if everyone prayed five times daily?

Almsgiving

According to the Koran, everything in the universe belongs to God and that whatever you are given – plenty or little – is held in trust for Him. God watches to see how the faithful use His gifts. Thus Muslims should show their thankfulness by praying often and giving alms. Setting aside a certain portion of one's wealth should help one feel joy for obeying God, not for praise or thanks from the beneficiaries.

Almsgiving is a blessing: the act of setting aside a specific portion of one's wealth for the poor and needy. Almsgiving is not limited to financial giving. Any act of kindness – a smile, kindness to animals, helping a friend or stranger – are acts that God approves.

Reflections

Do acts of kindness, such as almsgiving, help you feel better about yourself?

---

42. *Zakat* or Almsgiving. Sura 2: 110

In the Name of God, the Compassionate, the Merciful

Attend to your prayers and render the alms levy. Whatever good you do shall be recompensed by God. God is watching all your actions.

43. Duty to Give Alms. Sura 9: 60

In the Name of God, the Compassionate, the Merciful

Alms shall be only for the poor and the destitute, for those that are engaged in the management of alms and those whose hearts are sympathetic to the Faith, for the freeing of slaves and debtors, for the advancement of God's cause, and for the traveler in need. That is a duty enjoined by God. God is all-knowing and wise.

44. Be Charitable in Private. Sura 2: 271

In the Name of God, the Compassionate, the Merciful

To be charitable in public is good, but to give alms to the poor in private is better and will atone for some of your sins. God has knowledge of all your actions.

45. Forgiveness. Sura 2: 263

In the Name of God, the Compassionate, the Merciful

A kind word with forgiveness is better than charity followed by insult. God is self-sufficient and gracious.

Fasting

During the ninth month of the Muslim year (called Ramadan), while Muhammad was meditating, he received his first revelations. Each year after, during Ramadan, he would recite all that had been revealed until then. The anniversary of the night that the first words of the Koran were revealed is called Qadr, the Night of Glory. On this night the gates of Paradise are open, the gates of Hell shut, and the devil is in chains.

To commemorate this event, during the month of Ramadan, all faithful Muslims except pregnant women and travelers fast from dawn (as soon as one can distinguish a white thread from a black one) until sundown. From dark to dawn, one should take only enough food and drink to last the next day without feeling weak. Also, the faithful must not commit any unworthy act. One lie can make a day's fast meaningless. Some people who are sick or very young or old are excused from fasting in this period, but some must make up the missed days later.

Reflections

Would fasting help turn your worldly thoughts of clothes, food, and entertainment to spiritual thoughts of morality and goodwill?

---

46. *Sawm* or Fasting. Sura 2: 183–185

In the Name of God, the Compassionate, the Merciful

Believers, fasting is decreed for you as it was decreed for those before you; perchance you will guard yourselves against evil. Fast a certain number of days, but if any one among you is ill or on a journey, let him fast a similar number of days later; and for those that cannot endure it there is a penance ordained: the feeding of a poor man. He that does good of his own accord shall be well rewarded; but to fast is better for you, if you but knew it.

In the month of Ramadan the Koran was revealed, a book of guidance for mankind with proofs of guidance distinguishing right from wrong. Therefore whoever of you is present in that month let him fast. But he who is ill or on a journey shall fast a similar number of days later on.

God desires your well-being, not your discomfort. He desires you to fast the whole month so that you may magnify God and render thanks to Him for giving you His guidance.

Pilgrimage

Once in a lifetime, it is every Muslim's duty to make a pilgrimage (*hajj*) to Mecca during the month of *Dhu-I-hijja*. In Western terms this month usually falls in early summer. A person physically or mentally unable to make the trip may send someone as a substitute. No non-Muslim may make the pilgrimage or even enter Mecca. Pilgrims from every land approach the sacred city as members of the same family. All pilgrims – men and women, rich and poor – wear a seamless white garment, take no food or drink by day, harm no living thing (animal or vegetable), and practice celibacy.

For ten days the faithful follow rituals that remind them of the meaning of Islam. On the tenth and last day Muslims remember the obedience of the Prophet Abraham to God's command that he should sacrifice his son Ishmael. Such obedience is an example of Islam – to surrender oneself completely to God.

This yearly pilgrimage, when thousands of Muslims of every color and from many foreign lands come together to humble themselves before God, explains in part why Islam has no racial barriers. In Islam, religious ties are far stronger than blood relationships.

> **Reflections**
> Do you agree with the Muslims that spiritual ties are stronger than blood relationships?

47. *Hajj*: Pilgrimage to Mecca and the Kaaba. Koran 2: 197–198, 125, 130–131
In the Name of God, the Compassionate, the Merciful

Make the pilgrimage in the appointed months. He that intends to perform it in those months must abstain from sexual intercourse, obscene language, and acrimonious disputes while on pilgrimage. God is aware of whatever good you do. Provide well for yourselves: the best provision is piety.

We made the House [The Kaaba at Mecca] a resort and a sanctuary for mankind, saying: 'Make the place where Abraham stood a house of worship.' We enjoined Abraham and Ishmael to cleanse Our House for those who walk round it, who meditate in it, and who kneel and prostrate themselves.

Who but a foolish man would renounce the faith of Abraham? We chose him in this world, and in the world to come he shall abide among the righteous. When his Lord said to him: 'Submit,' he answered: 'I have submitted to the Lord of the Universe.'

Social and Moral Practices

In addition to the Five Pillars of Faith, the Koran gives rules for other activities.

Jihad

Commonly translated as 'holy war,' *jihad* actually means 'striving,' resisting evil. The greater jihad, said Muhammad, is the struggle against the lower self (ego and worldly desires) – the eternal fight between right and wrong, error and truth, selfishness and unselfishness. Through inner jihad, the spiritual person tries to awaken to true reality and behold divine beauty.

On the external level, jihad is protecting the way of God against the forces of evil. Jihad is often called Holy War in which the faithful defend Islam for the sake of God. The Koran teaches that Muslims should not be the aggressor in war. However, if an injustice has been done, they should fight until the enemy surrenders. If a soldier dies in a Holy War, he goes directly to Paradise.

Reflections

Do you believe that if someone attacks you or your country unjustly that you should fight back? Can you think of alternatives?

---

48. *Jihad* (Struggle, Holy War). Sura 2: 190–192

In the Name of God, the Compassionate, the Merciful

Fight for the sake of God those that fight against you, but do not attack them first. God does not love aggressors.

Slay them wherever you find them. Drive them out of the places from which they drove you. Idolatry is more grievous than bloodshed. But do not fight them within the precincts of the Holy Mosque unless they attack you there; if they attack you put them to the sword …

49. Reward for Fighting in a Holy War. Sura 47: 8, 15

In the Name of God, the Compassionate, the Merciful

As for those who are slain in the cause of God, He will not allow their works to perish. He will vouchsafe them guidance and ennoble their state; He will admit them to the Paradise He has made known to them.

… Therein shall flow rivers of water undefiled, and rivers of milk for ever fresh; rivers of wine delectable to those that drink it, and rivers of clarified honey. There shall they eat of every fruit, and receive forgiveness from their Lord.

Social Restrictions

Muslims may not eat the blood or the flesh of swine. They view pigs as scavenger animals, whose meat can transmit disease. Drinking alcohol is forbidden because of its association with violence and frequent addiction. They also must avoid lying and stealing. Gambling is forbidden because it is considered a dangerous waste of time. Addicted gamblers ruin their families. One may trade for profit, but not lend money for interest. In Muhammad's day rates of interest were unusually high, which often exploited and impoverished the borrower.

50. Eating, Drinking, Gambling. Sura 2: 173, 219

In the Name of God, the Compassionate, the Merciful

He has forbidden you carrion, blood, and the flesh of swine; also any flesh that is consecrated other than in the name of God ...

They ask you about drinking and gambling. Say: 'There is great harm in both, although they have some benefit for men; but their harm is far greater than their benefit.'

51. Theft. Sura 5: 38

In the Name of God, the Compassionate, the Merciful

As for the man or woman who is guilty of theft, cut off their hands to punish them for their crimes.

52. Speech. Sura 2: 42

In the Name of God, the Compassionate, the Merciful

Do not confound truth with falsehood, nor knowingly conceal the truth.

53. Business. Sura 2:188

In the Name of God, the Compassionate, the Merciful

Do not devour one another's property by unjust means, nor bribe the judges with it in order that you may wrongfully and knowingly usurp the possessions of other men.

Marriage

In marriage, though men are a degree above women, women may expect to be treated with kindness and justice. In traditional Muslim families, marriage is arranged by the parents and sealed by a written contract. The bridegroom's family makes an offer of money or property to the bride's family as a part of the contract. The marriage usually takes place in the home and is followed by a feast and festivities. The Koran says that God detests divorce, but if a man and woman decide to divorce, the woman receives her dowry back. Divorced men and women are free to remarry.

Men may practice polygamy to a maximum of four wives at a time, but only if he can treat them all equally; otherwise he should marry only once. Men are fully responsible for the upkeep of their wives and children.

Reflections

Do you agree that in a marriage men should have authority over women?

---

54. Men Superior to Women. Sura 4: 34

In the Name of God, the Compassionate, the Merciful

Men have authority over women because God has made the one superior to the other, and because they spend their wealth to maintain them. Good women are obedient. They guard their unseen parts because God has guarded them. As for those from whom you fear disobedience, admonish them, forsake them in beds apart, and beat them. Then if they obey you, take no further action against them. Surely God is high, supreme.

55. Polygamy. Sura 4: 3–4
In the Name of God, the Compassionate, the Merciful
If you fear that you cannot treat orphans [orphan girls] with fairness, then you may marry other women who seem good to you: two, three, or four of them. But if you fear that you cannot maintain equality among them, marry one only or any slave-girls you may own. This will make it easier for you to avoid injustice.

56. Modesty in Women. Sura 24: 31
In the Name of God, the Compassionate, the Merciful
Enjoin believing women to turn their eyes away from temptation and to preserve their chastity; not to display their adornments; to draw their veils over their bosoms and not to display their finery except [to members of the household]. And let them not stamp their feet when walking so as to reveal their hidden trinkets.

57. Modesty in Men. Sura 24: 30
In the Name of God, the Compassionate, the Merciful
Enjoin believing men to turn their eyes away from temptation and to restrain their carnal desires. This will make their lives purer. God has knowledge of all their actions.

Selections from the Koran

58. God's Animals. Sura 6: 38
In the Name of God, the Compassionate, the Merciful
All the beasts that roam the earth and all the birds that soar on high are but communities like your own. We have left out nothing in the Book. Before their Lord they shall be gathered all.

59. Right Speech and Forgiveness. Sura 4: 148
In the Name of God, the Compassionate, the Merciful
God does not love harsh words, except when uttered by a man who is truly wronged. God hears all and knows all. Whether you do good openly or in private, whether you forgive an injustice – God is forgiving and all-powerful.

60. Integrity. Sura 49: 6
In the Name of God, the Compassionate, the Merciful
Believers, if an evil-doer brings you a piece of news, inquire first into its truth, lest you should wrong others unwittingly and then regret your action.

61. Rely on God. Sura 9: 115

In the Name of God, the Compassionate, the Merciful

God has sovereignty over the heavens and the earth; He ordains life and death. You have none besides God to protect or help you.

62. Humility. Sura 31: 16–18

In the Name of God, the Compassionate, the Merciful

'My son, God will bring all things to light, be they as small as a grain of mustard seed, be they hidden inside a rock or in the heavens or the earth. Gracious is God and all-knowing.

'My son, be steadfast in prayer, enjoin justice, and forbid evil. Endure with fortitude whatever befalls you. That is a duty incumbent on all.

'Do not treat men with scorn, nor walk proudly on the earth: God does not love the arrogant and the vainglorious …'

63. Kindness to Parents. Sura 17: 23–24

In the Name of God, the Compassionate, the Merciful

Your Lord has enjoined you to worship none but Him, and to show kindness to your parents. If either or both of them attain old age in your dwelling, show them no sign of impatience, nor rebuke them; but speak to them kind words. Treat them with humility and tenderness and say: 'Lord, be merciful to them. They nursed me when I was an infant.'

Summary

Islam is the youngest and fastest-growing organized religion in the world today. Muslims acknowledge Judaism and Christianity, but believe the revelation given to the prophet Muhammad was the final and complete revelation.

Nothing in Islam is considered secular. Islamic moral principles guide the social, political, and economic decisions of all Muslims.

Muslims believe that God called Abraham, his wife Hagar, and son Ishmael to leave Palestine for Mecca and build a shrine called the Kaaba. According to Islam, Gabriel brought a black stone from heaven and placed it in the corner of the shrine. Mecca soon became a sanctuary where Arab tribes conducted business and worshipped their many gods in peace.

Later, according to the Muslims, God sent revelations to Muhammad via the angel Gabriel. One of the messages was to teach there was only one God and to worship idols was a sin. For twenty-three years the messages from God through Gabriel to Muhammad continued culminating in the Muslim Holy Scripture, the Qur'an (Koran in English). Muslims consider the Koran ('reading') untranslatable from its original Arabic, in which it has been carefully preserved. Muslims believe that all 114 of its chapters, called *suras*, came to Muhammad as revelations from God.

For Muslims, the Koran is God's eternal attribute of speech given in words and verbal images that can be understood by all people. It describes the creation, human fate in the hereafter, the last judgment, the garden of Paradise, and the terrors of hell. More important, it gives clear directions for human behavior in this world.

The Koran speaks of Muhammad's mission – to turn worshippers away from idols to the one true God. Muslims reject the Christian Trinity, which they consider polytheistic. They accept the virgin birth of Jesus, but consider him, like Muhammad and other prophets, a prophet only and not a god himself.

Angels, according to Islam, are God's messengers to help guide human beings through life. The first messenger was the first man, Adam, and the last messenger was Muhammad. According to Islam there have been 124,000 messengers in all. Twenty-eight of them are mentioned by name in the Koran.

For Muslims, the Koran is the purest and most authentic scripture in the world. It is the final and complete message of Allah to all humanity. The laws of the Muslim community are taken directly from the Koran.

Islam Today

In the last half of the twentieth century and today in the twenty-first century, Islam has become an increasingly important force in world politics. Many of the Third World nations are Muslim. Some of them control vital natural resources such as oil, natural gas, and minerals.

Islam continues to be the fastest-growing religion in the world. Though it was born in the Arabian world, it knows no national barriers or racial prejudice. All people are the children of God, thus Muslims consider their religious ties stronger than blood ties. And all Muslims, no matter where they live, learn to read the Koran in its original Arabic.

As Islam spread into the Western world, Muslims expressed shock at what they considered sexual vice and loose morality of these nations. They believed that the perceived moral decay had been caused by the separation of church and state. Thus many Muslims called for a return to the old ways and to nations controlled by Islamic culture. However, Islamic fundamentalism is particularly difficult for Muslims living in the non-Muslim world to follow. Consider, for example, the number of women who are participating in public life.

Timeline

c. 545 CE	Birth of Abdullah, Muhammad's father.
c. 570 CE	Birth of Muhammad.
c. 577 CE	Death of Muhammad's mother.
c. 580 CE	Death of Abdul Mutalib, Muhammad's grandfather.
c. 583 CE	Muhammad's journey to Syria in the company of his uncle Abu Talib. His meeting with the monk Bahira who foretells of his prophethood.
c. 594 CE	Muhammad becomes manager of Khadija's business and leads her trade caravan to Syria and back.

c. 595 CE	Muhammad marries Khadija.
c. 610 CE	First revelation in cave at Mt. Hira. Muhammad commissioned as Messenger of God.
c. 619 CE	Deaths of Abu Talib and Khadija.
c. 620 CE	Muhammad's ascension to the heavens.
c. 622 CE	Muhammad and followers migrate to Yathrib.
c. 624 to 631 CE	Holy wars to covert idol worshipers to Islam.
c. 932 CE	Death of Muhammad. Election of Abu Bakr as Caliph.
1095 to 1270 CE	Christian Crusades to the Holy Land.
1965 CE	Malcolm X assassinated.
1975 CE	Death of Elijah Mohammad, leader of Nation of Islam among African Americans in Northern America.

Study Questions

1. Explain the meaning of the words 'Islam' and 'Muslim.'
2. Discuss the statement, 'Nothing in Islam is considered secular.'
3. Explain the importance of the city of Mecca prior to its conversion to Islam.
4. What is the difference between Muslim and Jewish beliefs in the story of Abraham?
5. Clarify the significance of the Kaaba.
6. Describe the major revelation and mission given to Muhammad by the angel Gabriel.
7. Over a period of how many years did the angel Gabriel reveal the Koran to Muhammad?
8. What city do Muslims consider the navel of the universe?
9. How many suras (chapters) are in the Koran and how are they arranged?
10. Why do Muslims consider Christians polytheistic?
11. Why do angels such as Gabriel come to prophets?
12. Why do Muslims consider Muhammad the last of the prophets?
13. According to Islam, how many of God's messengers are there and how many are mentioned in the Koran?
14. In detail, give two of the Five Articles of Faith.
15. Name three of the social restrictions in Islam.
16. Explain each of the Five Pillars of Faith.
17. Describe the yearly pilgrimage that every Muslim must make at least once in his or her life.
18. Explain the significance of jihad.
19. Why do Muslims avoid gambling?
20. How many wives may a Muslim man have at a time? Are there any restrictions?

Suggested Reading

1. Ahmed, Leila (2000), *A Border Passage From Cairo to America – A Woman's Journey*. New York: Penguin Group.
2. Akbar, Ahmed (1994), *Living Islam*. New York: Facts on File.
3. Armstrong, Karen (2002), *Islam: A Short History*. New York: Random House.

4. Chittick, William C. (2007), *The Sufi Path of Knowledge.* New York: State University of New York Press.

5. Esposito, John L. (2004), *Islam: The Straight Path With New Epilogue.* Third edition, New York: Oxford University Press.

6. Hossein, Sevved (2002), *The Heart of Islam: Enduring Values for Humanity.* New York: HarperCollins Publishers, Inc.

7. Lings, Martin (1983), *Muhammad: His Life Based on the Earliest Sources.* Rochester, Vermont: Inner Traditions International.

8. Nasr, Seyyed Hossein, ed. (1989), *Islamic Spirituality 1: Foundations.* New York: Crossroad Publishing Company, 1987 and London: SCM Press.

9. Ramadan, Tariq (2007), *In the Footsteps of the Prophet.* New York: Oxford University Press.

10. Schuon, Frithjof (1963), *Understanding Islam.* London: George Allen & Unwin.

Sources

All selections from the Koran are from The *Koran,* translated with notes by N.J. Dawood. (1999), New York: Penguin (eleventh edition). Page numbers listed below after the semi-colon refer to this text.

1. Sura 3: 85; p. 50.
2. Sura 37: 99–110; p. 315.
3. Sura 2: 1–2; p. 11.
4. Sura 5: 15; p. 81.
5. Sura 87: 6; p. 424.
6. Sura 1: 1–7 (The Exordium); p. 9.
7. Sura 96: 1–5, 9; p. 429.
8. Sura 97: 1–5; p. 429.
9. Sura 53: 1–15; pp. 371–372.
10. Sura 11: 2, 10–11; p. 157.
11. Sura 93: 1–11; p. 428.
12. Sura 52: 30–49; pp. 370–371.
13. Sura 9: 40; p. 137.
14. Sura 33: 28–36, 39; pp. 295–297.
15. Sura 9: 2–5; pp. 133–134.
16. Sura 21: 34–37; p. 229.
17. Sura 34: 1; p. 300.
18. Sura 6: 96–99, 102–103; pp. 101–102.
19. Sura 15: 16–48; pp. 184–185.
20. Sura 112: 1–4; p. 434.
21. Sura 17: 111; p. 205.
22. Sura 59: 22–24; p. 389.
23. Sura 4: 163–165; p. 77.
24. Sura 18: 50; p. 209.
25. Sura 72: 19–20; pp. 408–409.
26. Sura 4: 136; p. 75.
27. Sura 5: 44, 46–48; pp. 84–85.
28. Sura 2: 98, 285; pp. 19, 42.

29. Sura 3: 30; p. 45.
30. Sura 39: 67–70; p. 327.
31. Sura 82: 1–5; p. 420.
32. Sura 2: 117; p. 21.
33. Sura 3: 73; p. 49.
34. Sura 10: 107; p. 155.
35. Sura 23: 62; p. 243.
36. Traditional.
37. Sura 1: 1–7; p. 9.
38. Sura 20: 14; p. 220.
39. Sura 7: 205; p. 126.
40. Sura 20: 130; p. 226.
41. Sura 2: 144; p. 24.
42. Sura 2: 110; p. 21.
43. Sura 9: 60; p. 139.
44. Sura 2: 271; p. 40.
45. Sura 2: 263; p. 39.
46. Sura 2: 183–185; p. 28.
47. Sura 2: 197–198, 125, 130–131; pp. 30, 22.
48. Sura 2: 190–192; p. 29.
49. Sura 47: 8, 15; pp. 357–358.
50. Sura 2: 173, 219; pp. 26, 32.
51. Sura 5: 38; p. 83.
52. Sura 2: 42; p. 14.
53. Sura 2: 188; pp. 28–29.
54. Sura 4: 34; p. 64.
55. Sura 4: 3–4; p. 60.
56. Sura 24: 31; p. 248.
57. Sura 24: 30; p. 248.
58. Sura 6: 38; p. 96.
59. Sura 4: 148; p. 76.
60. Sura 49: 6; p. 363.
61. Sura 9: 112; p. 145.
62. Sura 31: 16–18; p. 289.
63. Sura 17: 23–24; pp. 198–199.

Acknowledgements

Acknowledgement is made to the following for permission to reprint copyrighted material from the works listed below.

American Museum of Natural History, for extracts from *The Sun Dance and Other Ceremonies of the Oglala Division of the Teton Dakota*. Copyright 1917 by J.R. Walker, and *Notes on the Indians of the Fort Apache Region*. Copyright 1930 by Albert B. Readen.

Australian Museum, for extract from *Aunty Beryl Carmichael*, 2004.

Bernice P. Bishop Museum, for extracts from *Polynesian Religion, Bulletin 34*. Copyright 1927 by E.S. Craighill Handy.

Buddhist Publication Society, for extracts from *Three Cardinal Discourses of the Buddha*, translated by Nanamoli Thera. Copyright 1972. And from *The Word of the Buddha*, Nyanatiloka, ed. and trans. Copyright 1981. All used by permission.

Bobbs-Merrill Co., Inc., for extracts from *Buddhism: Selections from Buddhist Literature*, edited by Clarence H. Hamilton. Copyright 1952.

Cambridge University Press, for extract from *An Introduction to Confucianism* by Yao Xinzhong. Copyright 2000.

Crossroad Publishing Co., for extract from *Sacred Texts of the World: A Universal Anthology*, N. Smart and R.D. Hecht, editors. Copyright 1982.

Clear Light Publishers, for extract from *The Iroquois Book of Life: White Roots of Peace* by Paul Wallace. Copyright 1994.

Columbia University Press, for extract from *Sources of Japanese Tradition*, W.T. de Bary, editor. Copyright 1958. And from *Sources of the Chinese Tradition*, W.T. de Bary et al. Copyright 1960. Used by permission.

Dell Publishing Co., for extract from *African Myths and Tales*, Susan Feldman, editor. Copyright 1963.

Doubleday & Company, for extracts from *Zen Flesh, Zen Bones* by Paul Reps. Copyright 1981.

Dover Publications, for extracts from the *World's Rim* by H.B Alexander. Copyright 1953. And for extracts from *Jaina Sutras: Sacred Books of the East*, vols. 22, 45, Hermann Jacobi, translator. Copyright 1884, 1895. Claredon Press reprint, copyright 1968. Used by permission.

El Paso Norte Press, for extracts from *The Teachings of Confucius*, James Legge, translator, James Ford, editor. Copyright 2005.

Field Columbia Museum Anthropology Series, for extract from *The Arapaho Sun Dance* by G.A. Dorsey. Copyright 1903.

Gyldendalske Boghandel, for extract from *Intellectual Culture of the Igluik Eskimos* by Knud Rasmussen. Copyright 1929.

Random House, for extract from *The Analects of Confucius*, Arthur Waley, translator, copyright 1930, and *The Wisdom of Confucius*, Lin Yutang, translator, copyright 1943. Used by permission.

Rider & Co., for extract from *The Lion's Roar: An Anthology of the Buddha's Teachings Selected from the Pali Canon*, David Maurice, editor. Copyright 1962.

Smithsonian Institute, for 'Notes from the Bull Thigh, Sept. 4, 1910' by Truman Michelson.

Sunstone Press, for extract from *Songs of the Tewa* by Herbert J. Spinden. Copyright 1976.

University of Chicago Press, for extract from *The Religion, Spirituality, and Thought of Traditional Africa*, K.E. Martin and L.M. Martin, translators. Copyright 1979. Used by permission.

University of Nebraska Press, for extract from *The Old North Trail, or Life, Legends, and Religion of the Blackfeet Indians* (reprint) by Walter McClintock. Copyright 1968.

University of Oklahoma, for extracts from *The Sacred Pipe* by Joseph Epes Brown. Copyright 1971. Used by permission.

University of Utah Press, for extract from *Navaho Legends*, Washington Matthews, translator. Copyright 1994.

Vajirarama Publishing Co., for extract from *The Dhammapada*, Narada Maha Thera, translator. Copyright 1972.

Viking Press, for extract from *Book of the Hopi* by Frank Waters, copyright 1969, used by permission, and *Primitive Religion: Its Nature and Origin* by Paul Radin, copyright 1937.

Vira Shasan Sangha, for extract from *Reality*, S.A. Jain, translator. Copyright 1960.

William Morrow Publishing Co., for extract from *The Magic World*, William Brandon, editor. Copyright 1971.

Wisdom Publications, for extract from *Buddha's Words: An Anthology of Discourses from the Pali Canon*, Bhikkhu Bidhi, editor. Copyright 2005.

Index